A Little Book of
YANKEE HUMOR

A Little Book of
YANKEE HUMOR

Illustrated by Austin N. Stevens

Foreword by Marshall Dodge

YANKEE BOOKS

Yankee Publishing Incorporated
Dublin, NH

This book has been prepared
by the staff of Yankee Publishing Incorporated

Edited by
Clarissa M. Silitch

Designed by
Carl F. Kirkpatrick

Published MCMLXXVII by
Yankee Publishing Incorporated
Dublin, New Hampshire 03444

Fourth Printing, 1983

Library of Congress Catalog Card No. 77-80388
ISBN 0-911658-79-3

CONTENTS

FOREWORD

While the Texan makes fun of his audience, the New Englander likes to make fun of himself. "I don't know about your farm in Maine, mister, but I have a ranch in Texas and it takes me five days to drive around my entire spread," says the Texan. The Maine farmer replies, "I have a car just like that myself."

An overstated humor bowls an audience over with exaggeration. Humor directed at the humorist himself is said to be understated. The Texan overstates things perhaps because he feels expansive in the wide open spaces. Maybe the New Englander understates things because he feels constricted by the stone walls, the churches.

Nearly all the stories in this collection are understated. Even its title suggests modesty. Only three stories are overstated; "Captain Bob Bodden and the Good Ship *Rover*," "Antoine's Choice," and "Captain Ulysses and the Sea Serpent." Captain Bodden's story depends upon exaggeration for its humor, which is entirely appropriate to its early American setting when New England was the frontier. The characters in "Antoine's Choice" also appear to live in a frontier style in early Vermont. The sea serpent in Captain Ulysses is surely an exaggeration, but an exaggeration cut down to size by the creature's good-natured humanity.

A few stories in the collection, like "Trotting Race" and "Tim, Ben and the Horse," are neither under- nor overstated and hence are more melodramatic than comic.

Two of the cleverest pieces in the collection are "A Time for Forecast" and "Malcolm, My Horse." "A Time for

Forecast" spoofs the brainy New England intellectual and his bookish jargon. On a deeper level, Professor T. Gerald Foyp of Mentor, Maine, mocks the chaotic modern world and man's inability to cope with it. Even at this deeper level, the author, Bill Conklin, is laughing at himself.

"Malcolm, My Horse" is a delightful story of author Gayle Steed's defeat at the hands (hoofs?) of a foolish and ornery horse. The comedy derives from Malcolm's survival of defeat after defeat and in Gayle's acceptance of Malcolm despite her exasperation with him. Her final move to sell Malcolm signals not her rejection of him so much as her final acceptance of him as an equal.

The stories of this book, taken as a whole, more closely resemble these last two and hence bear out the contention that New England humor is understated and that understatement is characterized by the storyteller laughing at himself rather than at his audience.

Marshall Dodge
Bristol, Maine

1976: A Time

PROFESSOR T. Gerald Foyp, head of the Department of Geopolitics at Mentor College, Mentor, Maine, has just returned from places like Washington and Wall Street, getting what he calls "the heft of things." We were privileged to interview him in July, 1976, when his information and ideas were still fresh.

Can you tell us, sir, how you see the second half of the year shaping up?

It should move right along from where we are now. You'll have your early summer, and then your late summer giving way to fall, and after that the Holiday Season — Thanksgiving, Christmas, New Year's Eve. The idea of a seasonal, or if you will, cyclical year is pretty well established in our society. I don't foresee any great need or desire to change it, although adopting the metric system may usher in a surprise or two.

No comment on 1976 in terms of the election?

Well, there is this to say, and nobody ever seems to say it: a national election tends to make the end of the year a bit top-heavy, especially here in the New England states. That's probably due to the enormous numbers of people moving to and from the polling places and so forth. Things begin to tilt. You may find the salt and pepper sliding off the table, minor annoyances of that sort.

And the Bicentennial?

This year, definitely. But to a large extent it's already been discounted. I don't think it's any too soon to consider by Bill Conklin

for Forecast

that next year will be the 201st Birthday of the Republic, and to start planning for that. What you've got there is a year you just won't see again. There are committees to be formed, tours to be organized, medals to be struck. A lot went on in 1777, and kept going on right into 1778.

Will you be making any movies in the coming months?

No. I've never made a movie and I never will. There just isn't the time. I have to walk the dog twice a day, for instance, and I could go on from there.

Could you express an opinion on the economy?

I believe what we're seeing these days is that Nature isn't the only one that abhors a vacuum. It may be that — like a biorhebic engine — the economy must sometimes contract to expand, and it may of course be something altogether different. Sometimes it helps to visualize an inverted pyramid, the apex resting lightly in the sand. Pointing to what? Oil? Probably. One thing is certain: the letters GNP are being too much bandied about. The rest of

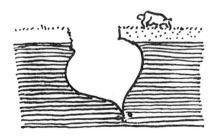

Figure 1 — *Alliaceous depression discovered near Vermont cowbarn.*

11

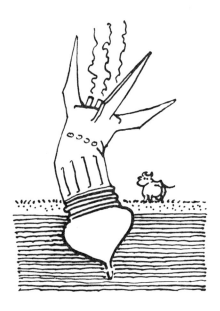

Figure 2 (left) — *Artist's reconstruction of putative onion-headed space vehicle.*
Figure 3 (right) — *The ancient Cathedral of the Dormition, Moscow. Note domes. Their shape, of course, is significant.*

the alphabet just sits there, and that's plainly non-productive. It wouldn't hurt a jot to talk about the TRF once in a while, or the WBD. Just before they took Uncle Silas away he said, "What this country needs is a good five-cent nickel," and I don't see what's so crazy about that.

What about investments over the next six months? Any advice?

Down on Wall Street they say the best time to buy your snowsuit is in July. I tried that once and was the laughing-stock of Lake Winnipesaukee. I've also heard a very profitable thing to do is get a corner on the market and squeeze the Big Boys. After that, there's mutual funds.

How do you plan to spend your own discretionary income this year?

On food, shelter, a good stout pair of boots. The way I see it, you only pass this way once. Why not go first cabin?

Considering Women's Lib, and the elections, this question may not be the cliché it once was. Do you think a woman will be president?

I'll tell you something, a woman has already *been* president. I can't say which one, but you'd recognize the name. Please don't press me on this, for obvious reasons of confidentiality.

All right, let's talk about détente.

Détente is just the tip of the iceberg. So many things are. The tip of an iceberg itself, for example. But look at it this way: if you turn an iceberg upside down, nine-tenths of it will be *above* the surface. Which is some tip. Or look at it this way: Neighbor Jones isn't going to build too big a fire in his fireplace if he knows I've got a pair of heat-seeking andirons.

That's an extremely pragmatic outlook. Do you also have some sort of faith that sustains you?

When I was six years old, I heard a very wise man say, "Tomorrow the farthest mountain will be not one step closer than it is today." I find that an idea with a lot of mileage in it.

Which might bring us to the so-called energy crunch?

Now there we've got to look beyond our fossil fuels, beyond our finite resources, and get our hands onto something big. I'll tell you where it's really hot. Up on the sun. You can fry an egg on the sun. That's simplistic, of course, but heat like that is just waiting to be tapped. Another good source of energy is friction. You've heard of rubbing two sticks together, certainly. But four sticks? Eight sticks? Sixteen sticks? Now you're getting somewhere.

What is your opinion of UFO's, ancient visits from outer space, things of that nature?

I can take you out behind a certain Vermont cowbarn and show you an impression in the earth that exactly matches the contours of a giant Bermuda onion. Now who is to say that at some time in our civilization we weren't visited by onion-shaped spaceships? There are rocks in

New England, minerals and the like, which geologists never have got a good fix on, maybe with reason. Also, we might want to consider some correlation with the onion-shaped domes of the Kremlin. Or the possibility that in this instance the past has quite literally paved the way for the future. Perhaps people wiser than we have prepared this particular landing spot in the knowledge that onion-shaped ships, or creatures resembling huge Bermuda onions, or even giant Bermuda onions themselves, will one day visit us. It's easy enough to scoff and mock, but far better to keep our minds — and our options — open.

There seems to be a continuing interest in what you might call frontiers of the mind, too. The feats of people like Uri Geller, for instance.

Listen, nobody can bend nails better than I can. I've never driven one straight into anything yet. And take this strange sensation psychologists call *déjà vu*. Only last night I walked into our old farmhouse kitchen, and had the uncanny feeling I'd been there before. And I have, you know — many, many times. The point is, it might be the same in Anne Hathaway's Cottage, or the Acropolis, or the Boston Armory. These things are cumulative; you can build on them.

What is your biggest environmental concern at this time?

The Equator. I read recently where they're taking a whole lot of heavy machinery down to the Equator —

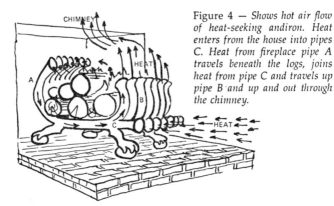

Figure 4 — *Shows hot air flow of heat-seeking andiron. Heat enters from the house into pipes C. Heat from fireplace pipe A travels beneath the logs, joins heat from pipe C and travels up pipe B and up and out through the chimney.*

14

rain-making equipment and earth-moving equipment and so on — and this is dead wrong. Now the Equator is where it is, and as it is, because that's how it's *meant* to be. I'm not just talking about latitude and longitude, I'm talking about a whole lot more. You listen to these smart fellows in Washington — politicians, engineers, what have you — and you get the impression what they're saying is, so what? It's just the Equator. Well, it's not. It's *the* Equator. Mess it up and nobody's going to roll in another one. That's it, boys. That's all she wrote. So we're back to the old qualitative-quantitative bugaboo. Do we want more of an inferior Equator — one that's been artificially rained on, and dug into, and pushed and pulled about — or just the right amount of the Equator Intactus? You figure it out.

On a more positive note, do you visualize any medical or scientific breakthroughs in the immediate future?

I think we're going to learn a good deal more concerning the curious state we call being awake. Science has determined that on the average we spend two-thirds of our life up and about, but nobody can say for sure why, or how, or exactly what good it does us. We're already learning there are several different levels of wakefulness, ranging all the way from wool-gathering to being totally alert. What we need now is for Harvard or Yale or Dartmouth to endow an Awake Institute. Then we'll have some major discoveries. Some people can get by on only three or four hours of being awake each day, while the rest of us seem to require much more. Why is this? We need to know.

One final question, because we see you stuffing things into your briefcase, and generally making leaving motions. If you had to define your philosophy of life in just one word, could you do it?

Certainly.   END

How Not to Run

MY mother never cared a damn about fancy names or titles. Ma and Pop Tolman, as they became known to several thousand who had been their paying guests at one time or another, owned a small inn and summer resort. It was probably, for its size, the best-known in New England for more than half a century.

All business decisions, and most other decisions as well, were made by Ma, who was a law unto herself and unto her ever-loyal husband. So the place never had an official name. Mail designed for the farmhouse, to this day, is variously addressed to Tolman Pond, Tolman Pond Farm, Tolman Farmhouse, or whatnot.

Ma couldn't have cared less. She didn't believe in advertising and never wasted any money on any of that "printed rubbish" such as letterheads or signs. There was never a typewriter in the house until after I was married and had invested in a second-hand portable.

No bookkeeping of any sort was ever done. Once or twice a year, when Ma wanted to know how much they had in their bank account, she would go down to Keene and ask Wallace Mason, the bank president. She wouldn't have trusted the teller.

Whenever guests were about to leave and asked for a bill — for a few days' stay or maybe for a whole summer — Ma would keep them waiting until she was sure she could leave the kitchen stove without burning something, find an old used envelope, and scribble some undecipherable

an Inn

figures with a well-chewed pencil stub. Then she'd say, "It comes to about a hundred and ninety-two dollars, I guess." If they wanted a receipt, they could whistle for it.

I first tried in earnest to improve some of Ma's operating methods when I was about seventeen, and had left school to help with the family business and the farm. I told her the law said that every inn must keep a register, and there was a big fine for violations. "Haven't any time for such nonsense," was all she would say.

I bought a register myself and set it up on a little desk, with pen and ink. Ma promptly took the pen and ink off to her own room and put the register in the pantry for writing down recipes, notes on when the cows were due to freshen, and for a handy source of paper on which to write letters to her friends.

Later efforts at keeping a register, over the years, fared no better. Finally we gave it up.

The more casually Ma treated the clientele, the more popular "Tolman Pond" became. By April, she would have received enough applications for the next summer to fill the place many times over — from people in about every state in the United States, and some from abroad. Most letters she would just say she didn't like the sound of, and heave them into the stove.

Occasionally some family would arrive and ask for a cottage they had reserved, for a month or whatever, long before. Ma would say, "Oh, did I write that you could have

17

it? Well, that's too bad. I must have forgotten. I told the Browns they could have it, and they're all moved in. Why don't you look around over Jaffrey way; there are some nice hotels and things over there." And she would go back into her kitchen, remarking how stupid some people were, coming all the way up from New York without telephoning first.

Perhaps I should say here, before going into detail later, that Ma's contrary nature extended into all other directions as well as the running of an inn. Much as people were attracted by her famous and enormously diversified and inventive cooking, probably they were more attracted by her company. She was a pillar of the church, but could outswear a teamster when it seemed appropriate; a totally undiscriminating reader; a tireless letter-writer; loved all sports; excelled at games, especially any card game known to man; and even in her old age was not above using a certain four-letter word when hard pressed at Scrabble with some of her cronies.

It seemed to put an endless number of people, of all ages and types, in good humor just to hang around her kitchen and the little sitting room adjoining it. Though many always refused when she offered them chocolates. People were forever giving her fancy chocolate assortments, and within the hour they would look as though the mice had been at them. She would have nipped off a bit from each one, just to test the filling.

In younger days, I used to wonder why Ma and Pop always got along so well and seemed so happy together, more so in fact than almost any other couple I knew. It seemed to me there were very great differences in their natures.

For example, Ma was a terrific liar when she chose — such a good one, it wouldn't take her long to convince herself that some outrageous fabrication was actually the truth, because she had decided it should be. She would say that each of the five Turner boys, over in the other end of town, had a different father, because she didn't approve of Mrs. Turner and her ways. Actually, all the boys had squeaky voices, exactly like old Jim Turner's, and they resembled him unmistakably; but this cut no ice at all with Ma, and she stuck to her story for the rest of her life.

Pop, on the other hand, was known far and wide for his scrupulous honesty. Some of his sharper relatives used to imply that he was too honest ever to amount to much, in fact.

Ma's best friends said Pop let her do much more than her share; that he was shiftless, easy-going, and so on. But Pop's intimates thought Ma was domineering and unreasonable, and stingy with their money.

Now, on looking back, I conclude that their great secret asset was an enormously robust sense of humor on both sides. Both could almost always find something funny in almost any situation, however disastrous. And they were as capable of laughing at themselves as at each other.

They had little else to keep them going in the early days, back around 1900. They had fallen in love when Ma came to teach the village school and boarded with Pop's parents at the farm. Barely twenty, she was a popular belle of Milford, her home town, but bent on a teaching career. The wilds of Nelson, with its one-room school of thirty, including some rough and intractable backwoods boys up to eighteen years old, were a challenge. She soon had them licked.

When Ma married my father, she had found a man who had at least a *few* of the qualities she thought any upstanding husband should have. He was handsome, fairly tall, enormously strong with a prizefighter's figure, a local champion at boxing and wrestling and swimming, and good at most other sports. An expert hunter and fisherman. Sang a good bass, played first cornet in the town band, and danced a fine Money Musk. Knew all the tricks of farming and wood-and-timber cutting. Was a skilled carpenter, cabinetmaker, and builder. Inventive and had a knack for machinery. Never lost his temper and had no excessive bad habits. But more important, he never seemed to mind being given enough commands by his wife, every day of his life, to keep three men busy.

Still, Ma always found plenty to criticize — why hadn't he fixed the hen house roof yet, and when was he going to build a new cold frame for her kitchen garden, and why hadn't he finished hauling sawdust to pack the icehouse? And he smoked his pipe too much, spent too much time telling stories to the boarders, and so on and on.

However, Pop was in plenty of good company when it came to Ma's criticism. For nobody escaped it. Friends, relatives, neighbors, even characters in the books she read. Even the paying guests. Ma could find something to criticize about anybody in the world, except herself.

The wonder is, how seldom anybody objected. The guests she complained about most often and openly were likely to be those who came back year after year.

Their first several years on the farm must have been a life of unimaginable hardships for Ma and Pop. The cultivated fields had long been abandoned, and the barns and outbuildings were mostly beyond repair. The only way Pop could pay off a $500 mortgage was by working ten-hour days in a sawmill, five miles down the road, for a dollar a day.

Ma worked on the farm at times, besides doing the housework. She could milk five or six cows, split hardwood for the kitchen stove, and pitch hay. Pop built a big new barn, cutting and sawing all the timber himself. Ma used the four bedrooms and the attic for the boarders in summer, and often had a few in winter too, in spite of no plumbing and few comforts of any kind. And so began what Ma called (to the embarrassment of my brother and me, when we were growing up) "the boarding business."

In those days Ma had a fine figure, though, in terms of a later day, rather full; thick, wavy hair, waistlong; a marvelously fine-featured face, with perfect teeth, wide blue eyes, and a natural peaches-and-cream complexion she would retain into her eighties.

Few guests at the farm could equal her at swimming, tennis, horsemanship, snowshoeing, even mountain climbing over on Monadnock. Evenings, she would lead off in the social activity — games, singing, amateur theatricals, dancing, or whatever. She must often have shocked the puritanical and prim ladies of the town beyond words. But as she also outdid them in church affairs — choir, Sunday school, church suppers — they seldom dared to be heard even grumbling in her presence.

It would be interesting to hear Ma's reaction to the welter of sexual-study books of recent years, had she lived to read them. To Ma, any and all forms of sex presented no problems whatsoever, so long as people had "common sense." (For that matter, all the world's problems, in her view, were caused solely by lack of common sense; though she herself, in several ways at least, possessed none at all.)

Besides having to help with the breeding and the births of the farm animals, the facts about human sex were never concealed from my brother and me in our infancy. It was just "common sense." And this was at a time, in local society, when a typical neighboring farm-wife would refer to their bull, in whispered tones, as "the creature."

Ma and Pop always slept in a double bed, until Pop died

at near eighty. When I was small, sometimes in winter my bed would be placed in their room to save space. Ma never bothered about blowing out the lamps until they were completely undressed and climbing into bed. Sometimes in the night I would hear Ma's voice, which though of a very musical and pleasing character, could be clearly heard even when she thought she was whispering. "Wayland, wake up! Move over here to me, my back is cold . . ."

But though Ma's language could be frank regarding sex, it was never what she called "coarse talk." Grammie Harris, who worked for us in times of sickness and other emergencies, had only one fault in Ma's opinion — she used "coarse expressions." And indeed, when Grammie would regale us at mealtimes, telling all the details of how she caught her ne'er-do-well husband up in the haymow with one of the Grady girls, her terminology was gamier than a Norman Mailer story.

Ma would never say anything to Grammie, but afterward she'd tell us that if we ever used some of those words, she would wash out our mouths with soap. And she would add that Grammie was a wonderful, fine woman, but just didn't know any better because she "came from a very low family in Fitchburg."

One spring, Ma positively refused to renew the lease on a cottage occupied the summer before by a highly popular New York family, of the sort who would be regarded as "ideal clientele." When I intervened with all the heated persuasion I could manage, it turned out Ma hadn't liked the way the kids' nurse — a very nice girl, incidentally — had "cottoned up" on the beach to one of the boys who worked at the farm. Ma wouldn't budge, and the cottage was rented to somebody else, whom nobody liked very well.

In contrast, another incident occurred some time after Pop's death, when Ma was in her late seventies. An attractive young divorcée had been spending some winter months at the farm, and was soon having a passionate affair with a chap who lived nearby.

One week they would be planning marriage, and the next they wouldn't be on speaking terms. Both were quite temperamental and what might be called rather unstable emotionally.

One night, after Ma had been asleep several hours, the girl crept into Ma's room and waked her. "I'm so scared I just don't know what to do, Ma," she said, weeping. "Bob says he's going to kill me — he hit me, and I ran down here, and he's looking all over the house, trying to find me . . ."

"That's all right, dear," Ma said. "Just crawl under my bed and stay quiet."

So the girl crawled under the bed, and Ma went out and called to Bob. There was nobody else in the house at the time. When he appeared, still yelling and stamping around, Ma told him she thought the girl had got her coat and gone out for a walk, and added, "Now you shut up and go straight home, and please don't wake me up at this hour again, chasing around the house!"

"Okay, Ma, I'm sorry," he said meekly, and left.

Telling me about it afterward, she said, "I guess they were just having one of their little tiffs, you know — it didn't amount to anything. Anyway, I got her all dusted off and cheered up after she came out from under my bed, and then I told her to go upstairs and forget all about it."

By the mid-30s, there had been many changes at Tolman Pond since the first automobile arrived in 1900 (a Stanley Steamer bringing the Titus family from Lynn, Massachusetts, for their first summer vacation at the farm). Various ells and wings had been added over the years, connecting the original house, with its big central chimney, to the barn. On the front side, the general Colonial character of the place had been kept; but from the rear it looked like the House of a Hundred and Seven Gables, with several more chimneys and all sorts of dormers added.

There were a dozen summer cottages, most of them housekeeping units. There were nine winterized bedrooms for guests, a dormitory, about three and a half bathrooms, and a ski lounge. My brother had installed a rope-tow on the ski slope I had cleared some years before. He had built his house up in the old pasture, and I was leaving the business to build my own house on another part of the farm.

The place was now filled to capacity much of the year, with a never-ending waiting list, and Ma was feeding from thirty to sixty. She had grudgingly, at long last, consented to hiring a regular staff to help her; this usually consisted of one woman-of-all-work, a stalwart character named Mabel. In summer, there were tenants whose grandparents had once rented their cottages, and whose own grandchildren would also be doing so in years to come.

Ma's methods, however, had not changed in the slightest, nor would they ever. Still no register, no prepared bills, and no bookkeeping. She would invariably address Dr. Knight as "Mr. Day," the Gillespies as the "Gellipsies," and similarly mangle many another name. Long-term guests who happened to go away for a night or two were likely, on returning, to find their beds occupied by total strangers.

When Mabel, irked at a woman who kept coming into the kitchen to complain about something, hit her in the rear with a well-aimed piece of stovewood, Ma took Mabel's part in the ensuing hassle. The woman left.

"Dinner" was still served in the middle of the day, old

farm-style "supper" at 6:30. Many guests had complained loudly about this for a long time, as had my brother and myself in our utterly futile efforts to "modernize" the establishment. But such was the genius of Ma's cooking, probably no guest actually ever left because of her arbitrary schedule. As for breakfast, if you missed it at 8:00, you could forage around in the kitchen for whatever you could find — but Ma wouldn't give you much help.

One spring a chauffeur-driven limousine pulled up at the farm, and an enormously stout and stately dowager emerged. She was looking for a possible lodging for some friends she was expecting later, and Ma told her to go ahead and look around as much as she liked.

The poor woman happened to step on a rotten board in a neglected section of the porch. One leg went straight down, just about to the hip, while the other slid forward. She was cast as solidly as our old mare the time her hind leg went down through the stable trapdoor. The chauffeur couldn't budge her, and there was nobody else around the house. Ma finally found Al, a painfully shy farm boy of around eighteen, who was working nearby.

"Come quick, Al," Ma yelled at the top of her voice. "There's a fat woman stuck in the porch — get a saw!"

When Al appeared with the saw and beheld the awful prospect of the task he was supposed to perform, he nearly defected, but Ma spoke firmly. "Just saw around her leg, Al," she commanded, "and then get her out of there!"

So Al started sawing, and when the woman was freed, he and the chauffeur and Ma heaved her up on her feet.

"It only scratched her leg a little," Ma said afterward. "I told her she should thank her lucky stars she hadn't been really hurt, but she went off in a huff. Good riddance." Then she added, "But oh, my goodness, she did look *so funny*, with that big flowered hat, sitting down on the floor

— and I had to keep telling poor Al to open his eyes, so he wouldn't saw right into her leg . . ."

Ma could afford to say good riddance, when she took the notion. We were starting to get reservations a year or more in advance. We had many doctors and professional people of all sorts — well-known writers, artists, musicians, movie stars, business people; there were also generals, admirals, ambassadors, and even Rumanian royalty.

Ma was not in the least impressed by such clientele. And to prove it, she would frequently turn away someone willing to pay three times what she usually asked, and accept some character like the Brooklyn ward-heeler we called, for some reason, Old Eaglebottom. He was a Damon Runyon type who wore shirts minus their collars, murdered the king's English, and pained the old Bostonians at the dinner table with off-color jokes.

Or again, Ma would refuse an offer of $400 rent for a cottage, and let it go to some impoverished school teachers for $200, "Because they're such nice people." Whenever I tried to remonstrate, she would say, "Well, it's my business, and I'll run it my own way. I won't have much longer to live anyway, and after I'm gone you can do as you please." Thirty years later, long after I had given up on trying to take an active part in the business, she was saying exactly the same thing.

Ma, though strong as a horse, was something of a hypochondriac. She was forever taking endless pills, patent medicines, and horrible-looking brews of various herbs which sat around on the pantry shelves between bowls of sauce, cake icings, and homemade cottage cheese.

Her only physical ills, actually, came from being greatly overweight. She could never resist, between meals, frequent tastings of all the rich dishes she was concocting. Not to mention the chocolates.

During and after World War II, Ma heard often from sometime-Tolman Pond guests who had run into others, in Europe, Africa, and the South Pacific, and just about everywhere else. No traveler herself, she was no more interested than as if they had met at the post office in Harrisville, New Hampshire.

Ma always had a number of kids of all ages around the place, sent by their trusting parents either to board or work part-time, and she usually took one or two city kids who couldn't afford to pay.

She certainly had a way with kids, but it wasn't derived from reading books in this field. To begin with, she never treated any two alike — she always played favorites, and blamed anything that went wrong on the ones she liked least, whether they were guilty or not. Any sort of plan or rules agreed upon in advance, she would often change without notice.

Complaints were never listened to. The most Ma would ever say to a kid with a grievance was, "Just use a little common sense, and you'll be all right! Now don't bother me, I'm too busy." Except for the rather haphazard work program, the kids all did just about anything they pleased.

In 1928, Danny McKay, thirteen, was sent up from New Jersey to spend the summer. Danny was a precocious little genius and full of hell. He arrived wearing only shorts, sandals, and a vivid pink shirt he had dyed himself. He was smoking a meerschaum pipe, and carrying a small bag and a huge round can full of tobacco.

He announced that he was a Communist, and whenever he was within earshot of the older and stuffier guests would launch into long diatribes against the evils of capitalism. This was obviously a routine he had thought up to enliven his summer, and it worked quite well. People were soon complaining to Ma about that terrible boy. But

Ma's only reaction (she didn't know nor care what Communism was all about) was to remark that anyone silly enough to let a spoiled brat of thirteen upset them, deserved it.

It seems symbolic of Ma's many-faceted nature that she was known by different names to her old friends, depending on their preference — Sarah, Sis, Sally, Saidie, Sade, Ma. Ma and Pop were not displeased when their small grandchildren took to calling them "Waylie" and "Sade." And when finally there were great-grandchildren staying with her, she was alternately scolding them and spoiling them, contrary as ever.

It is now several years after Ma's death and the end of Tolman Pond as an inn, a place of food and lodging, and whatever else it was called under her regime of more than 60 years. Yet we still get occasional letters from people who want to come back and stay at the farm. They seem to think it should have gone on forever, just as it was when Ma was there.   END

by Dwight Tracy

Please Send Eighty Thousand ...

IT was the time of unparalleled excitement throughout our otherwise drowsy Connecticut hills. The seed catalogs were starting to come in. Families who hadn't exchanged complete sentences since first snow united again to haggle over hybrids. Plant flats were resurrected from cellars; seedbeds were prepared; and hothouses were shoveled out and cleaned off.

We get pretty worked up about the annual catalog arrival on a couple of counts. Most of all it means that somewhere, somebody out there sincerely believes that winter is going to quit. He's even willing to bet money on it. And secondly, most of the frost-bitten residents genuinely look forward to once again putting in more vegetables than they're ever going to be able to use. But this year, above it all rose one stolid, disinterested figure. Me. After the succession of blight, bug, and bog disasters that have befallen every planting attempt at our place, Barren Acres, I'd had it. In fact I didn't even intend to *open* this year's catalog. Unfortunately, I was to weaken in the resolve. Its colorful cover proved irresistible, and I — sadly — opened. But though foolish, I hadn't turned completely stupid, for the opening was carefully gauged to miss the vegetable section. Instead of exposing myself to that temptation, I looked only at the back section of the lure.

Great heavens! Why hadn't I studied those rear pages years ago? Right there below my trembling finger was the perfect answer to land utilization, a plethora of profit for the pocket and pleasure to the eye. Said the sure-to-be-honest copy:

"From *this* (picture of hand holding skinny seedling) to *this* (photo of man being overwhelmed by monster Christmas tree) in just four to five years."

All remembrances of past failures instantly evaporated. In my mind row upon unbroken row of handsomely shaped Christmas trees stretched out over the property. Looking down what passes for our driveway, I could see a stampede of wealthy tree seekers and wholesale buyers charging the house. They were, of course, waving money and shouting bids.

Two thousand trees to the acre was the recommended planting. Well why hold it to an acre? Why not plant the entire back 40? The minor fact that the back 40 is indeed the whole property made little difference. Nor was I dismayed because the ground already contained trees — big trees, like solid woods. I had never done any clearing to trees, like solid woods. I had never done any clearing to speak of. But, after all, our fathers had obviously been able to do a heck of a lot of it, and with considerable less equipment than I owned. No, in the face of the vast promise of the great Christmas tree project, any petty problems such as the removal of some woods were beneath consideration. I immediately placed an order: Please send 80,000 Scotch pines.

Figuring to have a month or two to cut down the existing trees, I set to work the following Saturday. Perhaps the chain saw wasn't feeling well that day. Certainly I wasn't too healthy by about noon myself. But at any rate the day's work amounted to three multi-trunked soft maples cut down and sawed into firewood length. And that still left the brush to be dragged. The total area cleared measured 11 by 18 feet. That left approximately 17,486 trees still standing on the property. Several things became apparent. We would have a surplus of firewood. We would face a superfluity of brush. What we would not have would be the space to plant 80,000 Christmas trees.

Two days later a card arrived from the nursery people announcing that exactly 80,000 trees were on the way. A frantic call brought the frosty news that the trees, once shipped, could not be returned. Some lightning calculations revealed that I'd have to plant at least an acre of trees, have them grow from that to this in four to five years, all mature beautifully, and all sell for top dollar just to break even on the project. And what I had was our 11 by 18 area. Or at least I would have it if somebody dragged the brush away.

But never mind, I assured my now alarmed family, we still had space for the break-even trees . . . the lawn . . . the flower beds . . . that strip beside the driveway reserved for a future rock garden . . . and the dog run. Anyway, who was to know that the trees would be shipped so promptly, or that removing 40 acres of woods would prove so time consuming — to say nothing of impossible.

A few fast evenings of sawing and I had enlarged the initial planting area to 11 by 23. Also I had built nine brush piles for the birds and other wildlife and singed my eyebrows and used up a not-too-bad set of snow tires burning the remainder. Good thing I wasn't one of my forefathers. Boy, would we have had a small farm!

Next, as forewarned, the trees arrived. Does anyone out there have any idea of what 80,000 future Christmas trees look like? Well, to save your patience and cut down on my wordage, they look like 80 shipping boxes, each labeled IMPORTANT! PLANT AT ONCE! Had I planted at once each unopened box there wouldn't have been enough room for all of them.

After removing all the seats from our four-wheel drive, we were able to get all the trees back home from the express office in only eleven trips. Admittedly, there was a bit of cheating. I gave the agent 1,000 trees to plant outside his office. Haven't been back since, but if he got them all in, the effect must be amazing.

Anyway, it took two days' hauling to simply get the trees to Barren Acres. When we opened the boxes (which in itself took three hours) the trees appeared somewhat parched. Noting their condition with the usual command of a forester, I ordered my wife to soak down all the boxes with a hose. The result was 79 soggy boxes. The trees looked as if they didn't care much one way or another.

First we set out to plant the intitial area. Even the children were present to help with putting in the first tree. They absented themselves by the fourth. By planting a scant three by three feet apart, we tucked 45 trees into the space, leaving only 78,955 for the lawn et al.

The planting system for four-inch-high pines is simple.

A drawing on the shipping box explains all. One has only to dig a shallow V trench, stick the tree in one side, and stomp back the divot. Fine. Except the idea doesn't work well when there are huge stones close to the surface of the ground. There are, we discovered upon digging shallow V trenches, huge stones close to the surface of all our ground. Many of our trenches came up shallow indeed. Planting a tree in one half inch of soil isn't difficult. But convincing oneself that it is supposed to be lying flat on the ground with half its root system exposed after planting gets a little tough.

Sticking trees into the lawn proved considerably easier. That is, it proved considerably easier than convincing my wife that the house would look great in the middle of a forest.

"Temporary inconvenience," I assured her. "Why in just four to five years they'll grow from that to this (arms spread to maximum extension). Anyhow we have to put them somewhere in a big hurry."

Fortunately the lawn itself was kind, and spacious. It accepted 756 trees. That left us with a mere 78,199 unplanted. The ex-lawn proved to be the biggest taker. The flower beds beside the parking area held only 71 trees. The driveway strip went for 193, and the dog's run took 36. They'll grow faster, though So that left us with 77,899 Scotch pines about to shuffle off this mortal coil. They're hardy trees, and it was a good nursery, but everything has its limits, and we'd just about exceeded the little trees'. Toward the end of the organized planting some of the weaker trees fell by the wayside even as they were being planted. It was the stomping back of the dirt in the trench that did it. Stomp. Crash, all the needles fell off — instant miniature hatrack. Maybe I had let the little trees get a bit dry after all.

While my wife continued to hose down the ruined remnants of the remaining 77 boxes, I staggered off into the woods clutching bailed bushels of the survivors, searching for likely clearings. At first I planted trees only in large, woods-less areas. But as the woods filled and my bushels emptied, I became far less persnickity. If I could wedge myself and my baskets between two tree trunks, the resulting path came to count as a clearing. I planted them in the middle of blackberry patches, between giant roots, underneath barberry bushes, next to stone walls and even in the moss-filled crotches of a couple of dead elms.

Altogether we got rid of 11,718 Christmas trees in the woods. And inside of a week that's just about the number of Christmas trees the deer, or somebody, ate.

Of the remaining 66,181 trees, 10,000 were given away to unsuspecting neighbors, and 56,181 were quietly interred in a large peaceful pit beside the bulldozer that dug it.

With chaos and ruination raining down upon me, I figured there was little else to do but take darn good care of the 1,101 trees actually safely in the ground. Accordingly, I spent every spare minute carting pots, pans, and buckets of water out to the living. Spring came on full blast, and under the impetus of the extra water the grass and weeds grew splendidly. But the trees didn't. After awhile it began to look as if they were waiting for that fourth or fifth year to make the spurt that would bring them to their legendary size. The fact was that they were going to have to go some just to reach viewable size, for before we were even out of May the little trees had become invisible in the grass. In some desperation I commenced weeding around them. In the process I inadvertently plucked the limbs of 22 of the midget pines, thus diverting their future status from Christmas trees to possible telephone poles.

And so it was that we had 1,079 known survivors at the beginning of the Week of the Great Rains. The V trenches along several slopes hadn't healed, and before long erosion was taking its toll of sod, soil, and Christmas trees. We lost 349.

Forty-one more of the existing 730 trees succumbed to natural causes during the following month. And one, located directly under the bird feeder, was pecked to death by a confused hairy woodpecker after a lump of suet fell next to it.

Most of the remaining 688 Christmas trees were in fairly good shape. And they might have remained that way, hidden as they were deep in the waving grass of our former lawn. They would have stayed, that is, if we hadn't left the house and property in the care of some well-intentioned but uninformed friends while we took a much-needed vacation, away from the watering duties. Because we didn't like to talk about the project, we neglected to say why the lawn was so high. Seeking to please, our guests mowed it.

And that is why there will be no Christmas trees for sale at Barren Acres in the appointed four or five years.

In fact there may not be a Barren Acres by then. My latest calculations concern the annual cost of failures versus the return from describing them. According to the figures, I'm due to become extinct in three years. We've bought a vinyl tree to hold us until then.   END

A Trotting Race on

"THE most exciting harness race I ever saw? Heck, young fellow, they've *all* been exciting!"

Jed Parker produced a slab of eating tobacco, keen blue eyes twinkling at me as he stuffed his lean gray-bristled jaw. "I've seen 'em all, trotters and pacers alike, county fair and Grand Circuit, for nigh on to sixty years now. *Any* good horse race is the most exciting you ever saw, far's remembering's concerned. Because every good race is a battle of speed and wits, and every race is different. Now if you'd asked me what race gives me the most *fun* remembering —"

Jed paused to splatter the exact center of the glowing chunk stove with an amber stream of tobacco juice. I held my breath, waiting. In the mood, Jed was a gifted story teller. Pure magic to a harness-horse lover, these winter afternoons in the little "office" tucked away in one corner of the veteran trainer's horse-barn.

"Happened way back in ninety-seven," Jed went on after a moment of dreamy introspection. "First time I ever see the best horse lose the race — though not the last time, by a long shot. I was just a young buck working around the country as a hired hand in them days, and in the fall of ninety-six I got a job with this fellow Lonny Frazier over on the Connecticut River. He had a nice place right on the water, and a couple of darn good trotters. Blacks, both of 'em. About fifteen hands each and slick as trout. Lonny made some of the best applejack brandy I ever tasted —

by Norman B. Wiltsey

the Connecticut

though I wan't never what you could rightly call a drinking man.

"Long about the middle of December that year the
weather got real cold and stayed that way for three weeks.
The ice got good and thick on the river, and right away
Lonny got the itch for some ice racing. Settin' around Ase
Hopkins' store nights, he started blowing away loud and
reckless about his two trotters, Black Star and Midnight,
and I knew 'twas only a matter of time before somebody
called him. 'Why,' says Lonny, 'there ain't a horse in this
here whole county that stands a chance against either of
mine on the ice. And I got a hundred dollars that says so!'
Then he'd look around for somebody to contradict him,
but for more'n a week nobody did.

"Brad Myers drove in to the store one Wednesday night
and was settin' there behind the stove when Lonny and me
dropped in around eight o'clock. Brad owned a big bay
trotter called Iron Duke that was real fast from all accounts, and I looked for some fun when Lonny started
bragging about *his* horses. I wan't disappointed. Pretty
soon Lonny got off his spiel about owning the two best ice
trotters in the country, and Brad looked him over
scornful-like. 'Big talk, but I don't hear any money mentioned,' says Brad.

"Lonny liked to choke on the cracker he was eating.
'Would a hundred dollars interest you?' he wheezes
finally.

" 'Chicken-feed,' grins Brad. 'Make it two hundred and I'll race you.'

" 'Done — before you get cold feet and back out altogether!' snaps Lonny. They kept yapping away at each other till Ase shut up the store at nine-thirty and told 'em to go hire a hall if they wanted to argue all night. Lonny was still fuming and stewing when we got home. 'I got to beat that blow-hard, Jed,' he says over and over. 'I got to beat him, no matter how!'

"Next morning Brad shows up with his team hitched to a scraper, and I got out Lonny's team and went along with Brad to the river. The agreement was that both parties had to share equal in the work of scraping a half-mile straight track on the ice. They was to race half a mile to a red flag set up in the ice, turn, and race back. There was to be a half-hour rest period between heats — race to be decided best two heats out of three.

"The race was set for the following Saturday afternoon at one o'clock. By eleven on Saturday morning folks began coming in — on foot and in cutters and sleighs. News of the match race and the two hundred dollar bet had spread around the township, attracting people from miles around. Brad Myers drove in early so he could rest his horse awhile before the race. Iron Duke was real trim and racy-looking and some of the fellows thought he'd have too much bottom for Lonny's smaller Black Star. Others figgered the Duke was too long-legged for ice racing. The two horses had never met and neither had a mark, so you couldn't get a line on 'em that way. Of course Lonny and Brad each claimed *his* horse was a world-beater on the ice, and that didn't make the picking any easier. Soon there was plenty of betting and arguing goin' on all over the place.

"By noon there was near thirty men gathered in Lonny's

barn, waiting for the race to start. Some of 'em had brought flasks along, and seeing the drinking seemed to give Lonny an idea. 'Jed,' he says, 'sneak down into the cellar by the outside stairs and fetch up that keg of apple-jack we ain't opened yet. Don't let Priscilla hear you or she'll chase you out of the cellar with a broom.'

"I knew enough about Priscilla, Lonny's wife, to be mighty careful about making noises in the cellar. Priscilla was a big husky woman and a real hard-shell Baptist who believed horse racing and applejack drinking was sinful. Lord, she had a tongue like a bowie knife! Many's the time I'd heard her bawling Lonny out for wasting his time mak-ing brandy or fooling around with trotters when he should have been working his land. Lonny kept his mouth shut while she was jawing at him, I can tell you that. Priscilla outweighed him by more'n forty pounds and he wan't taking any chances!

"I lugged the keg up the outside stairs without Priscilla hearing a thing. I carried it out to the wagon-house where everybody was hanging around, and Lonny bustled over and says hearty-like, 'Set it up here on the work-bench, Jed, so all my good friends can have a warming drink on this cold day.' Knowing how Lonny loved his applejack I thought he'd lost his mind for sure, but I did what he said.

"At quarter to one the keg was maybe half-empty but everybody was feeling fine, hooting and laughing and having one hell of a good time. Everybody but Brad and Lonny and me. I'd had one jolt of that liquid lightning and neither Lonny nor Brad had touched a drop. We started for the river at ten minutes to one, and Lonny himself brought along the applejack.

"The temperature was well below freezing and some of the crowd built a fire on the river bank opposite the start-ing line, which was also where the hosses would finish.

The boys put the keg in the back of a sleigh near the fire. I saw Brad toss off a quick snort just before he climbed into his skeleton sleigh for the first heat. Lonny still hadn't tasted the stuff. I couldn't make him out. He kept jogging Black Star around in a circle and watching Brad like a hawk.

"They got away from a standing start at the word GO! Right off the bat Lonny shot Black Star into the lead. All the way to the flag he led Brad and the Duke, first by one length, then by two. The little horse skittered around the flag like a rabbit with a hound on his tail. Lonny straightened him out in a hurry and started fanning his hide with the gad. Back they come a-whopping — Lonny driving like a wild man and swinging that whip like his arm was a piston on a steam engine. Brad's big horse closed fast in the last eighth of a mile, but Lonny had grabbed too long a lead and Black Star lasted to win by half a length. Nobody had bothered to clock the heat, but they must have stepped that mile in close to two-thirty. Real good time, considering that they'd got away from a standin' start and had to slow up to round the flag at the half-mile mark.

"Lonny had practically stole the first heat by getting the jump on Brad and belting the stuffing out of a good game trotter to keep it. Now he had a mighty tired horse on his hands and I couldn't see how in thunder he could win another heat with him. It was doggone certain that Iron Duke was in better shape right now than Black Star. I figgered that Lonny's two hundred was good as gone. Still, the foxy old cuss had taken one heat and you couldn't tell what new trick he had up his sleeve for the next one. The crowd seemed to feel that way too, for there wan't much betting going on now. Them fellows that had bet against Lonny seemed pretty uneasy and they watched him right respectful-like as he drove past 'em.

"The drivers pulled up their horses and swung back toward the fire. Brad — looking mad as hops — climbed out of his sleigh, tied the Duke, threw a blanket on him, and made a bee-line for the applejack. Lonny jest set there in his sleigh watching Brad and smiling to himself. Brad had one shot and come back to his hoss, untied him and started jogging him around to keep his legs limbered up. Lonny scowled and drove off, swearing under his breath.

"In the second heat Brad was ready for Lonny's smart trick of stealing a winning jump at the start. At the word, he hit the Duke a gosh-awful belt with the gad and kept his nose pinned on Black Star's tail right through to the flag. The rangy bay lost a length on the turn, but once he got straightened out he come storming on like a champion. Half-way to the finish line he caught the tiring Black Star and come away fast to win by four lengths.

"Brad hopped out of his sleigh like a boy, laughing out loud. 'Hey, you old buzzard, how about slapping another hundred on that slow freight of yours?' he yelled at Lonny. Damned if Lonny didn't take him up! Seeing him throw away good money after bad on a played-out trotter made me sick to my stomach. Nobody was afraid to bet against him now. Men crowded around his sleigh shaking greenbacks in his face and the old fool covered 'em all till his money run out. Then the boys headed back to the keg to celebrate their sucker bets. Everybody, including me, thought that poor old Lonny had gone crazy, laying nearly a thousand dollars on a beaten horse.

"I noticed the boys had begun to tip the keg to get a drink, so I walked over to have one more nip while I could. Lonny tied and blanketed his hoss and come after me. The weather was fast getting colder but a slug of that brandy made you feel like you'd swallowed a hot brick. Lonny downed half a cupful, then poked me in the ribs. 'What's up?' I says.

" 'Shut up, you long-legged fool!' he whispers. 'Walk back to the horse with me — and keep quiet about it!'

"Now the old man's gone completely loony, I thought to myself. Might as well humor him — some day I'll be old and childish myself.

"We walked back to where Black Star was tied to the back of a cutter. Lonny took the rope off his bridle, folded up his blanket and climbed into the sleigh. 'Get in,' he says, 'don't stand there gawping!' I got in, settin' almost in Lonny's lap, the speed sleigh was that narrow. We went dashing back toward the barn and Lonny starts talking — fast. 'Listen careful now and don't say a word till I get through. I can't win this race with this hoss I'm driving, so I'm changing to Midnight for the next heat.'

"I was flabbergasted. 'Gosh, Lonny, you can't pull a trick like that! Why them blacks of yours ain't marked alike. Black Star's got a blaze in his forehead —'

" 'So's Midnight now!' cackles Lonny. 'I painted one on him early this mornin' before the folks arrived. Didn't think it was really necessary, but I hate to take chances where money's involved. Brad's got enough jack in him now so's he won't notice any difference. Leastwise, that's the way I figure.'

"I was plumb dazed at the old rascal's deviltry. 'It — it ain't exactly honest —'

" 'Honest, hell!' Lonny roars. 'Them tinhorns back there was fast enough to bet *me* when they figured *I* was the sucker. 'Tain't *my* lookout if they get so likkered up that they can't tell two hosses apart. All's fair in a horse race, young fellow, and don't you ever forget it!'

"I didn't agree with him — then — but I needed a job till spring, so I kept quiet.

"We had Black Star back in his stall and Midnight hitched up in his place in about three minutes flat. We got back to the river well before the half-hour time limit was up, and I swear to Goshen that not one of that hooting, merry crowd had even noticed that we'd been away! They was all too busy squeezing out the last few drops of apple-jack and adding up the money they was due to win from Lonny soon as his hoss lost one more heat.

"Lonny got Midnight off in front in the third and deciding heat and the snappy-going little black hit the flag a good length and a half ahead of the Duke. The big hoss was stiffened a mite from the cold, but comin' back he warmed up and fought his way up even about a quarter of a mile from the finish. He didn't get past, for this time he was racing a fresh trotter. Head and head they stepped for two hundred yards or so, while the boys went hog-wild with excitement. Then, little by little, game old Duke dropped back and Midnight come on under the gad to win."

Jed stopped to select a ruddy Northern Spy from the ever-present bowl of apples on his ancient desk. He bit into it hugely. I waited while he chewed, slowly and appreciatively.

"Did Lonny get paid off on his bets?" I ventured finally.

Jed's blue eyes crinkled with silent laughter as he swallowed. "Sure did — nine hundred dollars worth! Damned old scoundrel wasn't a bit ashamed of the way he won it, either. Matter of fact, he felt so all-fired good about it he shelled out twenty dollars to me and gave Priscilla ten to buy herself a new dress for church!"   END

Grandmothers

GRANDMOTHERS were an early invention. Originally a baby had no fun. Father was afraid he would break, and Mother was afraid he would get smothered. They had each read a book about the care of infants and they wore clocks strapped to their wrists so that they would not speak to Baby except at proper intervals. Life was dull for Baby. He needed a pal. So grandmothers were rolled off the assembly line.

Grandmothers are made of guardian angel, cookies, new permanent waves, clean handkerchiefs, pennies and laps. They vary in seating capacity but all of them, summer and winter, keep two quarts of guardian angel ready for emergency.

When Baby cries Grandmother says one of three things.
1. "I think he's hungry."
2. "I think he has a pain."
3. "I think he has a pin sticking into him."

Grandmother and Baby make an antiphonal dirge out of his crying and her explanation of it. They wear down Mother's determination to let him "cry it out."

Then Grandmother and Baby chuckle together as they rock.

When Baby is three years old, he decides to spend his nap-time either making a pinhole in his hot water bottle and squirting streams around his crib, or emptying the talcum powder into the shoes in the closet, or throwing the bottles on the bureau out the open window into a snowbank.

by H.L.D.

Grandmother becomes a priority need. Baby looks at Mother and yells for Grandmother.

She says just one thing. "I don't think the child is well."

Usually it helps.

Aged ten, Baby brings his gang to clean up the cookies, he keeps a snake in his room, experiments in the cellar with chemistry, learns to play the clarinet by ear, brings home stray puppies, collects cuspidors, discovers the use of stink bombs, breaks a window a month in the house next door, borrows the typewriter to run a newspaper, buys candy with his Sunday School money, makes three-cornered tears in new pants, will not wash his ears.

Mother says, "???"

Father says, "!!!!!"

Grandmother says, "Boys will be boys."

When Baby is thirteen years old and five feet, seven inches tall, he washes the front of his ears only. He will not study and he is too lazy to answer the doorbell and he argues and he argues and he argues.

Father is sure the baby is a good-for-nothing with criminal tendencies.

Mother still loves him, but she lies awake nights.

But not Grandmother. She knows better. She says, "He has grown *so* fast."

Baby has a cake with sixteen candles. He is five feet, eleven inches tall, and he gets a license to drive.

Two weeks later when a cop gives him a ticket, Mother says, "It's a good thing. He drives too fast."

Grandmother says, "I love to ride with him."

Father says, "Will he *ever* learn to be decently polite?"

Grandmother says, "He is very thoughtful of *me*." And she slips the baby a smile with a dollar bill in it.

His teachers say, "He's a bright boy, if he'd only study."

Grandmother says, "When he passes his College Boards I'm going to give him something pretty nice."

Baby is nineteen.

"Did you ever dream he'd belong to your fraternity?" Mother asks Father.

"Not since he was two," says Father.

"At the Club I am told that the girls think his manners are wonderful," says Mother.

"I suppose he might actually make the Dean's List," says Father.

Grandmother doesn't say a word, but she hides a smile with her knitting.

Suddenly the baby is Graduation Orator at Hale and voted the most popular man in his class.

Seven girls are hoping he will take them to the Prom.

The newspaper prints his picture.

Baby's mother looks as if she would burst with pride. Father looks as if he were trying not to look as if he would burst with pride. Grandmother is proud to look proud.

"What did I always tell you?" Grandmother says. END

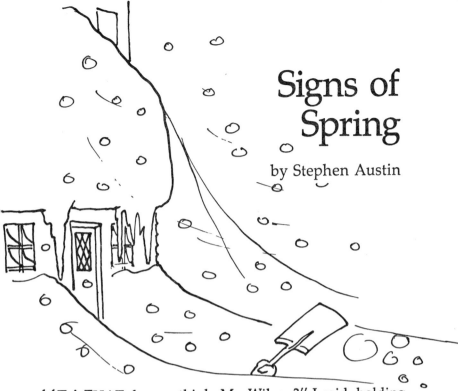

Signs of Spring

by Stephen Austin

"WHAT do you think, Mr. Wilcox?" I said, holding my hand up and catching two lazy snowflakes. "Do you think we're in for a storm?"

I'd just come back from my 11:00 class at Tufts. It was March in the year 1956, and Mr. Wilcox was out sweeping the light dusting of snow from his steps. Mr. Wilcox was my neighbor in Cambridge — a misplaced countryman of some sixty years — a pure type, complete with a hand-me-down philosophy, and a nature of illimitable goodwill, lightly glazed with a layer of crustiness.

He set his broom down against his house and straightened his back, as if he'd been chopping wood for hours. He lifted his head back like an old bear and sniffed once, shortly.

"See the smoke coming out of Cranston's chimney?"

I allowed as how I did.

"Well, when you see smoke actin' like that, it means it's going to clear — won't amount to a thing," he said. "I'd give another fifteen minutes — maybe half an hour." And with that he went back to his work.

It snowed all afternoon.

And it was still snowing hard at 4:00 when my wife asked me to walk down and get some groceries at the corner store.

Mr. Wilcox was out shoveling his steps.

"Hi, Mr. Wilcox," I said. "Really coming down to beat the band, isn't it?" He didn't say anything. He kept at it, taking nice clean bites with his shovel. He was working the bottom step, but the top step, the one he'd started on, was already white again.

"Do you think it's going to keep up like this?" I asked finally.

Still no answer. I wondered then if he'd heard me. The wind had come up a little, and he had his hunting hat on with the ear flaps down — you couldn't be sure.

"No," he said, suddenly, "no, it's about played out."

"How can you tell?" I asked.

He stuffed his shovel in the bank and straightened his back again, just like before.

"Well," he said, "you see those gulls up there? Circling?"

"Yes, I see them."

"When you see gulls circling like that, it means it's going to clear — in another hour or so ..."

"Oh yeah?" I studied the gulls. It would be good to remember a thing like that.

When I reached Mt. Auburn Street and our neighborhood grocery store, I could see people were beginning to have trouble handling their cars. The street hadn't been plowed yet, but salt had been put down and the road was like white grease. The parked cars were spinning in place, and there was a truck trying to rock itself out of a rut, holding up a whole line of cars. Traffic was backed up all the way to Harvard Square. I tried helping with a push, but it was no use.

By the time Cynthia and I finished supper that evening, there were six inches of snow on all the window sills facing south. But the wind was fierce and there were four feet of snow piled up on our front steps. It was still coming down, in fact harder than before.

Reports on the radio were hair-curling. Boston's main streets were jammed with stalled or abandoned cars. Thousands of commuters were stranded along state and local highways. Storm refugees filled churches, hospitals and police stations, and nobody could remember such a terrible storm. It was hard to tell how much snow had fallen because, according to the Weather Bureau, the wind velocity had reached fifty-five miles an hour. The announcer said he didn't think there'd be a St. Patrick's Day parade tomorrow.

I thought I'd better go out and do my steps — while it was still possible to get out my front door. All Gerry Street was buried under a graceful valley of snow, its banks arched like cobwebs against houses. Some drifts were stacked as high as first-floor windows. The wind howled down our road, whistled along the eaves of houses and screamed in the power lines overhead. For moments, for minutes, you couldn't see a thing — snow driving in every direction, even lifting from the ground in swirling white frenzies — and then, suddenly, it would settle and there would be quiet — a calm that might last thirty seconds.

During one of these interludes, I heard Mr. Wilcox's shovel scrape along his walk. I couldn't see him because his bank was now ten feet tall. I made my way across my

49

yard by rolling and wallowing, and when I got to his mountainous pile, I crawled up it and peered over the side.

"Hey, Mr. Wilcox," I shouted, "this is really some storm, isn't it?"

"I've seen worse," he said, and suddenly the wind hit us again, and he dissolved behind a curtain of snow.

We waited in this stew — he standing there, somewhere on his walk, and I sitting there on his bank — and when it had settled down, I said that I had never seen such a storm.

He told me about a storm in 1923 — laid down twenty-one inches in one fall, and drifting too, terrible drifting.

"Now that was a storm," he said. And I said that this one was good enough for me.

"Well, it won't last much longer," he bellowed, and then it began to blow again and he disappeared for another minute or two. When it calmed down once more, I shouted, "How can you tell?"

"Haven't you noticed?" He held his hand up in the air. "The wind's changed."

That night Cynthia and I lay in bed listening to the radio reports.

A big ship had capsized off Scituate and thirty men were battling for their lives. Winds of sixty miles per hour had built drifts at Logan Airport to more than fifteen feet. The whole Northeast was shuddering under the impact of the storm, and the Cape area was being hit by a ninety-mile-an-hour tempest. Two thousand motorists were stranded in one ten-mile stretch between Charlton and Sturbridge. Whole communities were isolated. All available men and machines battled to clear city streets. The Red Cross was on a round-the-clock alert.

At 6:00 the next morning, St. Patrick's Day, it was still snowing and, faith, what a mess! There were seven feet of snow piled high and wind-packed in my yard. It seemed to be coming down faster and thicker than before. And Mr. Wilcox was up early shoveling snow — frantically, as if to hide the evidence.

I shouted out our bedroom window, my voice loud and biting, "Hey, Mr. Wilcox, what do you think?"

I was immediately sorry I had done that. His shoulders sagged, and when he looked up at me there was something lost in his face, that firm certainty which was so much of the man, and in its place I saw undiluted bewilderment.

"My God!" he wailed, "I don't know!"

"Neither do I," I said under my breath and closed the window.

Well, as badly as I felt about everything, it was a good thing I made him confront the storm. I mean, it might have gone on forever. As it turned out, however, it stopped snowing about a quarter of an hour later. And after he finished shoveling his steps and walk, Mr. Wilcox went inside his house.

The next day was Sunday, but he didn't come out once. The only sign of life was the thin curl of smoke from his chimney. I kept my eye on his place because I wanted to talk with him. Smooth things over. He wasn't outside Monday, either, or Tuesday, and by Wednesday I felt terrible.

But in the afternoon, when I was coming back from another class, I found him in the yard cutting an approach to his bulkhead. He seemed himself again. In fact, standing there in his path, with its seven-foot banks on either side, he was the prophet Moses between the walls of a divided sea.

"Hi, Mr. Wilcox," I said. "That sure was some storm, wasn't it?"

"Yes, sir, it certainly was. But you know," he said, "I knew it couldn't last." END

51

Captain Bob Bodden and

Copyright © 1951 by Elizabeth Coatsworth Beston

BOB Bodden was an old man who lived in our town in a little house down by the wharves. Bob wasn't fond of work. He liked to sit in the shade, and whittle, maybe, and talk.

All the boys in town came to see Bob Bodden and listen to his stories. But no one liked to hear them quite as much as a little boy named Tom Mathews.

One afternoon Tom found old Bob Bodden under his maple tree, whittling as usual.

"Good afternoon, Mr. Bodden," he said.

"Good afternoon to you, Tom," said old Bob Bodden.

"I wondered if you would tell me more about the good ship *Rover*," said Tom, coming in at the gate.

"I'd be glad to," agreed Bob Bodden, whittling away. "But there's one or two little chores a boy like you could do first to help me out. You might fill the woodbox by the stove, and get a fresh pail of water from the well, and pick a box of cherries from the tree out back, if those pesky birds haven't got them all. Then you come back and maybe I'll find something to tell you about the *Rover*."

Tom hurried to fill the woodbox and get a pail of water from the well. It sloshed over his bare legs as he carried it, but that felt nice. And then he fought the birds for a little box of cherries.

Old Bob Bodden thanked him when he was done and put the box of cherries between them on the grass.

"The *Rover*," he said, looking at Tom, "was a wonderful

52

by Elizabeth Coatsworth

the Good Ship *Rover*

vessel. Don't know as there ever was such a vessel on the seven seas. Why, when the *Rover* was at the Bangor wharf, her bowsprit reached way out over Aroostook County and made a shade for the potato pickers as they worked. Picking potatoes all day in the sun is a hot job, and those potato pickers were real glad when the *Rover* was in port.

"She was certainly a large vessel. I remember I first went aboard her when I was about your age. I was cabin boy. But one day the Captain sent me up to the bow with a message to some of the sailors there, and by the time I got back I was a grown man with whiskers."

Old Bob Bodden stopped to eat a couple of cherries and spit out the pits.

"After that, I always rode Spud, my white horse."

"Oh, I didn't know you had a horse," exclaimed Tom, in surprise.

"Sure, I had a horse," Old Bob went on. "I was Captain, then, and I had to be able to get places. Captain Bodden of the *Rover* out of Bangor. That was my name and hail in those days."

He paused and Tom asked, "Where did Spud come from?"

"Well, now," said Bob Bodden, "that was funny. You know in them days we bought all the hay in Maine and took it down to New York and Boston and them other cities for the horses that pulled the street cars. We certainly shipped a pile of hay. And one voyage two or three horses got kind of overlooked in the cargo. Most likely they'd been hauling the hay and their masters lost them in that big hold. When some of the crew came across them, I liked the look of this one I called Spud, and I saw it would make getting around deck easier, if I rode. Of course that was before we had the railroad."

"Did you have a railroad on deck?" Tom asked. He was by now too interested to eat any cherries until Old Bob Bodden stopped talking, and then they both ate some cherries before Bob went on.

"Yes, we had a railroad and a telephone, too. Oh, we had all the modern conveniences on the old *Rover* before we got through. But with a ship that size we needed them, I can tell you."

"How big was she, Captain Bodden?"

"Now, I can tell you best how big she was by what she could do. I remember one time we were taking on pine lumber at Portland. But we never seemed to get her hold anywhere near filled. You know why?"

Tom shook his head. "No, sir."

"It was this way. Half the crew took it into their heads to unload the cargo t'other side of the vessel at the Liverpool docks. Fast as we took on the lumber at Portland they was unloading it at Liverpool. That was how big she was."

Old Bob Bodden ate another cherry, but Tom was silent.

"Or put it another way," Bob Bodden went on. "One time we heard a great thumping along one side of the *Rover*. Never heard such a thumping and bumping. Seems that some whales had taken it into their thick heads to make a hole in the side of the vessel. There's nothing as obstinate as a whale. When one of them whales takes a notion to do a thing, you might as well give up trying to persuade him not to. Well, they made the hole and in they come. It took all my carpenters to get that hole closed up.

54

And there we was, with four-five whales swimming around in the bottom of the hold. Fortunately, we was bringing the *Rover* back, empty, and the seawater didn't hurt anything."

"But what did you do, then?"

"Oh, with all that crew aboard, we was glad to have whale steaks. And we had oil enough for all our whale-oil lamps for a long time. That was before we put in electricity. When the *Rover* was all lighted up, she looked like the Milky Way. She was a sight to see, nights."

"She must have needed a lot of men to sail her," suggested Tom.

Bob Bodden nodded.

"You're right, Tom. We couldn't get all the sailors we needed from any one nation. We had to sign them aboard from all the nations of the world. Yankees, Mexicans, South Americans, Africans, Spaniards, Italians, French, English and Chinese, just to name a few, they was proud to sail on the *Rover*."

"But could you talk all those languages, Mr. — I mean, Captain Bodden?"

The old man ate another cherry and then said solemnly, "All orders were given in English. And understood in English. I never troubled about what they talked the rest of the time. But there was another funny thing about the sailors. At least it would seem funny on any other ship but the *Rover*. You see, Tom, the masts were so tall, you couldn't rightly expect a sailor to go aloft. I had to have a crew of ring-tail monkeys to climb into the yards and for the maintop, there was baboons."

Tom was staring up into the sky, trying to imagine what the *Rover's* masts must have looked like. He even forgot to eat a cherry when old Bob Bodden ate one. Old Bob went on. "Yes, those masts were all-fired tall. The *Rover* carried such a pile of sail, that when she hove in sight of shore, people thought a big storm was coming up and ran for their umbrellas.

"I remember one time we'd been having a lot of wind and those ring-tail monkeys and baboons had shortened sail. I don't know what I was doing, but my attention must have been on something else, for those ring-tail monkeys and baboons hadn't furled the mainsail right and proper. Along came a lot of rain and ran down into the canvas. When I saw how careless they'd been, I kind of lost my temper. I said things to them ring-tail monkeys and baboons in a way I wouldn't usually say to them. They was so upset, they dumped out the water on the wrong side. Instead of dumping it out into the Atlantic Ocean as I meant them to, they dumped it all on the land. Up to that time there'd been no ponds in Maine, just rivers, but after them ring-tail monkeys and baboons acted so careless, the water they dumped, ran into all the hollows of the land and that's why to this day Maine has so many ponds."

Old Bob Bodden and Tom ate two-three more cherries. Tom was beyond saying anything, but soon Old Bob went on, in a dreamy kind of way.

"The *Rover's* mainmast, you could really say was tall. I remember one day I noticed something big and round and shiny sticking right on the top of it. Land's sakes, if it wasn't the moon! That mainmast had sort of got under it and then along came a wave, and zippee! the top of the mainmast went right through that moon and carried it away. It didn't make no difference daytimes. I rather liked seeing it there. But at night there was so much moonlight it excited the crew from the West Indies, and they all got out their guitars and played music and sang and danced their kind of dances all night. The others complained that they couldn't sleep and after a while I had to order the baboons to cast the moon loose. They did, and she floated back where she belonged, but I was sorry to see her go."

Old Bob Bodden sighed deeply and then began turning over what was left of the cherries to find a good red one.

"Of course," he said more cheerfully, "you'd often find a star or two stuck on the yardarms. But no one paid heed to *them*. That moon was something different. Never heard of that's happening to any other vessel but the *Rover*."

Old Bob Bodden was silent for so long that at last Tom said hesitatingly, "What happened to the *Rover*, Captain Bob? Was she sunk?"

Old Bob Bodden roused himself to stare at Tom indignantly.

"Sunk?" he demanded. "The *Rover*, sunk? There isn't water enough in the whole Atlantic Ocean to sink the *Rover*. And yet, you might say she *was* lost, I suppose. Yes, one time I was cruising far to the south and she struck on the South Pole. That was a sad day. The pole must have gone right through her, for we couldn't work her free. She settled down, as far as the *Rover* could settle, and we couldn't budge her. There weren't tugboats enough in the world to pull the *Rover* loose once she'd settled down like that. So we had to launch her boats and sail back to South America. We made a regular fleet, and each ship's boat was the size of an ordinary schooner. One had the Yankees aboard, and one the Mexicans and another the South Americans and a fourth the Africans. Oh yes, there was a big ship's boat for each nation, including the ring-tail monkeys and the baboons who shared a brig.

"We all got safe to shore, but I was so broken-hearted I gave up the sea. Sometimes I dream of the *Rover* abandoned way off there with the South Pole stuck through her. They tell me now she's pretty well covered with snow and those little penguins live on her, you know, the birds that wear dress-suits and bow all the time. Explorers go down there, they say, and they report there's a continent there. Good grief! There wasn't any continent before the South Pole stove up the *Rover*. I should know, shouldn't I? I was her Captain and I'll never sail another ship like her. I doubt if you'll see her equal in all your life, Tom."

Old Bob Bodden had stopped his whittling and sat, brooding, with idle hands. All the best cherries were gone.

Tom said timidly. "Don't you feel too bad about the *Rover*, Captain Bob. I'll see if I can find some more good cherries on the other tree."

Old Bob Bodden looked up, and a smile came to his weather-beaten face.

"Now, that's a good idea, Tom," he said, "a real good idea. Of course I always had a nice little orchard abaft the pilot house on the *Rover*. These cherries aren't so good — don't get the sea air, I suppose — but still, they're good. And they serve to remind me of the finest vessel that ever sailed the sea." END

Author's Note: This tale is based on a paragraph from "An Old River Town" by Ada Douglas Littlefield, Calkins and Co. 1907, which gives a short account of an elderly stevedore of Winterport, Maine. Her study forms the basis of the first half of this version. The rest, beginning with the moon on the mainmast, the author has added. If, as I believe, Bob Bodden's tales have the true authentic ring of folklore, I shall be only the first of many to repeat, embellish and enlarge upon them. — *Elizabeth Coatsworth*.

No Vermonters in Heaven

I dreamed that I went to the City of Gold,
To Heaven, resplendent and fair,
And after I entered the beautiful fold
By one in authority I was told
That not a Vermonter was there.

"Impossible, Sir, for from my own town,
Many sought this delectable place,
And each must be here, with a harp or a crown,
And a conqueror's palm, and a clean linen gown
Received through unmerited grace."

The angel replied, "All Vermonters come here
When first they depart from the earth,
But after a day or a month or a year,
They restless and lonesome and homesick appear,
And sigh for the land of their birth.

"We give them the best that the kingdom provides,
They have everything here they could want,
But not a Vermonter in Heaven abides —
A very brief period here he resides
Then hikes his way back to Vermont."

The Perfectly Proper Pig

by Louise Dickinson Rich
and L. Thomas Hopkins

L AST week Peter's picture was on the cover of a national news magazine, but the story inside didn't mention Pa and all the pains he'd taken to develop Peter's personality. It seemed unfair; so I'm writing the full, true story of summer-before-last.

We — Pa and Ma and I — spent that summer in an old farmhouse we rented in New England. It was real boondocks: just a lot of farms around a little village, over fifty miles away from the nearest city. We went there so that my parents could have peace and quiet to work. Ma's an editor of children's books, and she had a mess of manuscripts to get ready for fall publication. Pa's a Profes-

sor of Psychology in New York, and he was working on
his doctoral thesis. We found the farm through Dr.
Haskell, a colleague of Pa's who has a summer place about
thirty miles away. He's not a pill doctor. He's a Ph.D.,
which is what Pa was aiming to become.

I was a little lonely at first. I didn't know anybody, and
Ma and Pa were pounding their typewriters most of the
time. But Fourth of July changed that. The village held a
big celebration on the Fair Grounds. Ma and Pa couldn't
go, because the Haskells were driving over for the day, but
they said it would be an opportunity for me to meet members of my peer group and maybe form some meaningful

and rewarding relationships. Holiday camaraderie and all that good garbage. So I went.

The minute I got there, I knew I was dressed wrong in my best J. Press slacks and my prep school blazer. Everyone else had on T-shirts and dungarees. I hacked around a while looking at exhibits of jelly and watching ox-pulling contests, with everyone giving me a pretty wide berth. I'd just about decided to cut out when someone bellowed that the contests were about to begin on the oval of the race track. First would be the greased pig race, everybody welcome, entrance fee fifty cents, proceeds to go to the Village Improvement Association, come one, come all.

I asked a man what a greased pig race was, and he said they turned loose a shoat (young, weaned pig, he explained) covered with grease, and whoever could catch and hold it got to keep it. "Wouldn't cal'late 'twould int'rest you," he added, eying me up and down.

"That so? Just point me in the right direction." He laughed scornfully, but he pointed me.

The announcer said the pig would be let loose when a gun was fired and the race would be on. Nothing was said about rules, so I assumed everyone else knew them and I'd have to figure them out as I went along. Two seconds after a skinny and mucky-looking little pig was let out of a crate, I realized that rules weren't mentioned because they were non-existent — no penalties for clipping, tripping, unnecessary roughness or general mayhem; I found out the hard way. When I picked myself up, the pack was down at the other end of the field after the pig, who was running and dodging like a maniac.

The next few minutes were confusing. A couple of times I thought I had him, but he slid out from under like an eel. He was greased plenty, and he was terrified. Then the pig came right to me, the mob hot on his heels. I feinted, he dodged wrong, and I had him. I caged him under my stomach between my knees and elbows and tried to ignore a ton of country boys on my back.

They gave me a gunny sack to carry my pig home in, and the farmer who'd donated him said he was pedigreed, but the runt of the litter, which accounted for his skinniness. Another man told me that in spite of appearances I was a gutsy little bustard. After that, I was In. Nothing like a greased pig race to level barriers. All the rest of the summer I had plenty of friends.

When I got home, Pa and Dr. Haskell were having their usual argument, which they prefer to call a discussion. It was pretty well along. They were calling each other Doctor and Professor instead of Ed and Bill. These arguments are about heredity and environment. Dr. Haskell believes that you inherit character traits that can't be changed any more than inherited blue eyes can. Pa believes that surroundings and influences can change the direction of character development.

Pa was saying, "Presupposing an active intelligence in a sound body, Doctor, the potential is unlimited."

"My dear Professor," Dr. Haskell said, "you can't make a silk purse out of a sow's ear."

This seemed a good cue to come on stage with my pig. I dumped him out of the sack onto the living room floor, and Ma hollered, "Get that thing out of here, Steve!" The pig had calmed down or just given up. He lay there limp with his eyes closed. He was not an appealing sight. Let's face it; a pig doesn't have the prettiest face and figure in the world at best, and this one wasn't at his best. Besides being underfed, he was filthy.

I gave a rundown of events, and Ma said, "One thing we don't need around here is a pig, even pedigreed. Shut him up in the shed and I'll get on the phone. Some farmer will be glad . . . ."

"Not so fast." Pa took my pig in his lap and went over

him thoroughly. "Fundamentally sound, I'd say. Good stock, which implies at least average intelligence. An ideal subject for experimental work on the effects of environmental change." He scratched behind the pig's ears, and it opened its eyes, looked at Pa and relaxed. "We're keeping him," Pa announced. "He's going to prove something for me."

Dr. Haskell laughed. "And when you've concluded your experiment, Professor, you'll still have a pig with pig traits — greediness, uncleanliness, stupidity . . . ."

Pa said coldly, "We'll see about that, Doctor. And you will please not refer to him as a pig. His name is Peter. I'll grant that physically he will remain a pig, but he will also be an acceptable member of society, clean, mannerly, responsive."

"Hogwash." Dr. Haskell cracked up over his own crummy joke.

That's how Pa and Peter became involved.

After the Haskells left, Pa said, "This poor little fellow is both physically and emotionally exhausted. He's had a highly traumatic experience, separated from his mother and siblings, subjected to a shocking ordeal, and transplanted to alien surroundings. We've got to build up his sense of security with reassurance, understanding and affection."

Ma sighed. "Then before we go further, I'd suggest you give him a bath."

Pa was against this. One more strange experience could easily shock Peter into neurosis, psychosis or even irreversible clinical depression; but Ma said, "Oddly enough I know what I'm talking about. We did a book on farm animals two years ago. Pigs are actually fastidious creatures. They prefer to be clean. Circumstances allowing, they even choose one special spot to empty their bowels."

Ma's store of random information is amazing. She never forgets a book she's edited.

Peter enjoyed his bath in the kitchen sink. He gave low little grunts as Pa soaped him gently, talking to him all the while. He turned out to be pure white, rather surprisingly.

Ma cooked a kettle of oatmeal which Peter ate with milk and honey. Then Pa took him out and they decided between them that a spot behind a syringa bush would be his toilet. Peter showed his appreciation, Pa informed us, by performing more than adequately.

Ma wouldn't allow Peter upstairs to sleep and Pa wouldn't leave him alone downstairs for fear he'd wake up frightened or hungry. So Pa slept on the couch in his study with Peter beside him in a box. I heard Pa rattling pans in the kitchen a couple of times and making trips to the syringa bush. Peter looked fine in the morning, rested and even a little fatter. Pa was rather heavy-eyed, but full of beans.

"I'm going over to Peter's old home and talk to Mr. Hodge," he told us at breakfast. "I need Peter's case history, and I want to check the rest of the litter. We'll use them as controls to measure Peter's progress, and it's important to evaluate them at once. Then I'll call the State Agricultural College. I know a man there." He wouldn't let me go to the Hodges' with him. I had to baby-sit Peter, who couldn't go either. A return to his former environment would confuse him and might cause him to regress. Or so Pa said.

While Pa was gone, I fed Peter, took him to the syringa bush, and weighed him on the bathroom scales, entering his weight — nine pounds — in a notebook. When Pa got home with a sack of pig meal and a pocketful of notes he'd taken, he was dismayed. The average weight of Peter's siblings was eighteen pounds.

"Malnutrition can be a factor in mental retardation," he said. "We'll have to build him up physically as well as emotionally and psychologically." Then he placed a call to his pal at the college.

Guided by the FSA (Foremost Swine Authority), Pa put Peter on a schedule. Three regular meals a day, followed by trips to the syringa; morning bath and weighing; morning and afternoon walks around the farm and house; naps beside Pa while he worked on his thesis; evenings in Pa's lap being petted and read interesting items from the paper; and so to bed. That was the routine.

Peter had a special high, distress call when he had to use the john. When we heard it, we'd let him out; and after a while he'd ask in again at the door. When we were sure we could trust him, he had the run of the house, like any normal pet. We were well enough integrated to think nothing of this; but the first time Ma's twice-weekly cleaning woman came, we had a crisis on our hands. All unprepared, she ran head-on into Peter coming out of Pa's study. She shrieked, "Steve! There's a hog wandered in here! Help me drive him out!"

Pa flew out of his study. "Don't scream at him, Mrs. Abbott! He's not used to it and it upsets him." He picked Peter up and started soothing him.

Mrs. Abbott sniffed and took off her apron. "I've heard of folks who kept pigs in the parlor, but I never expected to meet up with them. You can't pay me enough money to clean up after a pig."

Ma hurried in. "It's all right, Mrs. Abbott. He's housebroken. You know I wouldn't tolerate . . ." She eased Mrs. Abbott out, talking persuasively, and I went into Pa's study.

Pa was holding Peter in his lap, stroking him and Peter was nuzzling Pa's neck and giving soft grunts of pleasure.

They looked pretty silly. Pa peered over his glasses at me. "What was your reaction to Mrs. Abbott's attack on Peter, Steve? Sympathy? Amusement? Surprise?" I was used to Pa's analyzing reactions, so I was ready. "Surprise, mostly, I guess. Maybe some shock."

Pa nodded. "Good. You accept Peter as a personality in his own right. That will help enormously in the development of his potential. Mrs. Abbott's attitude is common. Each individual works out his own identity in relation to a group that he respects; say his country or race or religion. He supports his group by putting down all non-members. Mrs. Abbott was abusive of Peter because he's not a member of her group, which is people. I hope she won't quit her job. Discriminating against any living creature on the grounds of group membership is sick. Learning to embrace Peter in her philosophy would help Mrs. Abbott far more than it would Peter."

On my way out, I saw Mrs. Abbott with her apron on again washing windows. Ma'd talked her into staying.

When Peter outgrew the bathroom scales, Pa took him down to the Feed Store once a week and put him on their platform scales. The first time he was worried that the change of scenery might disorient Peter, but decided that a wider variety of experiences was essential to the development of a well-rounded personality. After that Peter was a car freak. The minute he heard a motor start, he came running. Ma wouldn't allow him in her car, and whenever she took off without him he'd sulk and grumble until Pa broke down and rode him to the end of the lane and back in the station wagon. At first Peter lay on the floor, but Pa thought he was being deprived by not seeing the interesting sights along the way; so he built a seat so Peter could sit beside him and look out the window. Peter loved it; but I know of at least one case when the driver of a car they met put his vehicle into a brook because he was so shook by what he couldn't believe he was seeing.

Mrs. Abbott was the first to realize how fast vacation was flying. One morning she asked me, "Steve, what happens to Peter when you folks leave?" She looked really worried. She and Peter had developed a very good relationship. She always said "Good morning, Peter," when she came to work; and he always inquired about her health. I know, because often I heard her answer a series of grunts with, "Oh, I'm fine. And you? Putting on a little weight, aren't you? Better watch that, Peter." She communicated with him almost as well as Pa did, and better than Ma and I did.

"Gee, I don't know," I told her. "Take him back to Hodges', I guess."

"You can't do that!" She was aghast. "It would be murder! Hodge would send him to the slaughterhouse along with the rest. I wish — but Abbott would never hear of my taking him."

I spoke to the parents about it, and they were concerned, too. "We can't take him to New York," Ma said. "They forbid even dogs in the apartment. Maybe your school, Steve? Some of the boys are allowed riding horses."

"No, ma'am," I said firmly. It's okay to be eccentric at school, but not downright weird.

"Peter's very popular in the village," Pa suggested. "Maybe some family with children . . . ."

We left it that we'd try to find a suitable home in the village.

The next Saturday Ma said we had to go to the city and get me squared away for school: underwear and all that. We left Pa and Peter at home. In spite of its being Saturday when everyone in the country was shopping in the city, by mid-afternoon we were all through and headed home. We didn't get far. On Main Street, we ran into a complete traffic jam. Cars were bumper to bumper, horns were hooting, traffic officers were blowing whistles, and people were coming out of stores and running down the sidewalks. We couldn't move an inch. Ma asked a policeman who was hurrying by what the trouble was, and he said something about some nut with a pig, and ran on.

"Dear Lord in Heaven!" Ma said. "Steve, get out and see. I can't leave the car. Oh, no, it can't be!"

It was, though. I wormed my way through the crowd, and pretty soon I could hear Pa shouting over all the racket and confusion, "He's my pet and I'm taking him shopping."

"Don't get funny with me!" the Law shouted back. "Get him out of here or I'll run you in for disturbing the peace."

Pa shouldn't have argued, but as I said, he lives a sheltered academic life, the life-blood of which is argument — or discussion. "Officer, I'm not disturbing anyone. These people are disturbing me and my pig. We just want to go into some stores and make a few purchases, and they won't let us move."

"None of your lip. I'm taking you in."

"On what charges?" Pa's a champion of civil rights.

"You'll find out." The cop started to clear the area.

I ran back to Ma and gasped, "They're arresting Pa and Peter!"

"Stick with them and I'll find you when I've parked the car. Get going, for Pete's sake!" Ma was too upset to have joked on purpose.

Pa and Peter were on the next block, standing with three officers beside a paddy wagon. Pa was saying, "The steps are too high and he's not used to being shoved by unsympathetic hands. He's been looking forward to the nice outing I promised him, and I won't have him disappointed. Why can't we walk to the station and perhaps do a little shopping on the way?"

"Are you crazy?" the cop asked as if he really wanted to know. "All right, we'll walk. But no going into stores."

The sidewalk was fairly clear now, thanks to a riot control squad, and Pa and Peter were escorted along it. I followed, along with about six hundred other people. Pa was talking reassuringly to Peter. "Don't worry. Just stay close to me. I know you're disappointed about not seeing the stores, but you're having a much rarer experience. Even I have never been taken into custody before, and I'll admit I didn't anticipate it. But we can discuss and analyze this whole business later, to our mutual benefit. Any new intellectual experience is educationally rewarding." And so on.

I guess Peter understood, but the cops didn't. One asked, "Have you been drinking?" Pa said that he had not, and that our society was in a bad way when a law-abiding citizen couldn't walk his well-behaved pet on a public street without being accused of drunkenness.

After they had disappeared into the police station and the crowd had been dispersed, I came out from where I'd been hiding in a doorway, sneaked into the station and sat down on a bench against the wall. I figured correctly that nobody'd notice me. They were all too busy trying to book Pa and Peter. The desk sergeant was asking the arresting officer the charges.

"Disturbing the peace, obstructing traffic, creating a nuisance, inciting a riot, possession of an unlicensed pet, and disrespect for the Law, for starters."

The sergeant said "Wow," and Pa said, "Just a minute! Any rioting, obstructing or disturbance was done by others, and I doubt the existence of any ordinance requiring the licensing of a pig. There was no disrespect shown the Law, I assure you."

The arresting officer said, "Sarge, you know as well as I do what they call us. Pigs, that's what. I may be a dumb cop, but I got feelings, too. Walking a pig on my beat is disrespect."

"Okay, okay," the sergeant said and got down to business. "Name, address and date of birth." By now the room was jammed by personnel from the different offices.

"Occupation?" When Pa said he was a college professor and got out his ID, everyone started muttering things like "Parlor pink" and "Investigation" and "Crazy egghead," and it looked as if another riot was brewing. Then the door of an office opened and a voice of capital-A Authority demanded, "What's going on here?"

Instantly everyone froze. You didn't have to be told that

this was the Chief of Police. He was Chief, all right. No one dared to breathe. Only Peter. In the middle of the deathly silence he announced loud and clear that he had to go the john.

"What ails him?" the Chief asked. "Is he sick?"

"He's saying that he has to use the toilet," Pa told him.

"Get him out of here quick," the Chief ordered; and they all began to hustle Peter to the front door.

"Not that way," Pa protested. "The way things are going, you'd probably charge us with littering. Isn't there a back door?"

"This way!" The police couldn't get them out fast enough.

When the mission was safely accomplished, the Chief ordered Pa and Peter into his office. "I want to talk to you," he said, tough. The other officers went about their business, and I sat down where I could monitor what went on in the Chief's office and where Ma could find me when she came in.

The Chief turned out to be not a bad egg. He'd been raised on a farm and knew something about pigs. He even unbent enough to scratch Peter's back and comment that he'd never have thought it possible to train a pig so well.

Pa bristled. "Peter is not a trained pig! Training is conditioned responses to specific stimuli. Peter has been helped and encouraged to use his natural intelligence to improvise in any situation, however unexpected. There's a vast difference, Chief."

A possibly disastrous discussion was shaping up, but luckily Ma came in then, looking out of breath and harassed. She sailed into the Chief's office with me in tow, and when Peter saw us he began making plaintive little whimpering sounds.

"Poor Peter," Ma said, all sympathy. "You've had a

long, hard day, and it's way past your suppertime. So if you'll excuse us, Chief." Talk about graciousness and self-assurance!

She almost got away with it, too; but not quite. "Hold it!" the Chief snapped, hard-nosed. "There are a few matters to be cleared up. I can't overlook your conduct this afternoon, Professor. You probably meant no harm, but common sense should have told you what would happen if you took a pig into a crowd of Saturday shoppers. The traffic jam and sidewalk congestion seriously inconvenienced the merchants and caused my department great embarrassment. We've been swamped with calls of complaint. I can't ignore them. I'm going to have to fine you and issue an injunction against your ever — repeat ever — bringing that pig into this city again. Understood?" Pa said he understood.

Peter was a very tired pig when we got home. He'd been on his feet and under stress for five solid hours. He showed his emotional strain by clinging to Pa's side and responding to petting in a much deeper tone than usual. He sensed for the first time, Pa said, the size and possible hostility of the world, and this intensified his need for security, belongingness and affection. We must find a suitable home for him at once, so he'd have time to adjust before we left.

There was a fairly accurate report in the city paper of Peter's arrest, headed "Pigs pinch Prof and pig." Pa cut it out and added it to Peter's dossier. Two days later Mrs. Abbott's nephew, whose five children were in love with Peter, offered to take him. Pa cased the joint and decided it would do. He took Peter down there with all his paraphernalia — harness, seat, ivory back scratcher, personal dishes and security blanket. Pa spent more time at the nephew's than he did at home for the next ten days. He said he was making sure that the transference was complete and satisfactory, without latent anxieties.

We meant to keep in touch with Peter, but we got involved with other things. After a couple of postcards from Mrs. Abbott saying that Peter was fine, the correspondence petered (whoops!) out. The next thing we knew, a year later, he was all over the cover of the magazine.

The cover story was really more about police programs to improve public relations than it was about Peter. His picture was on the cover mostly to call attention to the story, I guess. Anyhow, some Police Commissioner in a mid-western city with a high crime rate had read the item about Peter in the newspaper. He was planning a campaign for better police-public understanding and decided Peter'd make a good trademark or mascot. You know: if you can't lick 'em, join 'em. His investigators tracked Peter down and persuaded the owners to give him up in the name of public service.

Then they went to work promoting him. They had bumper stickers and decals made saying "Support Your Local Police" under Peter's picture; and they rode him around in prowl cars, stopping in trouble areas so that Peter could get out and mingle and make friends, the way he used to do in the village with Pa. He sat on platforms at schools and Rotary Club meetings whenever an officer gave a talk on safety or crime prevention. I imagine he loved that.

Oh sure, it was a gimmick; but it worked. Pretty soon Peter was being flown to other cities to perform. Since I started this, I've seen him on TV, riding in an open car in a ticker-tape parade. He looked great — bigger than ever, groomed to the teeth and smug as an alderman. He was touring the country in a special air-conditioned unit with two cops assigned to keeping him well and happy while he did his PR stint. All this was paid for, the authorities made clear — avoiding charges of graft, pork-barreling or wasting tax money — by royalties from Peter sweat shirts, bubble gum, toys and whatever. The balance goes into Youth Centers in slum areas. Peter's got it made.

So has Pa. It came out that Peter had been tutored by a psychology professor, and Pa began getting requests for articles and lectures from all over the country. I saw him on the ETV channel at school, and he wasn't half bad. In hard times like these, he said, when there are enormous economic and political tensions and a great deal of anxiety, people welcome anything to alleviate the common condition. That's why fads like streaking or eating goldfish sweep the country. So Peter, he said, plays an important therapeutic role in our society. It staggers you when you remember that his siblings are long-gone spare ribs and sausages.

There was even some talk about Pa's taking a sabbatical to organize a kind of Academy for Police Mascots. Pa turned the idea down. He'd got his Ph.D. by then, and Ma asked him if he considered it beneath the dignity of a Doctor of Philosophy to train pigs. Pa overlooked the fighting word *train*. He just said no, it wasn't that at all.

"Not enough of a challenge," he said. "Anyone who wants to take the time and trouble can develop creative intelligence and social orientation in a pig. I prefer the more complex problems presented by the human young."

I was home on vacation, and the way he looked at me made me very nervous. For once I was glad to get back to school where they don't worry much about our personality potentials.   END

A Doughnut at the

HALF a century ago when my mother, a bride, came to Providence, she was by all accounts both pretty and pleasure-loving. My great-uncle recognizing this, promptly took her hand.

"I am giving you my seats at the Boston Symphony, Kate," he announced as he ate his customary breakfast of fruit, hot cereal, tenderloin steak, coffee, toast and marmalade. "As you know, my appetite is so poor, and I am going to Florida. Doctor Philbrick will escort you. Old Phil has gone to the concerts with me since the Boston Symphony started coming to Providence. Going with him will be a liberal education."

How liberal my mother was to find out.

On the night of the first concert she was ready, her long kid gloves buttoned, her Paris opera glasses in a little velvet bag when the Doctor arrived. Elderly and distinguished looking, he would have seemed a suitable escort had it not been for what hung over his left arm.

At first glance, my mother thought it was a monstrous doughnut. It had a hole in the center and was much the color, but on closer inspection, she was horrified to discover, it was a rubber ring, not too different probably from what Sir Osbert Sitwell's father carried daily to the British Museum. That, of course, she could not know, nor would the knowledge have allayed her much.

"For my back," the Doctor explained, noticing my

Boston Symphony

mother's stricken look. "The seats in Infantry Hall are very hard."

My mother's brown eyes grew enormous as gradually it became evident he intended to take the ring to the concert. The idea was horrible, unthinkable. She would as soon have carried exposed the unmentionable requisite of every Victorian bedroom.

"Shall we start?" asked the Doctor, holding my mother's evening wrap. "It takes a little while on the horse cars."

This was another surprise, for my mother had supposed a hired hack waited outside. Wanting to protest but not knowing how, she let herself be guided to a seat on the horse car, which was filled with concert goers. There, she stared fixedly ahead, endeavoring not to see anyone she might know. The Doctor, on the contrary, studiously inspected the passengers, bowed to his acquaintances and proceeded to tell my mother about the program for the evening.

The liberal education fell, as so often happens, on inattentive ears. My mother heard only the whispered comments and suppressed giggles around her. Her cheeks, habitually porcelain pale, began to match the salmon pink of her leg-of-mutton sleeves. Thus, they arrived at Infantry Hall.

A vast barn of a hall on North Main Street, capable of holding a poultry show and a Symphony concert in rapid succession, it climbed, as most things in Providence did, up a hill. With a door on its upper level, Benefit Street, and a door on its lower level, it served both sides of the city.

Uncle James' seat was in the dead center of the Hall, on the broad main aisle through which most of Providence passed and upon which the balcony looked. From the viewpoint of conspicuousness, the seat was unsurpassed.

My mother could not listen to the orchestra. The flutter of interest which their arrival had caused, had passed. The Doctor, seated on his ring, was absorbed in the music, but my mother could not keep her mind from visualizing the moment, when the concert over, the Doctor would deliberately arise and slip that extraordinary object over his arm. Anticipation, so often keener than realization, ruined the evening.

When my father heard about the performance, he tried to console my mother.

"Everyone knows old Phil. They probably didn't pay too much attention."

"But they did!" protested my mother. "They laughed on the horse car. It was dreadful!"

"You must have the carriage for the next concert," my father said.

"But that awful ring. Tell him not to take it."

"I can hardly do that," my father said.

"Then I refuse to go," said my mother.

"That would be a pity. You would miss good music and hurt the feelings of two old gentlemen."

"Well then," said my mother, who was always resourceful, "I'll make a bag to cover the thing and it will look more like a cushion."

"That's sweet of you, Kate," said my father, kissing her.

So it was arranged. My mother made a neat black bag, which tied with a cord.

On the evening of the second Symphony Concert, in a plum-colored Worth gown with a wisp of tulle around her slender throat, she happily awaited her escort. My father's carriage, a brewster green station wagon, drawn by a pair of light bay Morgans, was at the door. The bag lay on the sofa. All was ready.

Old Phil seemed surprised at the suggestion he should put the rubber ring in a bag, but once he discovered my mother had made the bag, he hastened to comply with the request.

"How kind of you," he said, endeavoring to force the ring into the bag, which my mother held open. "I am afraid, it won't go."

"O dear!" cried my mother, who had been obliged to make the bag without measurements. Her distress was evident.

"Soon remedied," cried the Doctor cheerfully. "I'll just let the air out." And he did. "A perfect fit," he remarked gallantly offering his arm to my mother.

In the carriage, he explained the program and she was able to listen. In excellent spirits, they arrived at Infantry Hall. My mother bowed happily to friends, even stopping to chat on her way to her seat. The black bag, she felt, made her entrance if not inconspicuous, at least, unobjectionable.

The orchestra was making those sounds, which my father felt musicians should learn to do without. The air of expectancy, which immediately precedes the arrival of the conductor, prevailed.

My mother sat down and opened her program. Doctor Philbrick after disposing of his coat and overcoat, proceeded to remove the deflated ring from its bag. Somehow, my mother had not foreseen this. As the conductor came upon the stage, greeted by the customary ripple of applause, the Doctor succeeded in getting the tube of the ring between his lips.

The music began to sound and Doctor Philbrick did, too. He blew and blew. My mother stared straight ahead, unwillingly hearing the whoof of old Phil's breath more clearly than she heard the orchestra.

Ruddier and ruddier grew the Doctor's face, as the ring began ever so slowly to swell. First, it resembled a worm, then a snake coiled. As red as a turkey's wattles were the Doctor's cheeks. The snake shrank a little. The Doctor had reached his limit. He stopped blowing. There was the sickening sound of escaping air. Vainly, he tried to cover the vent as he took it from his mouth. The ring wilted.

Not all of the audience had been able to gaze straight ahead, as my mother had done. Most had turned to stare in stupefaction and fascination.

The Doctor concentrated anew on his task. He inhaled deeply and began again from the beginning. My mother felt a tide of mortification burning her throat, her face, surging to the roots of her lovely dark hair. Her lips trembled. Her chin quivered, but she forced herself to sit erect, her hands clasped in her lap.

As the orchestra played, the Doctor blew, rested, blew, the tube clenched firmly in his teeth. The ring again began to assume major proportions. The circle of interest in the venture widened. Those people not fortunate enough to sit near the Doctor, were obliged to crane and peer — which they did.

The conductor gradually sensed some inattention on the part of the musicians, who noticed a diversion taking place in the audience. With added zest, he waved his baton but produced no fervor.

True, the audience had come to hear music, but they could not afford to miss Doctor Philbrick's inflation. It was as exciting as a balloon ascension. Twice the ring almost became a doughnut. Twice, the air escaped viciously in a serpent-like hiss before the Doctor could manipulate the valve.

As the Doctor started on his third attempt, the attention of the gallery had become engaged. Some of the musicians had discovered what the rival attraction was. Only the conductor was completely mystified. His irritation mounted with the whispering tide. "Look — look — he's going to get it — watch —"

At the end of the movement, the conductor swung suddenly and fiercely faced the audience. He was a split-second too late. The Doctor had just sat on the doughnut.

When my mother recounted the evening's horrors to my father, tears and laughter mingled.

"I'll never go again," she declared.

"Yes, you will, Kate."

"Never," she stoutly maintained. "I couldn't bring myself to. It wouldn't be right under the circumstances — in my condition."

"Is your condition interesting?" my father quizzically inquired.

"Maybe not now," she honestly admitted, "but —" she added brightly, "I'm sure it will be before another Symphony Concert."   END

I Am What I Ate

A S I'm sure everyone has noticed by now, we are in the throes of a nostalgia fad that may have no parallel in recorded history. Every time we turn around, we are assaulted by a slightly demented obsession with quaint music, jargon, fashions, hairstyles, and life-styles of the '30s, or '40s, or '50s, or even the '60s. Any day now, I expect to see a magazine article or television program trot out the nostalgic delights of that time we all knew and loved called "last month."

The '40s have recently come in for perhaps more than their share of this sometimes wretched excess. I am a child of the '40s; born in 1936, I reached the age of reason in 1943, and by the time that sex was more important to me than anything else I could think of, the decade was over. So I have a certain fond remembrance for the period. Yet in all the rising literary and mass-media gorge about the '40s, I have not seen a single discussion of the one thing that can bring tears to my eyes or a lump to my throat: namely, the food I knew and loved as a boy.

Now, I'm not talking about good old Mom's cooking — although I remember much of that with affection (the memory of my mother's baked spaghetti, for example, can still inspire a clutch of hunger in my belly). No, the food I remember best was the food I did up with my own little hands, the food crafted to meet the precise demands of my appetite, the food whose creation soon acquired a list of ingredients, proportions, and procedures as complicated and

by T.H. Watkins

rigid as the most sophisticated recipe in the *Larousse Gastronomique.*

After researching the subject with some diligence, I know I am not alone; everyone I've talked with can remember some little tidbit out of his childhood that was uniquely his own invention, as toothsome in memory as it was in fact. However, unlike most kids, whose over-protective mothers forced them into sneak attacks, my mother gave me a more-or-less free hand in the kitchen, provided I cleaned up after myself. This was especially true on Sunday mornings, when I was frequently allowed to bring my mother and father breakfast in bed (two eggs over and hard, with crumbly bacon, and dark toast so loaded with oleomargarine that its center hung down like a hammock). As a result of this freedom to learn, to express myself, to use my young imagination, I soon progressed beyond the somewhat primitive efforts of my contemporaries. I was, in fact, a master of kiddie cuisine.

In the interest of illuminating this little-known segment of life in the '40s, then, I offer a few of my better creations. Some of these recipes will doubtless be familiar to many people of my generation, but many I believe to be unlike anything anyone else ever ate — with or without relish.

IN THE FRYING PAN

What most mothers are incapable of grasping — and what nutritional experts religiously ignore — is the function of simple grease in the food patterns of childhood. There is something in every child that craves grease, an atavistic need for the warm, reassuring, salty, slick *messiness* of the stuff that must go clear back to the days when our ancestors were roasting leg of mastodon over an open fire, then tearing at it with their bare hands and sucking liquefied fat off their fingers. The importance of grease to the following recipes will be self-evident.

Hamburger Knots

Two things are of primary importance in the preparation of proper hamburger knots: the quality of hamburg used and the method of cooking. It is necessary, first, to obtain about a pound of the cheapest kind of hamburg available in, say, 1946. That was pretty cheap hamburg, since it had, I believe, a ratio of about ten ounces of suet and shin-scrapings to every ounce of genuine meat, some of it beef. (Since it was also just about the most expensive meat we could afford at the time, there was always an abundance of it around.)

Take the pound of hamburg, split it roughly, shape into patties, and place in a frying pan over a very hot flame (the only temperature control you need to worry about when cooking in a frying pan is "highest"). No added grease will be necessary. Standing as far away from the stove as possible (a long-handled spatula is welcome here) so that you sustain no second-degree burns from popping grease, shrink the patties; not so much cook them, mind you, but *shrink* them. When you have distilled about half an inch of boiling grease, flip the patties (flip and jump back, flip and jump back). When the patties have formed a nice black crust and have shrunk to the size of a pair of gently flattened ping-pong balls, your hamburger knots are done.

Placed on a single slice of bread (for the proper kind of bread, see below) with lots of mayonnaise and rolled up like a hot dog, hamburger knots can supply you with enough calories to last anywhere up to two hours. Dried out on a paper towel and stuffed in the pocket of your blue jeans, they have all the durability of the mountain man's pemmican, and every bit of the nourishment since the long cooking reduces them to almost pure meat. They will keep for nibbling purposes for a good week, and are very handy if you get into a rock fight and run out of rocks.

Fried Bread Balls

I claim full credit for fried bread balls — perhaps the finest after-school dish ever invented. Not just *any* bread will do, however. In fact, for any of these recipes there is only one kind of bread — *real* bread, the thin-sliced, white, enriched sandwich bread that can be purchased in any grocery store, anywhere.

There are two tests you can use to determine if your bread is real bread; both should be done in private. The first is this: It is the kind of bread you can roll up into little gray pellets in the palms of your hands and then use in a beanshooter. An even better test is to place a slice on the table and poke your index finger into the center; if the impression remains, it is the right bread — and if you can see your *fingerprint* in the impression, it is prime.

Making fried bread balls is not simple. Moisten a slice of bread with just the right amount of water — too much water, and the bread will disintegrate; too little, and it will lack the proper adhesion for shaping. Once you get it just right (it may take three or four practice slices), wad the slice into a neat ball, rolling and squeezing it between your palms until it holds together all by itself. Drop into an inch or two of hot grease (preferably leftover hamburger knot grease), and fry it until the outside is crisp and crackly, leaving the inside moist and tender.

It is best to eat fried bread balls soon after they cool, before the grease in them starts to congeal. After a couple of days, they will begin to go funny around the edges, so they aren't nearly as durable as hamburger knots. Yet they are perfect for nibbly-munching, and filling enough to sit in your stomach for quite a long time — almost until dinner.

SANDWICHES

Sandwiches! The word is too anemic to evoke the sheer authority of what I managed to create by putting something between two slices of bread. Massive in weight, bulk, and gustatory satisfaction, each of my favorite sandwiches was an elegant construction engineered with the dedication and enthusiasm only a hungry ten-year-old boy can muster.

As noted earlier, the bread used in these sandwich recipes *must* be of the white, enriched, thin-sliced variety. Also, it should be noted that *only* oleomargarine can be used — no butter. Unfortunately, it is not possible today to obtain *real* oleomargarine — the kind I used in 1946. That margarine came in a clear cellophane package. It was dead-white, thanks to the lobbying efforts of the butter cartel which persuaded Congress to outlaw the manufacture of imitation butter that actually *looked* like imitation butter. The oleomargarine people got around this by equipping each package with a little plastic bubble of food coloring. You popped the bubble and kneaded the package of margarine until it had achieved a pale yellow consistency.

I hated that yellow butter-colored margarine. My

mother maintained that the color was flavorless, but I insisted that it made the stuff taste throw-uppy. My technique was to sneak open a fresh package of margarine before it got kneaded, slit the end of it, and scoop out enough to use on my sandwiches.

Almost any of today's cheap brands — even though yellow — will give much the same effect, provided they are the kind that sweat when you leave them out of the refrigerator too long. But remember — none of this poly-unsaturated junk. The margarine should be *crawling* with saturated polys, otherwise the subtle nuances of flavor will be lost.

Peanut Butter Tear

Up until a couple of years ago, it would have been impossible to make a proper 1946 peanut butter sandwich, because the market has been glutted by easy-to-spread homogenized peanut butter, one of the more depressing technological excesses of our era. However, the "organic" food mania at least brought *real* peanut butter back to us — more expensive, since it's easier to manufacture, but worth every penny. You can always tell if it's real peanut butter by the inch of oil that lies on top of the stuff.

The important consideration here is that the peanut butter must be kept in the refrigerator at all times, so that it retains the spreading qualities of modeling clay. Too, you must ignore the instructions on the jar which enjoin you to stir the oil into the body of the peanut butter; this is absolutely the wrong way to go about it, since it takes longer, makes the peanut butter easier to spread, and dilutes the oily taste which is essential to a proper sandwich.

There are two schools of thought regarding the correct sequences involved in peanut-butter-sandwich-making. One holds that a thick layer of oleomargarine should go on the slice of bread first, and that the peanut butter is then spread on top of it in equal proportions. Except for the fact of equal proportions (an inflexible rule) this theory is nonsense. The only way to make it right is to mash the peanut butter into the bread first, ripping, tearing, and shredding the bread as you go along until it looks as if it had been passed through an electric fan. With the base coat applied, you then heap on one or more additional layers of peanut butter, and on top of this pile an equal amount of oleomargarine. When finished, the sandwich should weigh no less than eight ounces, and with a little extra effort can be made to tip the scales at close to a full pound. To test for the proper weight, simply hold the sandwich by one end: if it doesn't bend at right angles, it is not heavy enough.

There are those who maintain that grape jelly or even strawberry jam can replace the oleomargarine. Some people will eat anything.

Strawberry Ooze

A school lunch favorite. Here again, both quality and quantity are important. Cheap strawberry jelly will not do, for it is not quite liquid enough, nor will the really expensive strawberry jams, for they are too full of fruit chunks. Only the bargain-rate supermarket brands are exactly right for this sandwich — the ones that use about one cup of fruit to every three or four pounds of sugar, together with lots of artificial coloring so that the semi-liquid jam is bright red. Spread four or five tablespoons of this between two pieces of white bread, wrap the sandwich in waxed paper, place in the bottom of a paper sack, and drop a couple of red apples on top of it. After four hours of sitting in your school locker, the bread will have turned pink.

DESSERTS

I can't claim to have developed many skills along the lines of dessert-making; there were too many rich goodies you could simply go out and buy. Such things as vanilla ice cream with a generous topping of Hershey's canned chocolate, cream-filled Hostess Twinkies with a Coke on the side, gelatin fruit pies and cream soda, or ice-milk sandwiches were enough to satisfy me under normal conditions. Yet there was one dessert which I frequently made that was unlike anything one could buy anywhere. No one else in the household would eat it, but that was all right by me — I made it in servings of one.

Chocolate Dribble

I'm not at all sure it is possible these days to buy chocolate pudding in the packages requiring that it be cooked in a double boiler for upwards of half an hour. The puddings I see around today come in little cans: all you have to do is yank the pull-top ring and dig in with your fingers. Awful stuff. Assuming that such packages are available, however, it is important to remember that the cooking instructions are a pack of lies. Most maintain that one package of chocolate pudding will serve six. Ridiculous. Properly made, one package of chocolate pudding will serve no more than one small boy. Also, the instructions regarding quantities and length of time in cooking are fraudulent. A decent chocolate pudding should have *substance,* and only by ignoring these instructions can you avoid the glutinous confection they attempt to foist off on you.

Use only *half* the milk specified, and cook the pudding at least *twice* as long as the package recommends. This will make it pretty hard to stir, which you must do constantly in order to eliminate lumps, but nothing worthwhile is ever achieved without effort. When the pudding is done, the spoon will not only stick up without support, it will vibrate if you give it a sharp thwack! with the flat of your hand.

Scoop the pudding out into a glass bowl and refrigerate for a few hours. If you have followed these instructions to the letter, you will be able to turn the bowl upside down, shake the pudding out in one mass, and throw it to the floor. If it bounces back, dribble it around the kitchen before eating.

When some magazine or radio program recalls Bogart and Bacall, Frank Sinatra and Glenn Miller, bobby-sox and Pearl Harbor, my mind wanders to thoughts of Strawberry Ooze and Hamburger Knots. I don't make such things now, of course; the layers of civilization have grown too thick on me, and my taste buds have become jaded by too many years of rare prime rib, green salad, and buttered croissants. END

by Barbara Clayton

It Could Happen to Anyone

IT was the dead of winter, six o'clock in the morning, and Charlie was trapped in a snowbank, twelve miles from town on an isolated highway in northern Maine. Cold? It was so cold that Charlie swears the night before a cat had frozen solid in mid-air over his front lawn.

Frigid to his toes, Charlie was reflecting that he might well follow in the footsteps of the unfortunate cat when he heard the chains of a heavy van. He was out of the car like a shot.

"Hey!" he yelled, waving his arms.

The van stopped, a sleepy driver poked his head out the

window, assessed the situation, and produced a chain. "Have you out in no time," he promised. "Tow you to town."

With the station wagon secured behind the van, they started off along the road. At the second curve the van accelerated and the car skidded sideways. Charlie's relief turned to alarm.

"Slow down!" he shouted, blasting the horn.

The van accelerated more.

Lurching and swaying in his car, Charlie flicked the lights, blasted the horn, and yelled his head off.

The van went faster.

The station wagon careened from snowbank to snowbank. Charlie gripped the wheel. When the driver slowed at the next curve, Charlie was going so fast that he almost came alongside the van.

"Slow down, you maniac!" he howled.

With a look of terror, the van driver stepped on the gas. Like lightning, they zigzagged in tandem along the slick icy road. Sweating, frozen to the wheel, expecting each spectacular moment to be the last, Charlie leaned on the horn.

The van went faster.

Scared? Charlie had never been so scared. Until he saw a car approaching in the opposite lane. The car came to a dead halt, but the van never slowed a whit. Rocketing sideways, Charlie spun the wheel, and by one coat of paint skinned past the car.

Too spent to yell, too numb to blow the horn, Charlie ricocheted madly behind the van. Mile after mile, farms and houses boiled past. Town, thought Charlie. Now the van would *have* to stop.

It did.

With a screech of brakes and not the slightest warning,

the van slammed sharply into a driveway while the station wagon, with Charlie hanging on for dear life, bowled crazily along the street. When it reached the end of the tow chain, however, it snapped around violently, and the wagon yanked the van backwards out of the driveway and onto Main Street.

Charlie couldn't move.

Leaping out of the van, the driver stared at the chain, the wagon, and finally Charlie. "M'God!" he breathed. Charlie pried his fingers from the wheel.

"M'God!" White and shaking, the driver peered at Charlie. "Forgot you was behind me. Been workin' all night. Had the radio up loud so's to stay awake. The chains was thumpin' on the road, and . . ." His voice trailed away.

Charlie managed a nod.

"Clean forgot about you," the driver rattled on. "Thought some damfool lunatic was tryin' to pass me on that greasy road. Kept blowin' his horn, flickin' his lights. Almost got me on one curve. Hard's I tried, couldn't get away from that maniac. I'd speed up, he'd speed up . . ." The driver lost all words.

Carefully Charlie considered the twelve homicidal miles. He moved an arm, found the handle, and opened the car door. With deliberation, he placed both feet upon the ground and rose to his full five feet nine inches. Eyeball-to-eyeball he faced the driver of the van.

"I'm glad," he said, "that I finally managed to attract your attention."

As Charlie says, it could happen to anyone.   END

Sermon at Sea

by M.A. Tyler

MANY years ago, when I was a young man aboard a big four-masted bark bound for England, an incident occurred which demonstrated quite clearly the qualities possessed by many of the captains commanding those romantic Cape Horn windjammers. It all began as a result of a brief period of mental gymnastics on the part of the crew as they sat around the forecastle during one Sunday free watch.

The west winds were "late" that year: that is, we had to keep driving south in order to fetch up with them. And meet them we must before heading east to round the cusp of the Horn for our long trek north for England.

Terrific winds, often reaching hurricane force, Cape Horn Current, and drift ice, all combine with the bone-chilling cold to make this particular stretch of water rather nasty as a general rule, and thereby, in part, lies the humor of the tale.

Our trip thus far had been a fast one: thirty-one days from Port Victoria, South Australia, to Cape Horn.

The "Old Man" was a driver. This we knew before signing on and that was one of the reasons many of us were there. His consistent record for coming in first, days and even weeks ahead of the rest of the fleet, made his command more desirable on which to serve. Of course, it meant more concentrated hell, but for a shorter period of time.

Then, too, we were there to become sailors, and a finer man to bring about this transition could be found nowhere in the fleet.

As stated before, the trip down had been fast. Knots were piled up only at the expense of long grueling hours spent aloft handling sail and pulling on braces.

True to tradition, the "Forties" had roared, the "Fifties" raged, and with our position of 58°17'S, 75°45'W, we had better meet the Westerlies soon, or the "Sixties" would soon be climbing aboard to attack.

Fortune smiled that day. Three blasts on the Mate's whistle brought all hands. Braces were manned and the heading brought from a S77E to N71E. We were starting our run. We had met the Westerlies at last.

The dispositions of the crew, worn thin through weeks of working in cold wet clothes, living in a drenched forecastle with sopping wet bunks, and the incessant calls of "All hands on deck" to work ship during free watch, were in the pink of condition to tackle this toughest part of the voyage. They were, when not fighting canvas, fighting among themselves.

The topics of conversation of a group of men sitting around during free watch ranged from choice foods to women, feather beds, and opera, and invariably wound up the same way — in a scrap, verbal or otherwise.

How it started or who started it on this particular day, I don't remember, nor does it matter. But at last they were on religion — as fine a topic as one could dream up under the circumstances, especially with several hotheaded denominational advocates in the group taking a very belligerent self-centered attitude.

Fortunately, the discussion eventually swung to what turned out to be a more amusing angle. The point was brought up that the Old Man, among his other responsibilities and duties, was obligated to conduct Sunday services for Christian members of the crew, and were not all of us Christians? And why hadn't we had any services?

Well, as previously stated, the boys were prime and ready to tackle anything, even the Old Man — and they did.

A delegation of three was chosen by simply outshouting the most radical advocates for shipboard services, and sending them aft to demand our rights under the "Acts."

With our stomachs knotted in apprehension, we waited for the results, expecting most anything in a disciplinary line, and wishing we had not acted in quite such a hasty manner.

In due time, the three returned, wearing a look of credulous wonder on their faces, and reported the Captain was actually sympathetic about the whole thing. He apologized for his laxity in the matter, gave them each a drink of aqua vitae, and promised to carry out his responsibilities on the following Sunday.

Since we had entered the Cape Horn Current, our weather had been unusually fine. The wind's holding steady allowed full canvas and only an occasional Gray Back. (Gray Backs are a species of wave found only in these waters. These waves, presenting a wall, 10 to 30 feet and more high, rush at you with the speed of an express train. As you cannot ride over them, they break on top of you, dumping tons of solid green water, many feet deep, on deck. While these waves are dangerous, mighty wet, cold, and uncomfortable, they are standard equipment with the Cape Horn area. One soon learns to accept them and how to live with them. Yes — just hang on.)

Well, Sunday came as Sundays do, and at eight bells Kalle, the officers' mess boy, came to the forecastle and passed word that the Captain requested all hands to muster on the forward well deck at No. 2 hatch for religious services.

We took our positions on deck, all making certain we had something secure to hold fast to. I was sure I could detect an undercurrent of excitement when the Captain assumed his station behind the fresh water tank for the galley. This tank was located right in front of the half open galley skylight, from which one could see heat waves rising from the huge cooking range directly below.

The Old Man was all of eight feet above us on the break of the midship house and the tank came waist high, ideal for a pulpit: warm, dry, and comfortable.

He placed a large leather-bound Bible, with a massive brass clasp fitted with a small padlock, on top of the tank and opened it very slowly, placing his hands, palms down, on the outer edges to keep the pages from lifting. He looked down upon all of us, as if to count noses, took a deep breath, and said: "Let us pray." He gave thanks for many things, including his ability to conduct this service in each of the five languages represented aboard his ship, that all might benefit from this occasion.

I might say, without elaboration, that at this point, due to extenuating circumstances, there was not one of us who would not have been more than willing to excuse the Captain from further obligations of a religious nature after his most lengthy prayer. We would have welcomed the opportunity to scud back to the comparative warmth and safety of the forecastle. But there we were, and there he was; it was quite apparent that we were due for a sermon, come hell or high water. After all, we had asked for it.

He had concluded the Finnish section of the sermon when the first wave hit us, enveloping us in a solid wall of ice-cold water. Some of the boys were torn loose from their moorings and wound up under the lee pinrail, completely submerged and fouled in a tangle of lines, but the Captain politely waited until we were all settled, counted noses once again, and then continued with the business at hand without further interruption.

At the completion of the Scandinavian discourses, we were the most miserable, beat-and-bedraggled crew of Christians anyone ever laid eyes on — and the end was not yet in sight.

Still, no one dared to make a break for shelter. Just to add spice to the affair, the wind, which had been fresh, with all our sails set clean to the royals, was picking up noticeably. The ship had a list that put the freeing parts under by the time the Captain had finished the English portion, which, frankly, I missed in its entirety due to certain distractions. The Mates were by now casting worried glances up at the rigging, wondering how much more it would take.

I doubt if any of us really appreciated the unselfish and fair-minded attitude displayed by the Old Man when he reached into the voluminous pocket of his great coat and withdrew a black, flexible-bound, ecclesiastical publication of the Russian Orthodox faith and proceeded in his own inimitable way to recognize the two Russian members of our crew, the first sailmaker and an apprentice boy. At this point, we discovered that not only could the leerail go clean under and stay there, but that she would also sail quite well while dipping the ends of the lower yards in the crests of the waves. Each sickening roll brought the angry sea half way over the hatches, forcing all of us to the windward or high side of the deck and to hang on to each other for dear life. This condition did not promote our undivided attention to the Captain, but he seemed unaware of any impending disaster and droned on with no change of expression in voice or countenance.

By now, the Mates were not the only ones showing signs of alarm. We knew if canvas were not struck, and soon, we might have to swim around Cape Horn, a stunt we were not anxious to try.

The old windjammer was a shrieking bedlam of sound. The crash of the waters coming aboard, blended with the thunderous booming of the canvas, and the rattle and bang of the tackle blocks, tried to outdo the screech of the wind through the rigging. Only on a square-rigger could you obtain this tremendous, almost overpowering sensation of sound.

Although by now we were unable to hear a word of the sermon, I'm quite positive some of the boys were going along with the Captain, voicing their own little prayers.

No ship ever built could endure this punishment very long and, sure enough, ours didn't. Her first sign of protest came when the jibstay, weakened by rust in the splice at the top gallant mast loop, carried away with the report of a cannon, trailing sail, jibstay and all, over the lee side along the rail.

The Old Man, with as benevolent a look on his face as any preacher, finally reached and finished the Benediction, slowly closed the massive Bible, placed both hands, palms down on the cover, then raised his eyes and looked at us for several long seconds. "Amen! Mates, take the watch."

No crew ever tied into clew and bunt lines, or swarmed up into the rigging with greater alacrity than this one; nor did they require at this point the customary orders to accelerate them towards their appointed stations. Canvas seemed to dissolve from the royals down with only tacit command from the Mates.

Perhaps we were just too busy fighting our way out of those turbulent waters; or perhaps we realized we could learn more than seamanship from the Old Man. But no mention was ever made of continuing the Sunday sermons.   END

Go Fly a Monkey

by Joel M. Vance

IF someone had told me that a girl of golden curls and fathomless blue eyes and complexion of rosebud and milk would become infatuated with me and follow me around with liquid gazes, I'd have been as appalled as if someone had told me that John Wayne was giving up Western movies to become a band instructor.

Birch Lake summers were for fishing and swimming and exploring and kick-the-can. Not for mooing and bawling like a lovesick calf. Why I entranced Jeannie surpassed reason. At twelve, I was not exactly a Twentieth Century sex symbol. I owned the profile of a paper clip. I had snake hips and my ribs were countable from a block away. I preferred to think of myself as wiry, but everyone else said I was as skinny as a tomato stake.

Girls flustered me in general, and Jeannie, from the moment we locked stares in Thurston's Grocery Store, flustered me in particular. My blush threshold was subnormal. Talking with girls caused me to flame and sweat and drop such conversational gems, as "Yeah, well, I guess . . . ."

I knew Jeannie only as a girl of unusual charm who lived on the other side of town, sat on the other side of the classroom, and was as unapproachable as someone on the other side of the moon.

Then, one stunning day at Thurston's where we bought

ice cream cones, candy bars and gumballs, she fell in love with me. My cousins, Hal and Frank, and I wandered into the store one hot summer morning in search of a double dipper, chocolate on top, vanilla in the cone. Jeannie was standing by the soft drink cooler, bottle of Seven-Up raised within three inches of her rosebud lips, when our eyes locked (the view was slightly obstructed by a strip of flypaper).

"My mom said she'd tan my fanny if she caught me lassoing the chickens anymore," Hal was saying. Hal was studying to be the Durango Kid.

"Let's go over to the ice house and cool off," Frank suggested. "I'm about to burn up. You comin', Bobby? Hey, Bobby? Bobby, you comin'?"

I was adrift in sweet confusion, staggered by a Cupidal dart as keen as a new Gillette Blue blade. Jeannie's eyes were wide and astonished and her Seven-Up foamed and fizzed unheeded. Strengthless, we were unable to break the heavy stare which immobilized us. Had I not been with my cousins, I probably would have said hello, and she would have said hello, and we would have stumbled on into a jittery twelve-year-old's romance, replete with mushy notes and hand-holding and other innocences. But I had to have my mouthy cousins with me.

Frank, unable to get my attention, followed my moo-cow stare to its destination, then looked back at me. He raised his eyebrows devilishly and jabbed Hal in the ribs. "What's the matter, Li'l Sweet Bobby?" he simpered sickeningly. "Got somethin' in your eye?"

I tumbled off the meteor I was riding and fell to earth. Jeannie exhaled, completed her swig of pop and turned away, reddening. I remembered nothing from the past few moments. It was as if I had taken a dizzying trip around the moon, faster than light. I was weak all over.

Frank's buzz-saw voice nipped at me, like a small, angry dog. "Bobby's got a girrruulllllll!" he keened, guffawing coarsely.

Heat pulsed in my face. "Have not!" I shouted, shoving him against the gumball machine. "Let's go lasso the chickens!"

"You want my rope?" Hal sniggered. "Then you can go lasso that chicken." He and Frank leaned on each other and whooped.

"Ahhhhh!" I snarled, searching for a biting retort and not finding one. "Go fly a monkey!" I meant to say, "Go fly a kite" or "Go stuff a monkey!" but it came out all wrong. In that awful moment of embarrassment, I did a childish thing. I blamed Jeannie for it and thought I hated her. She had caused my embarrassment. Girls, for crying out loud, who needs them? Even as I scorned her, though, I remembered that melting look and I had a momentary feeling my chest was going to split like a ripe watermelon dropped on the ground.

After that, I avoided Jeannie as if she were threatening to beat me up: but she plagued me. I went down to the dam to swim, and she came along and looked soulfully at me. "Hi, Bobby," she said shyly. "Are you swimming?"

"No," I growled, like Billygoat Gruff. "I'm folding parachutes." She mistook biting sarcasm for humor and giggled helplessly. I gritted my teeth. All right, so I despised her. Then why was I hiding in water up to my neck, ashamed for her to see my corduroy rib cage and chicken muscles? "Look, Jeannie," I pleaded, "why don't you go home? I think your mother is calling you." I watched the road, panicked lest Hal and Frank come along and whisper and giggle and point at me.

"I think I'll sit here and watch the water," Jeannie said, blistering me with a thousand-watt smile. "You be careful and don't go over the dam." I growled and dogpaddled down the shore without looking back. When I put my feet down, she was right above me on the bank.

"You sure do dogpaddle good," she said admiringly.

"So do dogs," I answered shortly. She giggled.

Horror of horrors, Jeannie's mother and mine became co-chairmen of the annual Birch Lake Pie Supper. They were as close as sisters while they planned the event, and suddenly Jeannie was at our house incessantly, mooning around me and asking if I liked to read Nancy Drew mysteries. It was terrible.

On the second Saturday before the Pie Supper, Hal and Frank and I followed our normal schedule. We attended the matinee at the Birch Lake Rialto, a tin-sided movie theater, which offered a dirty screen, plush splintered plywood seats and the thick atmosphere of an old locker room. But it showed, and had been showing for a long time, the continuing western adventures of the Durango Kid. In Chapter 50, we had left our hero hanging from a cliff by one bleeding hand. A sinister character called Black Bart was stomping viciously on the Kid's clutching fingers. The Kid stared somewhat apprehensively into the yawning abyss and tried to ignore Black Bart's grinding boot.

But it was no go, and he fell free and began to plunge to certain death. The scene froze and the music came up dramatically.

"Will this mean the end of the Durango Kid?" asked the off-screen narrator.

"No!" we shouted in unison and whistled and stomped.

"And what of Brave Feather, the proud Indian companion of the Kid, now staked to an anthill in the desert?" our nosy interrogator asked.

"Let the ants eat him!" we screamed.

"Be sure to be here next week for Chapter 51, the Pit of

Death!" cried the voice. There was a vast clacking of rickety seats. We crunched through a summer's accumulation of popcorn fallout and squinted into the bright sun.

"Golly!" Hal exclaimed. "How do you suppose they're gonna get him out of that messup?"

"They'll probably have Brave Feather's people down in a cave somewheres down in that pit," Frank mused thoughtfully, for he was a student of movie serial technique. "You know, they'll be standing there when he comes flyin' by, and the best lassoing Indian will throw a rope over him, and they'll drag him into their secret hideaway where they got skulls of their enemies and torches and all that good junk."

And that is precisely what happened in Chapter 51, which ran the week before the Pie Supper. We were riding an emotional high when the serial episode ended and were suddenly stunned when our off-screen confidant announced, "Be sure to be here next week for the final installment of 'The Perilous Adventures of the Durango Kid!' Will the Kid escape the dreadful spring gun which Black Bart has fiendishly set in the anthill where Brave Feather is staked? See the savage uprising by Brave

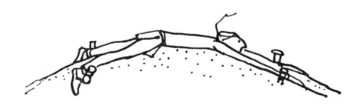

Feather's people. Will the President, riding the train from Abilene to Wichita, fall into Black Bart's trap and be kidnapped? And how can the Kid possibly survive the fall between the hurtling boxcars?"

"Whew!" Frank breathed, awestruck. "I can't figure *no* way out of that can of worms!" The final episode was the entertainment highlight of the summer for every kid in Birch Lake. Every kid in town was going to be there, come high water or chicken pox. Every one, it turned out, but me. On Thursday, my mother stunned me by announcing firmly that *my* Saturday afternoon would be spent helping her work on the Pie Supper. No amount of whining would change her mind. The Pie Supper chores were the worst possible fate, and I just knew old dumb Jeannie was behind the whole thing. Probably spend all afternoon reading me selected passages from Nancy Drew. I concentrated on hating Jeannie of the dumb bouncy curls and big old eyes.

Seething, I stalked toward town, kicking rocks. The last people I wanted to see were Hal and Frank, but naturally I met them. "Hey, Bobby," Frank said. "You got any ideas on how the Durango Kid is gonna wind things up?"

"I'm not going," I muttered. "I gotta help on the pie thing." They registered sympathy, and then a slow smile slithered over Frank's face.

"Hey! I'll bet you're gonna take little miss dolly curls to the dreat big Pie Supper. Bobby's got a girrullllll!"

I growled and shoved him, and he stumbled back and fell over his mother's prize Peace rose and howled in pain. "You leave my brother alone!" Hal cried, jumping on me. We crashed to the ground, scuffling and shouting inarticulate hate slogans.

Their mother broke it up and I stalked on downtown, brooding on man's inhumanity to man. Score another one for Jeannie. If I'd had a dog, she'd have figured out a way to make him bite me.

"Hi, Bobby." The shy, soft voice made me jump and I whirled to face dumb old Jeannie. She stood there with that melting, tender look on her big-eyed face. Don't tell me she didn't know how cute she was! For a moment I forgot how much I hated her. "My mother said you might go to the Pie Supper," she murmured shyly. Boy, that did it! The mention of the Pie Supper detonated me.

"Why don't you leave me alone, you dopey dope!" I shouted. "I'm not gonna go to any Pie Supper with you! I wouldn't take you to a dog show if I thought you'd win first prize! Why don't you go crawl in a hole and pull it in after you! Leave me alone!"

There was a terrible silent moment after I ran out of dreadful things to say, during which she merely looked starkly at me, her face gone white. "I thought," she whispered, "you liked me a little."

I felt my heart sliced with rusty hacksaws. I bit my lip and looked at the ground and wished I could sink into a muskrat hole with the rest of the rats. I tried to say, "I'm sorry," but my pride had a firm grip on my tongue and I couldn't get the words out. She turned and ran toward town, her shining curls flying in the sunlight.

Then my mother relented and said she wouldn't need me at the Pie Supper, and so it all was unnecessary. Saturday morning sparkled with the magic of summer and the day glittered with glory. Breakfast tasted like wet sawdust.

Hal and Frank and I stood around and dug our toes in the dirt and finally decided to make up. Everything was okay again. Then why did I feel as if someone were digging postholes in my heart?

The theater filled fast. This was the big one. I picked out a seat that seemed to be relatively free of old wads of gum.

About now, I thought, my mother and Jeannie's mother and Jeannie would be gathering across the street at the Town Hall before the Pie Supper . . . .

The house lights went out to a tumultuous cheer from the assembled youngsters. There flickered before our eyes the blurry title: "CHAPTER 52 — The Last Desperate Moment!" A piece of lint lodged on the projector lens and vibrated there.

"Hey, Projector Man, get your mustache outa the machine!" cried a wit somewhere on the other side of the theater, and everyone whistled and stomped. The lint flicked away and the Durango Kid swirled to a plunging halt. The scene changed to show Brave Feather staked to an anthill. I began to itch. About now, Jeannie would be unloading the pies and stuff across the street. Were her eyes still stricken, her cheeks white? I bit my lip.

"Brave Feather!" the Kid cried, sliding gracefully off his stallion to help his fallen companion.

"Hey, watch the spring gun, ya dumb bunny!" all the kids shouted. Then the great white stallion was there, whinnying and shoving the Kid away, pawing until he tripped the deadly spring gun harmlessly.

The two heroes galloped recklessly across a railroad trestle, intent on saving the President. This was it — Hal and Frank were transfixed, their eyes big. Big eyes. White, shocked face. "I thought you liked me a little . . . ."

"I gotta go!" I cried, leaping up. I shoved Frank out of the way. I pushed my way to the aisle, ignoring the shouted insults of those whose view I blocked, and stumbled up the aisle, wading through the rifted popcorn and cups. I ran across the street, scooted up the steps and through the door of the Town Hall.

The room was filled with women — plump ones, skinny ones, tall ones, short ones. Jeannie was on the fringe of this matronly forest, her back to me. She turned and her big eyes widened.

"I *would* take you to a dog show!" I blurted. "I mean — I'm sorry about everything and I didn't mean what I said and ... and ... would you go to the Pie Supper with me?"

I ran out of breath and courage and gulped and felt like running. She smiled tremulously and diamonds came into her eyes and she said, "I'd like to go with you."

For all I know, the Durango Kid and Brave Feather both fell off the train and got trampled by the great white stallion, and Black Bart kidnapped the President and lived happily ever after. I really didn't care .... END by A.T. Anderson

Benjamin Franklin Visits His Mother

ONE of the greatest men this continent has produced was Benjamin Franklin. He was so versatile and interesting, that he was in fact thirty men rolled into one, excelling in every role.

Ben had many ideas, theories, and sometimes, strong opinions. In any age he would have been extraordinary. In ancient times a temple would have been erected to his memory. If alive today, his great personal power, his uncanny gift of looking into the future, would have been astounding. He was always experimenting and inventing, sometimes right on the spot. One of the most curious and interesting of his experiments concerned his idea that mothers did not necessarily recognize their own children after an absence of many years.

Several years after coming to Philadelphia, he received word of his father's passing. After he had sold his business, in which he had prospered and amassed by careful thrift the sum of $75,000, he devoted the remainder of his life in unselfish service to his country. He became a beloved public figure, both here and abroad. But now he wanted to see his mother once again, whom he hadn't seen since he left his home in Boston, a slender youth of seventeen — round-faced, red-cheeked, with ample blonde hair falling to his shoulders. Franklin at forty-two was quite changed. He was now a robust looking man, balding on top, with shoulder-length dark hair greying at the temples. A humorous quirk to his mouth gave him an honest, open look, and his wide, grey eyes were friendly.

He had mentioned in conversation with friends that he conjectured that a mother might, by a kind of instinct or natural affection, recognize her children, even though she had lost recollection of their particular features.

To discover the existence of this instinct by actual experiment, Franklin planned to introduce himself as a complete stranger when he went to visit his mother. Thus he could watch and study her closely, waiting for the supreme moment in which she would discover her son's identity. Then he could determine, with the cool detachment of a philosopher, whether the Big Moment was due to a mother's instant affection, her intuitive love, or innate attachment.

On a cloudy, chilly day, sullen with storm clouds, Ben at last arrived in Boston, late one afternoon in January, at his mother's home. He rapped on the door, and he asked the maid who answered if he could speak to Mrs. Franklin. The maid led him into the parlor, where he saw his mother, seated before a blazing fire, calmly knitting. He introduced himself as Neb Frank and, looking at her pleasantly, said in his most winning way, "I have learned, madam, that you entertain travellers, and I wonder if I could prevail upon you to let me have a night's lodging here?"

Mrs. Franklin eyed him up and down coldly, insulted at his question implying she was a common innkeeper. Not a flicker of recognition came into her face, as she said coldly, "Sir! You have been misinformed ... I am a *lady*, and do *not* keep a tavern. I do keep some members of the legislature as paying guests during the session. All my beds are full, so GOOD DAY!"

With that, she furiously resumed her knitting, with intense application, trying to suggest he should take himself off as soon as possible.

Ben looked at her, and wrapping his great cloak about him, he pretended to shiver, and said, "Madam, the warmth of your fire makes me reluctant to leave right away. Pray, may I warm myself a bit before I go?"

Without answering him, she pointed to a chair close to the fire, and he sat down, extending his hands to the blaze. Just then the boarders began arriving, which stopped any further conversation between Ben and his mother. Coffee was brought in and served by the maid, and according to the good old custom of the times, a big plate of rosy pippins (apples) was brought out, along with pipes and a paper of McIntire's Best Tobacco.

Soon the men brought chairs from the dining room and formed a semi-circle around the fire. Mrs. Franklin left the room to see to the supper preparations. Franklin was now in his element, and never was there any occasion as rich as this, savoring just when or how the surprise about his identity would come. Ben was an incomparable raconteur, a well-read person, a gifted speaker, and now displayed his great powers of personal magnetism. He was full of amusing anecdotes, knew everything of the problems facing these men, and they on their part were so completely under his magic spell that they were surprised when the big clock in the dining room (another of Franklin's inventions) struck the hour of eight. Mrs. Franklin suddenly appeared in the doorway to announce supper was ready. She seemed disconcerted to see Ben was still there, assuming he had taken his leave after coffee in the parlor. She frowned when she saw him rise and follow the men into the dining room, uninvited. At the table, Ben again kept the conversational ball merrily rolling and none could remember having had such a happy mealtime.

After they had eaten, Mrs. Franklin called one of the older men, telling him she had something important to say to him. The others went into the parlor but Ben lingered a bit, hoping to eavesdrop, as he felt he knew what she had on her mind. He heard her complain bitterly about the rudeness of this stranger, as she related how he had gained entrance into her home. Then she told him she was greatly worried and wanted his advice as to the quickest way to send him off, before all the inns would be closed.

"He seems to be a most outlandish man," she finished, "and I am most suspicious about his intentions."

"Ma'am, we have been all amused and entertained by this happy stranger, who seems to be very well educated and a born gentleman. No doubt he has forgotten about the lateness of the hour; so I am sure if you will call him aside and advise him of it, he will leave with no trouble."

Mrs. Franklin stood a few minutes, deep in thought. Presently, she appeared in the parlor doorway. Summoning all the dignity she could command, she said, "Gentlemen, I am sure you are aware that the hour is late, and our inns will be closed unless the stranger betakes himself off immediately!"

"'Ah! madam, your indulgence, please . . . I should like to smoke just one more pipe with these congenial gentlemen, though I have no wish to discommode your family. One more pipe, and I will be gone."

He then proceeded to light his pipe, and with the first whiff, his powers returned with double force. He told of the hardships of their forebears, while he extolled their piety. One of the gentlemen mentioned a debate held that

114

day in the house of representatives. Thoroughly familiar with the problems, Franklin entered upon the subject and astounded his hearers by his logic, uncommon sense, and knowledge of their problems. His audience was so intent on all he had to say that they could have sat all night listening to him, but suddenly the big clock struck eleven. Mrs. Franklin hastily entered the room, and this time there was no mistaking her anger.

"Sir! My patience is exhausted! I feel myself imposed upon, and though I am but a lone widow, I have many friends who would protect me ... I bid you leave with no further tarrying!"

"My humblest apologies, ma'am," replied Franklin. "In such pleasant company, I confess I forgot the passage of time."

With that he arose, put on his greatcoat, and approached the street door, lighted on his way by a maid holding a lighted candle, with Mrs. Franklin nearby making sure he would leave at last.

All during the time Ben had been entertaining his audience, a tremendous January storm had filled the streets with snow knee-deep, and just as the maid lifted the latch, a roaring northeast wind threw the door forcibly open, bringing in drifting snow, and the wind howling in fiendish glee. The wind quickly extinguished the candle, and the maid hurried to the fireplace to relight it. Franklin cast a woebegone look at Mrs. Franklin, saying sadly, "Surely, madam, you could not possibly turn me out in this dreadful storm? I am a stranger here, and would perish in the streets. You look like a charitable woman, and you could not turn a dog out on such a tempestuous night."

"Don't prate to me about charity," angrily retorted his mother, now at her wits' end as she realized her plight. "It is your own fault that you tarried so long. To be perfectly frank with you, I do not like your looks nor your conduct."

While thus speaking to him, her voice had risen sharply, so some of the men from the parlor came to see what the trouble might be. When they saw the storm and snow, they prevailed on Mrs. Franklin to reconsider, and let the stranger stay at least until daylight.

"Well, no bed is to be had so he shall have to sleep in a straight chair in the parlor," she finished lamely. Not sharing her boarders' belief in her strange guest's honesty, she quickly began gathering her treasures, her six silver teaspoons, her pewter porringers, her pepper box, and put them all in a box and carried them to her bedroom. Locking the parlor door, she made sure he could not escape by sticking a fork over the latch to secure it. Calling a servant, she ordered, "Samuel, I want you to sleep here on the floor by the door tonight keeping your clothes on so you will be ready at the first move he makes. I will not have my house plundered while we are all asleep." She bade her maid to take her pallet into her bedroom so the two women would be prepared.

Long before sunrise the next morning, Mrs. Franklin arose, roused her domestics, and carefully unfastened the parlor door. She was agreeably surprised to find her guest sleeping on his chair, his head slightly tilted, his greatcoat draped over him. She went to him, saying cheerfully, "Good morning, sir! I trust you have rested well?" Glancing at her, Ben stretched, and answered that, yes, he had been quite comfortable.

"I always have my breakfast before my boarders rise and I invite you to join me," she said. The maid brought in a tray on which was a pitcher of hot chocolate, slices of bread, and a pat of butter.

Sipping her chocolate thoughtfully, and studying his

116

face, she asked, "You say you are a stranger here . . . pray, sir, to what distant country do you belong?"

"I, madam, belong to the great city of Philadelphia," Franklin replied.

"Philadelphia!" she exclaimed, and for the first time Franklin noted her face flushed with interest as she pursued her questioning. "Oh! If you live in Philadelphia, perhaps you know or have met my Ben?"

"Who, madam?"

"Why, my Ben . . . Benjamin Franklin . . . oh, he was the dearest child that ever blest a mother! He was my baby son, my fifteenth, and a smarter one never lived!"

"What?" answered Ben, as though delightfully surprised. "Is Ben Franklin the Printer, *your* son?"

"Yes, oh yes! Do you know him?"

"Why, he is my most intimate friend; in fact, he and I lodge in the same house," continued Franklin, now amused at this turn in the conversation.

"Oh, God forgive me!" exclaimed the poor soul, raising her watery eyes to heaven. "How I have wronged you! To suffer a friend of my Ben's to sleep in a hard chair, while I rested on a good bed."

Studying him more closely, she asked, "What did you say your name is, sir?"

"Neb, Neb Frank, ma'am."

"Neb? What kind of heathenish name is that?" She seemed to be pondering her next question, as she asked, "Tell me more, pray, about my Benny. It's been many years since he left home, poor lad, though I've been told he has made his mark in the world."

Chuckling to himself, Ben proceeded to tell her of many family incidents, of his inventions while still at home, one of which included a special surgical instrument which saved a brother's life.

117

"My! You must indeed be an intimate friend ..." and then she said, musingly, "Neb, Neb" ... ah! the light dawned!

Smilingly, and studying him closely, she asked, "I wonder if you're not playing a trick on an old woman, and your curious name, Neb, is Ben, spelled backward? ... *Are* you my Ben, my most beloved son, citizen of Philadelphia?"

Of course Ben admitted his deception, and what a joyous reunion was theirs! With tears freely flowing, his mother embraced him tenderly, kissing him on top of his head as she murmured her happiness, begging him to stay as long as he could with her.

Long after Ben had returned to Philadelphia, he maintained as a result of his experiment that a natural affection between mother and child did not exist after a many years' absence.   END by Steven H. Bamberger

Ho! Ho! Ho!

UP until my wife's brainstorm of last year, Christmas, to me, was the most cherished of all the holidays. Easter is always lovely, too, and so is Thanksgiving; but somehow Christmas, with tiny hands reaching for tiny toys and high-pitched voices raised in song, was my favorite. It was, that is, until last year.

It all started out innocently enough with a chance remark by my wife.

"This will be the last Christmas Junior will believe in Santa Claus," was what she said, and while she was only echoing the words of parents throughout the ages, it remained for us, I believe, to be the first parents ever to *do* something about it. Our "plan," if you can call it that, was for me to dress up as Santa Claus and climb up to my son's window on Christmas Eve. Exactly what I was supposed to do when I got up there was never discussed, and to this day I still can't imagine how I ever fell for the idea in the first place.

My son's bedroom, incidentally, opens onto the first staircase landing, which makes it not as high as some low-hanging clouds but high enough for me to have to borrow my neighbor's extension ladder. Also, there is a natural tendency for a house to grow taller at night — but I can't prove this.

Christmas Eve last year, if you recall, was a clear, crispy, moonlit night. We had trimmed the tree in the afternoon and, since we always exchange gifts the following morning rather than at midnight, Junior had little to look forward to after supper, to his knowledge at any rate, other than to hang up his stocking and go to bed and dream.

To save time, I set up the ladder while he was in his bath so that all we had to do after tucking him in and listening to his prayers was to race downstairs to the basement and dress me up.

The costume my wife had purchased was extra-large and consisted mostly of pillows, sewn in, to prevent slippage. There was one huge pillow in front and another huge pillow in back, and it was all I could do to buckle my patent leather belt into the first notch. The mask and peaked hat were conventional, as was the enormous toy-sack, also stuffed with pillows, that I was just about able to sling over my shoulder.

A touch of brilliance, though, was the two strings of sleigh bells which my wife, convulsed now and no longer able to talk, thrust into my free hand at the last moment. In other words, I was to be the sleigh as well as Santa. Undaunted, and giddy myself with the spirit of the occasion, I bounded up the cellar steps, shattering the stillness of the Holy Night with what seemed to be a million tinkling sleigh bells.

Bringing my knees up smartly (I blush to think of it now), as I imagined a reindeer might do at the gallop, I bobbed along the length of the house, taking short, mincing steps around the corner, then bobbed some more until I finally came to a halt beneath my son's window.

"Whoa, Prancer!" I roared, still jingling my sleigh bells frenziedly. "Whoa, Dancer! Whoa, Blitzen! Whoa, Snitzen!" and then, letting the bells slip to the ground, I approached the ladder with a hearty, "Ho! Ho! Ho!"

I had originally planned to laugh my way up the ladder,

but it immediately became apparent that there was nothing particularly funny about climbing a ladder, accoutered as I was, by the light of the moon. It looked as though I wasn't going to get up there at all until I discovered that my front pillow had wedged itself securely against the rung immediately ahead of it.

Dislodging it with a muffled curse, quickly followed by a "Ho! Ho! Ho!," I took my first step upwards only to have to go through the same procedure with the same pillow all over again, so that to Junior, in his room, I must have sounded like *two* people coming up the ladder, one swearing like a trooper, the other laughing like a maniac. I wasn't concerned about how I sounded, though. My only thought was to reach his window, before sunup, if possible, and the minute I did I made a wild grab for the sill, inadvertently disturbing the pull on his shade — which shot up out of sight with the crack of an M-1 rifle, scaring me half to death.

It must have scared him too because the first thing I noticed as my head hove into view was that he was no longer tucked under the covers as we had left him a few minutes before. Rather, he was sitting bolt upright in a rectangle of moonlight, and if you have ever heard the phrase "eyes wide as saucers," that's exactly the way his eyes appeared at that particular moment. Even his mouth was wide open in an expression that I mistook for one of sheer joy at seeing Jolly Saint Nick practically at the foot of his bed. "Ho! Ho! Ho!" I heard myself saying again.

What happened next, while it may take a little longer in the telling, actually transpired in less than a few seconds. Evidently the last "Ho! Ho! Ho!" did the trick, because the echo of it was still rolling down the valley when there came out of my little boy's throat a shriek so penetrating and so fearsome that I hope I never hear the likes of it again. There was stark terror in that shriek, and panic, and it was delivered with such wild abandon that I momentarily forgot where I was.

Sensing only that flesh of my flesh and blood of my blood was warning his Daddy of impending disaster, I pivoted around suddenly to fend off whatever ghastly thing might be headed my way and toppled headlong onto the holly tree below.

That's about all there is to tell about last Christmas Eve at our house. I have no idea what my wife has in mind now that another Season is upon us but, frankly, if it were up to me, I wouldn't even bother putting up a tree this year.   END by John Gould

The Bank Account That Grew and Grew

ONCE upon a long time ago a promising young man down-east on the coast of Maine took unto himself a bride, and she was not only fair to look upon but she had a great deal of sense. The match gave promise of long years of content, and it was even so. The years passed by even to the sere and yellow leaf, until at last the promising young man was old and alone, for the joyful years of the union had been fulfilled.

Now it happened that when they were first married he gave his bride a checkbook, saying, "This is for you, and when you want money you have only to write a check. I'll make the deposits, and you need have no concern about money."

He had gone to his bank, which was in a larger community some distance from the tidewater town in which he had his lobster business and packing plant, and he had spoken to the banker in this wise: "Set up a joint checking account for me and my wife, separate from my business account, and every time I send in a business deposit put some of it in the joint account. It's only for her household and personal use."

So there you have it. The lovely bride never had to come to her husband about nagging small expenses, nor did she

123

have to come to him about large ones. If she needed something for the house, whether pickling spices or a new rug for the living room, she had only to fare forth and write a check.

True, since it was a joint account the husband could have drawn checks on it too, but that was not his intent, and he never did. His business grew, and prospered, and it was the kind of personal pocket business that permits the owner privileges. If he needed money for himself, he could just go to the till and take it, or he would have his bookkeeper write him a check. One can readily see how an arrangement of this sort would spare a marriage the fretting of numerous fiscal matters that beset less ordered households. Furthermore, the wife was not expensive. She was quite happy to wear her old coat one more winter; she made do and did without. It was seldom she permitted herself anything to be construed as a luxury. She shopped wisely, and always waited for sales on canned goods. She never had a man come in to paper and paint, but would do it herself — getting the materials wholesale through her husband's business contacts. Thus, as the years rolled by, the joint account gained on her. She had no reason to inquire as to the balance, and on her husband's part he left the matter to his banker and his bookkeepers, and didn't inquire either. He knew the banker would notify him if the balance dropped, and since the banker never did it was proof that all was well.

The years unfolded and became extensive. When this good wife went her mortal way he grieved appropriately, and being elderly he merely adjusted and continued to operate his business as before. Although eighty-four, he was spry. Indeed, fourteen years passed, and at ninety-eight he was not only still active, but keen and physically fit. It was at this time that he received a cryptic letter from the bank. People who had retired had been succeeded by others who had retired, and the letter was from a come-lately whippersnapper the old man couldn't recall having met. The letter said that if the gentleman would stop in at the bank there was a financial matter that needed discussion.

It threw the old fellow. Unexpected, the letter suggested perhaps he was in business trouble, so in somewhat frantic mind he consulted his bookkeepers and had them make a trial audit. They assured him that everything seemed in good shape. But still concerned and with many a misgiving he called the neighbor boy who drove him about, and he hied to the town where the bank was located, and he went in. "Yes," said the young man who had written the letter, "we've been wondering about this special account you have."

Knowing how that account had been set up, and considering the long years since, we should not be astonished that the old man had long since forgotten all about it. He had never changed his original instructions to the bank, nor had his own bookkeepers bothered him by reminding him of them. The bank, caught up in its own uninspired methods, had ridden along. Not only had his wife failed to draw out anywhere near what he had put in, but for fourteen years since her funeral the deposits had been made as before, and nothing had been drawn out.

As stories go, there are different versions. Some say the balance in the joint account was only $879,000, but other legendary estimates go as high as three million. An officer of the bank, somewhat embarrassed at being questioned about it, said some thirty-five years ago that while he was not at liberty to disclose the precise amount, the balance was in excess of $500,000. When he was asked how a bank could possibly permit one of its better customers to get caught up in such an absurdity, he said, "Oh, I don't know — it's just one of those things, and it happened."

So, after fourteen years of widowhood, was this not a pleasant legacy from a loving wife? And shouldn't we all ponder what any of us would do if, at ninety-eight years of age, we suddenly found we had half a million dollars we'd forgotten?   END

Jason's Rules

by Stephen Austin

MOTHER always drove in second gear ... at 50 miles per hour, on the left hand side of the road. She was a small lady and as the seats of her big black Buick wouldn't go forward far enough for her to reach the pedals, she'd slouch and peek under the wheel and over the dip in the hood. Not being able to see the road, she'd sight along this view to the left gutter or ditch, and off she'd go, as I said before, doing 50 in second gear, the car screaming and the dust from the shoulder of the road billowing out behind her in mean-looking rolls like smoke from a locomotive. Everybody in the little town of Walton knew her and loved her, and when meeting her simply passed on the left hand side of the road.

It took practice though, making that small and sudden adjustment, and some people never quite got the hang of it ... like Mr. Henderson, our neighbor. When he saw her coming, he'd drive right off the road, no matter where he was.

"T-bone" and I assumed she was doing everything just right, and that Mr. Henderson was a lousy driver. That's why we used her driving technique as our only reference.

T-bone had come to stay with us that fifteenth summer

because his parents were in Europe on a business trip. It was his idea that we teach ourselves how to drive, offering it as a character-building experience and a good way to kill time while our voices changed. We called him "T-bone" partly because he was tall and spare, and partly because his real name was Henry T. Porterhouse, III, but mostly because it clashed so violently with his grave young nature. He never much liked the name, but he liked it a lot better than "Old Potato."

That summer the 1931 Plymouth was the spare car in our family and so, when the house was empty, T-bone and I would go out and start her up. And that's just about all we'd do — at first. The motor would chug in neutral and the car would rock us gently. With a little effort, one could imagine the whole countryside spinning by.

Between these dry runs, we made a careful study of my mother's driving habits and not being able to distinguish between technique and style we decided to play it safe and imitate everything she did.

At first our trips took us out into the fields and we bumped and rumbled along in first gear, both of us bouncing up and down inside the cab like dice in a cup. But this was not enough. We wanted the road and we wanted second gear. So one day we pulled out onto the main road and turned the old Plymouth down the hill, reasoning that we could more easily shift into second gear headed down than up. T-bone was driving, and he was intensely relaxed. That is, his mood was strained but his casual style was adopted from Mother's. With his left elbow sticking out the window, right hand on the wheel, his left wheels on the left shoulder of the road, and moving the car smartly down the road at approximately 10 miles per hour, he inspired confidence. Every muscle in his face and body was taut and ready for the shift. We were just passing the Bemises' place when I shouted "NOW!" and T-bone's hands and feet became a blur in motion. First, he jammed on the foot brake and I smacked my head on the windshield. Secondly, he tromped on the gas pedal, and our heads whiplashed backwards. Thirdly, he threw the car out of gear, and the engine bellowed mightily. Then down the hill we went in neutral, gaining speeds we had never dreamed of. The faster we went the louder I shouted, "THE BRAKE, THE BRAKE," and the harder he pushed the clutch pedal: 30, 35, 40, 45, and God in heaven, 50 miles per hour; but I had to hand it to him, he was holding her well over to the left.

It was at the corner of the foot of the hill where we met Mother. And we were by her before she even recognized us, she on her left, we on ours. Considering we went past each other at the combined speed of 100 miles an hour, it's not too surprising she didn't spot us.

After the corner, the hill levels out and even turns up, and it was here that T-bone finally got the car in second gear, but he stalled it and she locked on the grade, tinkling with heat in the summer sun.

* * * * *

About a year and a half later T-bone and I were ready to get our licenses. T-bone reached sixteen before I did, and for a period of two weeks after his birthday he lived within the pages of the rules-of-the-road book. He knew it upside down. What's more, having clocked twelve hours on the highway with his own mother and another thirty-two hours on the "back forty" with me, he could drive as well as any man. Getting his license should have been merely a matter of bureaucratic formality — and would have been, had we not made one big mistake.

We consulted my brother, Jason.

This was nothing new. Jason had always been an important reference point in our lives, because talking things over with him turned the dullest enterprise into a grand plan, a great adventure. In fact, Jason was so clever at wrapping up life in tinsel and satin packages I'm not sure he always knew himself where, in the gloriously colored excelsior, the small nugget of truth was hidden. He was a spellbinder, an elixir salesman, and, according to my father, the most dangerous man in the middle New England area.

Jason was home on furlough. On the very week of T-bone's test, we searched him out for any last-minute bits of information he could offer that would insure the promise of success. The first thing my brother did was to discredit the rules-of-the-road book by dismissing it as a "pack of nonsense," valuable only for the written portion of the test, which didn't count anyway. Warming to his work, he told us how to handle Mr. Barter, warning us that he alone could authorize the issuance of T-bone's Private Operator's Motor Vehicle License. He told us not to call him Mr. Barter . . . call him by his first name, Nial. Despite his advanced years and his dignity, he liked to be thought of as one of the boys.

Breaking down Jason's advice into two lists, it went something like this:

DOs

When you crack a joke and you get to the punch line, elbow Mr. Barter (Nial) in the ribs.

Address him occasionally as "Nial, you old potato." Be familiar, and don't let him put you on (see list of DON'Ts).

DON'Ts

If he asks you to stop on a hill, *don't* do it. It's a trick! You're not supposed to stop on hills and Nial just wants to

130

see if you know that. (Footnote) Generally, it's a good idea not to do anything he asks. It's probably a trick.

Don't drive too slowly. He'll think you lack confidence. Speeds around town should be kept in the high 30s or 40s ... faster, if you can pull it off.

Don't use the rear vision mirror when starting out. Instead, stick your head right out the window, sort of backwards, then let out the clutch and floor it.

Don't come to a full stop at stop signs. You'll lose your forward thrust and you could stall the car. Move smartly through the intersections at about 15 or 20 miles per hour. But (and Jason stressed this point), if you're taking a left turn at an intersection, remember to cut the corner to the left.

Jason gave us a lot of other valuable material. Stuff like handling the wheel with one finger ... "That's very pro and old Nial will be impressed." But above all, *don't* take the test seriously. If Mr. Barter pretends to get excited, he's just trying to rattle you. Laugh it off, and he'll know you've got the confidence it takes to make a good driver.

"Have you got all that?" Jason finally asked.

T-bone had been scribbling furiously and judging from his pile of notes, he'd gotten it down just as Jason had said it, almost word for word. I wasn't worried then because I knew T-bone would commit it all to memory, and armed with this kind of inside information his license was in the bag.

I got my bike and rode into town on the day T-bone was to take his test. We were to meet outside the I.G.A. store. Mr. Barter owned and operated this small grocery store and giving driving tests was just a sideline. I must have arrived late, for just as I was leaning my bike up against a porch post of the store, T-bone came out with Mr. Barter. He had his left arm thrown around Mr. Barter's shoulders and it didn't seem to me that Mr. Barter much liked it. He kept trying to pull away from T-bone, but T-bone fixed his grip around Mr. Barter's neck and hung right onto him until they reached the car.

T-bone climbed in immediately and fired up his mother's Hudson. When Mr. Barter started to climb in, I could see his face for the first time, and he sort of looked mad about something. He was just settling himself in the seat beside T-bone ... in fact, he hadn't even closed his door, when T-bone stuck his head out the window "backwards," as per instruction, and took off like a shot, slamming Mr. Barter's door and burning rubber for a good 15 feet.

T-bone could really handle that car ... right down the middle of Main Street at 40 miles per hour and looking backwards the whole time. It seemed like a tricky way of doing it and it must have impressed Mr. Barter. When they

132

got to the end of the street, I saw T-bone take a hard right, wheels screaming, and disappear down the New Post Road. And, I swear, it couldn't have been more than ninety seconds when suddenly he was coming up Elm Street from the opposite end of town. As they swung through town again, I could see Mr. Barter shouting something at T-bone, and it must have been pretty funny because T-bone was laughing. They went right around the fountain in the center then, leaving tracks in two places, and T-bone managing this whole maneuver with only one finger on the wheel! Boy, he was doing it just right! And then they were gone again.

Normally, it takes twenty minutes to run the course for the road test, but T-bone must have set a new record because in about five minutes I saw the Hudson coming towards the center of town via School Street, lickety-split, right past the Go-Children-Slow signs. When he turned left on Main Street, he remembered to cut the corner at the intersection and there was a near thing with a big truck. But he must have gotten a point or two for quick thinking, because he neatly avoided a head-on collision by driving up on Dr. Fenton's lawn. No one could have spotted it as he didn't let up on the gas a bit. I mean, he just drove right up over the sidewalk and onto the lawn, passing between the two elms there and then back over the sidewalk and onto the street again. It was as slick a piece of driving as I've ever seen and certainly nobody without a good deal of self-confidence could have pulled it off.

Now he was headed right for the store with a final burst of speed, but I couldn't see Mr. Barter at all! No sign of him, and I wondered if this was some part of the test Jason hadn't told us about. I didn't have time to think about it as he was coming on too fast and those of us there on the sidewalk all scattered.

That's when I heard him hit the brakes and saw the car come shuddering in sideways, lifting gently on two wheels before it finally came to rest on all four. Some of the townspeople began to gather around, because you don't see driving like that except in really good movies.

And then I saw Mr. Barter. He was coming up off the floor of the back seat area of the car, like a ghost rising out a grave — at least he was as pale as one. He was shaking badly, too. He climbed out of the car and walked kind of stiff-legged toward his store, taking each step very carefully.

"Well, Nial, you old potato," T-bone shouted from the car, "... what do you think ...?"

Mr. Barter stopped in his tracks. But he didn't turn around; he didn't even turn his *head* around.

"I think," he said in a voice we could all barely hear, "... I think you're a crazy man." And then he just walked into his store and shut the door, the door with the CLOSED sign on it.

* * * * *

That's about all of it. Oh, I may have left out a detail here or there, but you've got the gist of what happened ... certainly enough to see T-bone's side of the story, and why, after twenty years, his other nickname, "Old Potato," still rubs him the wrong way.

by Ralph C. Williams

Seed Potatoes

"IF you planted potatoes, they would loosen up the soil and the sod would have a chance to rot and then you could level this plot off and plant grass seed in the fall."

I had learned to have considerable respect for this 83-year-old farmer's advice. He lived down the road and had done odd jobs for me.

"Don't buy potatoes in town," he said, "they're apt to be scaly. You get out what you put in. I know where you can get some good ones. Anytime you say, I'll go along and show you where his place is."

A few days later I saw the old man preparing the ground and told him I was ready to go.

"I'll be with you in a minute," he said.

He disappeared into the recesses of the barn and emerged a moment or two later with his coat and hat on, suddenly transformed.

"Where is this place we're to go to get the potatoes?" I asked.

"Winchendon, Massachusetts," he said. "You go over to Troy and take the road past Fitzwilliam."

When we reached Winchendon, I asked where the house was. "You go down here, turn sharp right."

We cruised along after the turn for half a mile or more. We were going slowly for I was expecting to be told to stop at the next house.

135

"It's a white house. I'll tell you when we come to it. You'll see a road and you turn off to the left."

We were going along faster now, for there was no sign of any road. The old farmer seemed completely aware of where he was going, but I noticed that we had gone almost four miles beyond Winchendon.

"We used to work together on the same farm," he said. "We've been good friends ever since. That was well-nigh — let's see — thirty-five years ago. Here's where you turn."

We went down a road to the left and stopped in front of a large farmhouse with many outbuildings.

The old man got out slowly, muttering to himself about where he might find his friend. He decided to try the house. A woman in metal curlers tight to her scalp pointed to the barn, for the old farmer was extremely deaf.

In a few minutes he emerged from the barn with another old man, bent over with arthritis.

"This is my neighbor who lives in the old brick house," he said to him, and introduced me with a courtesy that was impressive. "He's come to see if he could get some seed potatoes. You had such a good crop last year, I thought mebbe you'd have some to spare."

"Come over to the house and we'll see. There ought to be some left. They're in the cellar."

The same gaunt woman received us in the big kitchen, still wearing, tight to her head, the metal clasps. Sitting rocking in a chair was almost an exact replica of herself, with hair curlers tight to her head and the same angular look. She rocked and rocked all the time we were there and never said a word.

There were no formalities this time other than asking me to have a seat. I was not introduced to the two women.

The two bent male figures were exchanging the usual

amenities about the drought, the state of the crops, the difficulty of making a go of farming these days. Our host related that last week he had found that it was getting too burdensome and had suddenly decided to sell off his livestock.

"I did all right on the sale," he said, "but the next day they were having an auction over at the Beale's place and I bought four Holsteins and a young bull."

"That's just like him," the gaunt woman put in, as she emerged from the cellar with a bushel basket filled with potatoes that had begun to sprout. "I didn't know how many you wanted, so I brought up a bushel."

"How many *do* you want?" the man asked.

"Not more than a peck," I said, and asked my farmer to pick them out, for I didn't know much about seed potatoes.

He had brought a burlap bag. He spread it open and bent over the bushel basket, slowly judging each potato, discarding some, putting others in the bag, until he stopped, saying he thought that ought to be enough.

The host, who had been watching the operation as he prattled on about things of interest to the farmer, said, "That'll be seventy-five cents."

"That's just about what I made it," my farmer said, as he closed the bag with a twist.

I paid the seventy-five cents and my farmer sat down again. I realized that this was a social call as well as a business deal and sat down myself. Our host started a lengthy story about his troubles with a tractor that needed repairs, which he would like my farmer's son to make. I had been waiting for the woman to locate the correct change and suddenly noticed that my elderly farmer had started to nod.

"Guess we'd better be going," I remarked to our host.

"Reckon you might as well," he said, with a glance at the nodding man in front of him.

The old farmer roused himself. I picked up the bag of potatoes and carried it out to the car.

He was silent all the way back. I glanced at him to see if he was asleep, but his eyes were open. It required such an effort to shout my remarks that I mostly remained silent also.

When he drew up in front of my house, I told him I would carry the potatoes into the barn.

"I'll carry 'em," he said.

I put the bag down outside the car. He slowly and painfully emerged, bent over, and hefted the burlap bag. Then he looked up at me with a twinkle in his eye and remarked with a smile, "There's more'n half a bushel o' potatoes, and, you know, they're four dollars a bushel anywhere round. You got a real bargain." END

The Day the Liberty Bell Came to Boston

by Richard Pritchett

THE Liberty Bell came to Boston on June 17, 1903, for the big Bunker Hill Day parade. It hasn't been back since! Actually the 2080-pounder arrived in Boston the night before, but it was allowed to rest overnight in a South Boston railroad yard just outside the South Station, where it was scheduled to make its grand entrance the following morning.

The most famous bell in America had departed Philadelphia at 7:30 Monday morning, June 15, for its epic train trip to Boston. It was guarded by four sturdy

139

Philadelphia police officers, plus several city dignitaries headed by Charles Weaver, mayor of Philadelphia.

At the time, there was a friendly agreement between the two cities. Philadelphia was supposed to ship the Liberty Bell to Boston for a day, and the Hub, in turn, was supposed to send Bunker Hill Monument or some other shrine down to the City of Brotherly Love for a visit. There had even been some speculation that the Bostonians might ship Plymouth Rock to Pennsylvania for an outing, if the town fathers down Plymouth way would let them rent it for a few days.

Be that as it may, after what happened on Bunker Hill Day, the budding friendship between those two old rivals, Philadelphia and Boston, went right by the board. And Boston didn't have to ship anything down to Pennsylvania, because the Philadelphians would undoubtedly have snubbed whatever was sent them.

En route northward to Boston, the special train carrying the Liberty Bell made several stops. In Princeton, New Jersey, for example, the special train had to halt so that former president Grover Cleveland could make a speech welcoming the cracked bell to town.

In New York there was another welcoming speech, and in Connecticut the bell was formally welcomed to about ten towns. In Providence, 30,000 people were on hand to say hello. By the time the bell finally got to Boston, the old historic relic must have been worn out from all that pomp and ceremony, and in the mood for a quiet night in that South Boston railroad yard.

Exactly at 11 A.M. the following day, Wednesday, June 17, 1903, an honor guard from the Ancient and Honorable Artillery Company showed up to escort the one-ton piece of metal through downtown Boston, and onward to Charlestown for the big afternoon parade there. In addition to the honor guard, about fifty Boston patrolmen were lurking here, there, and everywhere in the general vicinity of the South Station. During the night there had been a report that a group of angry Irish patriots planned to steal the Liberty Bell, ship it over to England, substitute it for Big Ben, and have it toll Freedom's Song in London as a protest against British rule in Ireland. But the great theft never took place. Exactly how the dedicated patriots were supposed to lug away the 2080-pounder remains a mystery to this very day. Nevertheless, Boston's finest remained on guard all during the Liberty Bell's visit to the city.

The great day had arrived and Boston planned to celebrate it in grand style. "Hallelujah! Hallelujah! For This Is Charlestown's Day," proclaimed *The Boston Globe* in its front page headline.

The bell was loaded aboard "a dray pulled by thirteen magnificent bay horses," and paraded through the streets of downtown Boston en route to Charlestown. Each horse was supposed to represent one of the thirteen original colonies. Thousands lined the streets to cheer the procession.

But it was in Charlestown that the largest crowds were waiting. Charles Emmon, chairman of the parade committee, estimated that "half the city turned out." Conservatively, this meant that more than a quarter million people were on hand.

And what a parade it was! There were dozens of big brass bands, and marching contingents from all the military branches. There were floats galore, and clowns, and dozens and dozens of local politicians. The Liberty Bell was exactly in the middle of the line of march, and naturally it was completely surrounded by politicians. At least, they were as close as they could get.

Directly in front of the Liberty Bell, which was still

aboard that dray pulled by thirteen horses, there was a strutting marching band from one of the Charlestown civic organizations. On either side of the bell was the Ancient and Honorable honor guard. And on the dray were those four Philadelphia policemen who had journeyed north with the bell to protect it. Directly behind the bell were those fifty Boston-patrolmen on the lookout for Irish patriots.

Next came Mayor Weaver of Philadelphia and his associates. After them came an army of local political celebrities. They were having a great time waving and greeting the populace. Behind the politicians there was another Charlestown marching band, and the rest of the parade.

Now there is a very steep hill leading downward from Bunker Hill Square where the monument is located. During the parade, the bell moved along on streets that paralleled the square, but it was not supposed to make its appearance at the monument until four o'clock when the parade was supposed to end. As the bell was headed down a steep hill, presumably Bunker Hill Street, toward Main Street, a lot of wild things happened all at once. Alas, the anonymous poor soul driving the dray lost control of the situation. He had the thirteen horses in front of him, and the bell, four Philadelphia patrolmen, and the dray pressing down behind him. The horses started galloping, and the driver tugged and tugged on his reins. His tugging caused the horses to veer sharply to the left. Fortunately there was a small side street on the left, and the Liberty Bell turned into it. As for the Charlestown marching band directly in front of the bell, that group went straight ahead.

When the Liberty Bell went left, so did the Ancient and Honorables running beside it, and the police guard behind it. So did the Mayor of Philadelphia, and all the Boston politicians. So did the second Charlestown band, and all the rest of the parade. Everybody wanted to be with the Liberty Bell that day. As a result, the latter half of the parade made a wrong turn.

The dray driver had regained control of the situation by the time he reached the end of the small side street. He had two choices: he could make a right turn, and head down another steep hill toward Main Street. The poor chap was most reluctant to do that. So he made a left turn, and paraded up a lonely thoroughfare — the cheering crowd

The dray driver was suspect for a while.

was someplace else — toward Bunker Hill Monument. Naturally he was followed all the way by the rest of the parade.

Once the Liberty Bell arrived at Bunker Hill Monument an hour ahead of schedule, Boston's finest took prompt action. Fearing the driver had made his sudden turn to escape those Irish patriots, police sealed off the Monument Square area and refused to allow anybody to enter it.

Down below on Main Street, several thousand people lost their tempers all at once. The much publicized Liberty Bell had failed to show up! Most of them went home snarling. Some did head towards Bunker Hill Monument, where it was supposed to be displayed for two hours, but they couldn't get near the thing — at least not until five o'clock. By then police had scoured the area, convinced themselves there were no Irish patriots around, and had accepted the story the dray driver told them. Unfortunately, he had "an Irish accent," according to the old *Boston Transcript*, and was suspect for a while.

That night the bell was displayed on Boston Common until midnight, "illuminated by calcium lights." About fifty thousand people saw it.

The next day it left town and headed for Plymouth, where an attempt was made to parade it through town to Plymouth Rock. The parade was called off due to "a heavy schedule" — the Philadelphia people weren't about to let the bell out of the train again until it got safely home. However they did allow Chairman Doyle of the Board of Aldermen to make a speech welcoming it to Plymouth. Then it was non-stop all the way home to Philadelphia.

Boston hasn't seen the bell since the day of the big parade. In fact, as near as can be determined, the Liberty Bell hasn't been allowed out of Philadelphia again without an armed military escort.
END

by Genevieve M. Darden

Nothing to Buy but the Life Preservers

IT all began with our having the bathroom painted. Towards the end of the job, the fellow in charge, an amiable, sixtyish Frenchman-turned-Yankee, heretofore a stranger to us, dropped the word that he had a boat for sale. Eighteen feet, fiberglassed, forty-horsepower motor newly overhauled, electric start, new lights, recharged battery, punt, and trailer.

"Seven hundred complete," he said. "I'll throw in an inside paint job."

We, or specifically I, had been in the market all spring. I'd wanted a boat of my own for as long as I could remember, and I'm old enough now to be a grandmother. The time was right. The price, about $600 less than anything else we'd seen, was right. We jumped.

"Nothing to buy but life preservers," said our painter friend (who likes to be called Len) as he rolled up the doors of her stall.

The fiberglass job was bumpy, the red waterline wavery, the wooden seat backs on the flimsy side, and the sanding under her inside paint hasty, maybe nonexistent. Her hull, however, was solid, and her eight-foot beam reassuring for choppy Buzzards Bay. My husband Hugh thought the motor looked spruce and clean, and our daughter Ann,

145

then 20, and friend Michael, also 20, who know more about these matters than we, said the whole package looked like a buy. On the third day after our first look, we patted her on the prow and gave Len a husky deposit.

That night he decided to keep the punt and the new lights and reduce the price to $650. We held out for the lights but sacrificed the punt; Len didn't want to be stranded on land, which was a feeling we understood. We settled on $675.

The next day he towed the boat up to the shade of our front yard and painted the inside and deck a gull gray. It wasn't his fault that a flock of pigeons spent the night in the trees and that boat and trailer arrived at our shack on the bay looking as if they'd been shoved through a polka-dotting machine. We scrubbed until dark; in the morning I repainted a good part of the deck, and the top of the motor.

On Saturday, in the fine quiet of 7 A.M., we launched her from the public ramp on Mattapoisett wharf. She slid in smiling, and I was so busy smiling back that I didn't realize until she was several yards from the pier that I had been elected to drive back to the shack in the car and row out to the mooring for Hugh, Ann and Michael, who were making the maiden voyage.

Through binoculars, I watched from the cabin porch as they rounded Ned's Point and headed for the mooring (which I'd just learned would cost $65 instead of $40). The boat looked exuberant to me, but Michael and Hugh, when we were within shouting distance, said she had no speed — seemed to be running on one cylinder. Climbing into the pram, Michael added that she felt closer to 16 feet than 18. Nevertheless we spluttered along the length of Mattapoisett Neck that afternoon, Hugh nervous, he told me later, and I, in my ignorance, exultant. I did not, I kept assuring him, care about going fast; the boat was to be an escape, not a wave skimmer. I did, however, admit that we had difficulty getting out of the path of sailboats, and there was some business with a red-haired youngster of 11 or 12 who kept cutting circles around us in a green skiff that looked like a toy.

Len, summoned, came on Sunday morning, fiddled with the motor for two hours, put in new plugs, gratis, and took us for a trial run. The result sounded splendid to me, but Hugh said the motor still had no speed, to which Len replied, motioning paternally in my direction, "Better for *her* this way." He also observed that we needed a boat hook and a horn, that "it wouldn't do any harm to buy a socket wrench," and that he'd like to go bass fishing anytime we cared to take him. Ann, rowing out to collect us in the pram, said our chock and cleat were far too small and should be replaced.

All the next day the boat sat on her mooring, and I admired her from shore, mulling about names. *Dido? Gretchen? Clytemnestra?* (I teach literature for a living.) Ann suggested *Funny Girl,* and Michael, coming for supper, said something about *Largo.* In the evening, braced with $20, I went to the marine shop to buy life-preserver cushions, an eight-inch cleat, and a chock. The cushions were reasonable, but the chock and cleat were made of the kind of bronze normally reserved for sculpting the head of Caesar — the bill was $39.60. Horns, I learned, started at $3.50, boat hooks of any respectable length, $8.95. And how, the salesman asked, about a mop?

We were, in short, in business, and sure enough of ourselves to begin to worry about underwater topography. So a couple of evenings later Hugh and Rick S., who bills himself as a veteran mariner, took the boat out to teach Hugh the locations of dangerous rocks and to "listen" to the motor. At 8:30, almost dark, I learned through the glasses that the motor had stopped — its top was off, tiny sparks were shooting from it, and the boat was washing rapidly ashore about 500 yards west of the shack. Hugh, it seemed to me idiotically, was waving in my direction to help.

With the aid of five neighbors, we kept her off the rocks while hauling her out, stowed the motor in a car trunk, disconnected the battery and nosed the poor stripped shell against a storm wall, on borrowed rollers, for the night. The sea pounded until dawn; we set the alarm for 5, but at 4:45 it was obvious that surf would keep us from rowing her back to the safety of her mooring. I walked up to look at her, naked, vulnerable, unsteady on the rollers, and forlorn.

By the end of the week, the motor had had $68 worth of work; we added a new $19.95 battery, $5 battery box, and a $7.95 boat hook, which by that time seemed only a bagatelle. Hugh and I lugged the motor from the car trunk to the boat (combined bills for back X-rays, $77), Michael arrived in time to help hook her up, and he and Hugh disappeared over the horizon.

An hour and a half later they reappeared, and I kicked off my sneakers, ready to swim out to see what the boat looked like from the inside (I was beginning to forget), but before I was up to my knees they shouted, "Going to boatyard." Len, they explained at lunch, had installed the wrong size plugs. I asked why the yard had failed to grasp this fact the first time, but I'm too inept in mechanical matters to transmit the answer.

In any event, plugs replaced ($11), the *Penguin* — as I had named her, largely because she is round, white, and despite ailments, endearing — came whipping around the point at what seemed to me an impressive rate of speed.

"Everyone's had a good run but the owner," Hugh announced as the pram scraped the shore. Revelation. "How about it?"

We rowed out, got aboard, the *Penguin* started, and stalled. The tide was low, the wind picking up, and the sky-blue cruiser of neighbors nearby. Hugh dove for the mooring, I panicked, recovered, threw over the anchor, Hugh crawled back in, and discovered a hole in the gas line. An hour later all seemed well again, but I had swum ashore. Not sulking, I insisted — just a routine appointment on land. Michael and Ann took the boat out for the afternoon and had a whirl.

On Sunday Ann piloted two guests and us into the choppy water off Strawberry Point, from which one can see the Cape Cod Canal; sea and sky were beautiful, and we had a respectable amount of speed. One seat back fell off and the floor board split, but the hull underneath looked sturdy; it was, relatively, a great day. To celebrate, I went shopping for a boat horn, found they were $13.98 and settled for a whistle for 42 cents.

By the weekend all, finally, was shipshape; we rowed out early on one of those clear, off-shore Sunday mornings small boat owners dream about, and turned the *Penguin's* key. Nothing happened. The new battery was dead.

Hugh climbed grimly back into the pram. "I'll get the battery from the car and put yours in to charge." The maneuver worked, and we were off by 9:00 in fine style. The wind had shifted to onshore, however, so we stayed out (and well in) only about an hour. Neither of us said anything about the frightening wash of water over the stern. That night we drove to our home in Fairhaven, ten miles away, emerged into the black summer night laden with laundry, groceries, and stuff from the freezer, and found the car battery dead as a stone.

I spent most of the next week wishing I dared to take the

Penguin out alone in the mornings after Hugh left, and admitting that I didn't and probably never would. I rowed out and bailed her three or four times, after summer squalls, but that was the extent of it. Motorboats were more complex than I had thought, which was some kind of understatement of the decade.

On August 1 a violent electrical storm, the worst in my memory, broke just before midnight and continued, with buckets of rain, for four hours. At 2:00 I sat up in bed, watching the lightning plummeting into the harbor like bolts from Olympus, and straining my eyes toward the *Penguin.* At 4:00 I dressed, got the pump, and headed for the pram. Ann mumbled that it was a grisly way to commit suicide so I went back to bed. At 5:00, as light began to filter through the heavy skies, a last torrent of rain fell like a giant curtain. In its midst a burst of lightning flared over the whole harbor and I saw the *Penguin* flip over like a plastic toy. All we could see when the murky sun came up was the red tip of her bow.

By noon she, and three others in the same plight, had been righted by the boatyard crew and their motors dumped into a tank for flushing. On August 2, 3, 4, and 5, while the summer winged by, I went to the yard to check progress.

"Have a heart, lady," the foreman said on August 6. "Look around." I did. Ailing motors lay on all sides and underfoot. I wasn't even sure which was mine.

Three weeks before Labor Day, it was ready, as was the bill for $193, which didn't include a new battery, battery box, etc. etc. etc.

"What year's this motor?" the mechanic asked chattily as he looked it up.

"1966." Len had said so. The registration, though smudged, said so.

"Checked the serial numbers?"

"No."

"Take a look sometime. It's a 1960."

"Oh."

"And all those barnacles stuck to the bottom and stern ..."

"Don't all boats have barnacles there?"

"Not those painted with anti-fouling paint."

"And mine is ...?"

"House paint, lady. Plain old red house paint."

I hit a piling on the way out of the boatyard harbor — gently, but still a disgrace — and Michael, a senior at Massachusetts Maritime Academy, said as we chugged into the channel that Hugh and I should probably take the Coast Guard's winter training course for rookies. I admitted, humbly, that he was right. But certainly the toughest part was over. Not much more *could* happen. We'd ordered a fitted tarpaulin from a sail loft to keep out the rains (we could have bought a half interest in the *Queen Elizabeth II* for the tariff, but never mind) and made plans to build up the boat's stern and look around for a lighter motor. Most important we'd agreed to haul her out until next year (hurricane season was approaching) and put her back in her stall. We'd gone the voyage to learn. Next season had to be better.

But the Fates. Ah, the Fates! The old Destiny Spinners. Always sitting there watching, waiting ....

Two mornings after we locked the stall doors came a letter which apparently had been chasing us around, from winter house to summer shack, for weeks. From the Massachusetts Division of Motor Boats, it read: "Dear Madam: We are unable to issue you a certificate of ownership of motorboat MS 6234 K as, according to our files, registration MS 6234 K belongs to someone else. If you will ask the former owner to send in his certificate ...."   END

Tim, Ben, and the Horse

by Philip Milton Carr

... the horse never did get used to it ...

IN another 200 years there would be a wide, paved road, tourist accommodations, and souvenir shops in the area where the two pioneers were now secluded in a small hunter's cabin deep in New Hampshire's White Mountain wilderness. They hadn't met the horse yet. He was secluded in a Lancaster stable, dozing undisturbed, after years of pulling and hauling in a mostly unsettled and unexplored territory.

On this cold and snow-swept winter evening in 1771, Timothy Nash and Benjamin Sawyer sat opposite each other, the stillness broken only by intermittent howls of wind outside, the snap and crackle of fireplace logs inside. Both were part of that canny breed of New Hampshire mountain men who knew that a fireplace could never be fully trusted, so a stone jug of O-B-Joyful, or what the Puritans called New England Fire, sat on the splintery table between them. Soon the poker resting in the fire would be white-hot and they could mix in the molasses, sugar, and pumpkin shavings, plunge in the poker, and the brew would become Black Betts, which was a better drink than cold rum for winter nights in New England.

They were hunters and wore the beards, fringed moose skins, and large skinning knives typical of their clan. When they worked, it usually meant that their provisions, or someone else's, were getting low and they sold meat and hides to effect a balance. Neither was lazy, but each was independent with modest needs, a taciturn disposition, and a deep knowledge of the meaning in each leaf, cloud, and whisper of wind that existed throughout the mountainous forest where they hunted. Though they were friends, they rarely hunted together unless one needed help; but they sometimes drank together though neither needed help.

That morning Tim had wounded a moose on the side of Cherry Mountain. It didn't drop much blood, so he climbed a tall pine hoping to catch sight of the animal and decide how best to cut him off and thereby save a lot of tracking. But when he peered south toward the White Hills he forgot about the moose altogether. What he saw could not be. Yet there he was, in the top of a tree looking at it. He came down out of the pine, skipping two and three limbs at a time, and hurried by dead reckoning to verify the strange sight. Satisfied, he quickly backtracked, slabbed a side of the mountain, and went straight to the crude cabin Ben had built earlier that year.

"It's there, Ben. I seen it, and it's sure 'nuf an Injun trail. But it ain't no ordinary Injun trail. I tell ye, believe it or no, it goes right *through* them mountains!"

"I reckon the Sokoki and Pequawkets coulda used it but it still ain't no road," Ben answered.

Tim then emphasized, "Benjamin [Tim always said

"Benjamin" when he emphasized], it don't gotta be no road! All Guv'ner Wentworth said it hadda be was a *pass*. He said 'Any man finds a pass through the mountains which'll shorten the haul to the Portland-to-Portsmouth trade route gits a tract of land fer his troubles.' Now you know he ain't give *all* the land in New Hampshire to his relatives yet, and land's worth money."

Ben poured rum straight into his cup, forgetting about the poker. He stroked his whiskers thoughtfully and finally agreed, "Okay, Tim, iffen ye say it's there, it's there. I'll go in with ye fer halves, but I confess to no real hankerin' to walk through the woods to Portsmouth."

So it was that they started early the next day to follow the "notch" through the White Mountains. The trail proved to be an ancient, secret Indian route, as Tim had suspected. At one point they even found an old, tattered piece of birch bark folded and wedged into the tomahawk slit in a dead ash. When they unfolded it, there were no inscriptions or picture-words, only a few beaver hairs. Many years ago a Sokoki trapping party had left the message for another group they expected to follow them. What they were doing was shown by the beaver hairs, and the direction they had taken was indicated by the way the folded message had pointed. But the Indians, with few exceptions, were gone now. When King Philip's War, the other conflicts that ensued, and finally Lovewell's War in 1725 had killed many of them, the rest moved to Canada where it was safer.

The trail was rough; in some places ledges rose or dropped 10, 20, perhaps 30 feet. Added to this, they had to cross the swift, white waters of the Saco River several times before they came to easier travelling. But on they struggled, through and over snow, ledges, brush, and deadfalls. At last they arrived in Portsmouth, where they

155

asked directions of a somewhat aloof and better-dressed citizen, and then went to the Governor's house to tell John Wentworth of their discovery. There they engaged in an argument designed to prove it was necessary to speak with His Excellency *in person*, and won their point with a long, hard, we're-jest-about-outta-patience-with-you stare.

When the beleaguered bureaucrat hustled off, there was an opportunity to view their surroundings. Ben looked about, wondering why he had ever left the rustic comfort of his cabin in northern New Hampshire. At the same time, Tim was scanning the executive splendor that encircled him and thinking, "Yesiree! This could mean a *sizeable* tract of land!" These thoughts were abruptly interrupted when a door opened and John Wentworth said, in a rather imperious manner, "Yes, gentlemen?"

Tim took the bull by the horns, and in a calm voice, just slow enough and just positive enough to excite interest, explained that a shortcut through the White Mountains had been found. He further explained that "natcherly, of course" a few trees would have to be cut and a few bridges built; but it was still a mighty fine notch which would save a great deal of time in reaching the trade route. Tim felt it prudent not to dampen the Governor's interest by telling him about the ledges. As the Governor looked at the seasoned and rough-clad pair he suspected, from their appearance if for no other reason, that should the route indeed exist it could not be all *that* easy. Yet, if there were a route . . .

His Excellency looked at Tim and Ben, and he thought. Then he looked more and he thought more. Finally, he had it — a way of determining not only if there really was a route, but whether or not it was worthy of being developed for travel. "Mr. Nash, Mr. Sawyer, I appreciate your discovery. Yet I'm sure you understand that I must verify such a find as this. Therefore, if you will bring a horse down through that notch, from Lancaster to Portsmouth, you will be properly rewarded with as fine a tract of land as either of you could desire."

"Bring a *horse*, Guv'ner?"

"Bring a horse, Mr. Nash."

"But Guv'ner," Tim replied, "we're jest mountain men. Hunters, trappers. We ain't got no horse. Don't use 'em. 'Cept fer that, we'd be happy to oblige."

In the brief seconds that followed, Tim's mind, used to "figgerin'," had rationalized that as long as the horse was Governor Wentworth's idea, it was only "fitten" that he should be the one to pay for it. And the Governor, sure he had outwitted the two, said that if there were no other costs involved, he would be glad to give them the expense money required to buy a horse. His donation was generous, perhaps because governors buy more elegant models than mountain men, and Tim and Ben started for home.

Ben was certain that the horse spelled the end of the venture; but Tim made mental notes of the river crossings, the drop-offs, small cliffs, and any other barriers or hindrances he saw. At the end of the journey he knew just what they would need for equipment to ensure a successful completion of the task.

With the "expense money" they went to a stable in Lancaster where they met the horse. His back was bent in the middle, as was his disposition, and the years had begun to tell on him. He looked raggedy, but he still had strength, forged from the endless hours of pulling Yankee timber and Colonial plows. As Tim and Ben looked him over, they knew he just had to be the cheapest horse in Lancaster. Ben hadn't been let in on Tim's innermost thoughts, and now he emphasized, "Timothy" [Ben always said

157

"Timothy" when he emphasized], "surely ye ain't goin' ter ride *that* down the notch ter the coast. It'll kill yer! And iffen ye don't break yer neck in the notch, they'll laff yer ter death in Portsmouth."

Tim looked at Ben as though he should have known better and exclaimed, "Ride! Who's goin' ter *ride* 'im? He didn't say trot, canter, er gallop. All he said ter do was *bring* 'im. Guv'ner John said 'bring,' and that's what we're a-gonna do — *bring!*" Now the plan became clear to Ben, and he couldn't help but agree with the moral aspect of the adventure. The notch was a shortcut — which Wentworth had asked for — and, if they did "bring" the horse, well . . . that was also what he had asked for. Fair was fair.

From the stable owner they purchased — with practiced haggling skill — a large pulley, a few hundred feet of stout rope, two wide leather straps, and an ax. They then told the uncertain stabler that as long as he had bested them in the deal for all the equipment, it was only right that he should throw in that useless horse to help carry it. The man wasn't convinced, but the horse was eating every day, not working, no one else would probably buy him, so he agreed. The last step in preparation was buying the provisions, which meant O-B-Joyful in sufficient quantity, and a little food.

When everything had been secured, it was all loaded on the horse, and early one morning the three started through the wilderness for Portsmouth. They called the animal "Hoss," which was good enough considering they were only going to use him this once, and the farther they went, the longer they lived with him, the greater became their "convincement" it would not be a lengthy relationship.

If the going had been tough before, it was rougher now. They frequently had to use the ax to cut brush and dead-falls to get "Hoss" through the woods. When they reached the Indian trail, they faced a 30-foot drop. Here, they cut three poles, lashed them together, and built a tripod from which the pulley was suspended. Then the leather girdle was passed under the horse's belly and secured to the rope which was run through the pulley. With the free end of the line snubbed around a tree, they put their shoulders to the horse's rump and forced the uncooperative animal off into space. Grunting and grumbling, they then lowered him as gently as possible to the ground.

The procedure was repeated at each place too high or too deep to negotiate. The horse never did get used to it, and he balked at each obstruction because he knew what was coming. Whenever they reached a drop-off, "Hoss" would brace his feet, dig in, and vote to go no farther. They considered building a fire under him, even giving him a snort of rum, but concluded that although the fire was an idea worth remembering, the rum was not, because it might make him even more obnoxious and hard to handle.

The horse was raised and he was lowered; he swung to and fro, and he bobbed up and down. He didn't like river crossings any better, and Tim and Ben would push him from behind, pull him from the front, or push and pull at the same time. Once, they had to make an "Injun bridge" by felling a tree across the stream, hewing the top side flat, and leading the horse over this while they swore at the injustice of having to walk in the icy water while *he* walked high and dry. "Hoss" was also an indiscriminate kicker: he kicked at the cliffs, kicked at the water, and kicked at Tim and Ben. The mountain men were more varied and conflicting in their response. They cursed the horse, and they congratulated him. He was insulted, encouraged, comforted, castigated, blessed and bullied, cheered and threatened — usually in colorful backwoods invective that flowed forth in a single breath. But on they went — over

the rises, across the waters, and down the notch. At night, by a flickering campfire, they enjoyed a kind of amnesty and rested up companionably for the next day's contest. And then, one bright and sunny morning, the contests were over. They were through the notch, the ground was smoother, and the way lay easier before them. A few days later, Tim, Ben, and the horse, walked into Portsmouth and strode toward the Governor's mansion.

It was late in the morning, and the Portsmouth gentry were up and about. They stared in awe and amazement at the trio that marched stoically and purposefully past them — the sway-back horse loaded with gear and the two mountain men who trudged on either side of him, dressed in moose skins and carrying muskets. When they reached the house, Governor Wentworth, having seen them coming, was standing outside to greet them. Tim officially declared, in what he considered his most refined and impressive manner, "Guv'ner, we brung yer horse." The Governor agreed they had, discussed details of the trip with them, and then assured them that, as soon as title could be drawn up and the land surveyed, they would receive an extensive tract of property to be called "Nash & Sawyer's Location."

After this, Tim inquired the name of a local citizen who "liked horses," and they set off for the new destination. On the way Ben prophesied, "Tim, he won't like horses *that* much." When they got there, it looked at first as though Ben would be right. But Tim, looking suspiciously over his shoulder to be sure they weren't overheard, confided to the man that, "This here ain't jest *any* horse. This here is *The Horse*, which is famous. He's jest come down through the White Mountain notch, fearlessly and bravely. Ain't no horse ever done what he's done. He jest looks a little peaked on account of his trials." When Tim added that, if the price were right and a good home "garnteed," he'd throw in the pulley and rope for free, the bargain was clinched.

With the proceeds of the sale they bought enough New England Fire to assure a proper and "fitten" celebration on the trip back. Working their way through the notch for the fourth time, they celebrated, congratulated, and reminisced. They knew that Wentworth's word was good, and they would receive their land. That day they crossed the Saco, camped early, celebrated, and slept well. When they arose next morning, each had a "swaller" of O-B-Joyful and, noting there was but a spoonful or two left in the jug, Ben selected the largest boulder he could find next to the river. Walking ceremonially up to it, he smashed the jug over it, declaring in what was a rare oration for him: "In memory of this here notable occasion and great accomplishment, yer name is now Sawyer's Rock!"

* * * * *

The boulder is still there and still called "Sawyer's Rock." Across the road, Route 302, is a picnic area with benches, tables, and fireplaces. Sleek, shiny, and fast automobiles pass the boulder every day, but few passengers, if any, notice the historic monument. Some are on vacation and some are hurrying from this problem to that complexity; but most all are unaware of the trying and triumphant adventure that took place there over 200 years ago. Perhaps, in late evening or early morning hours, when everything is quiet and no one travels, when stars are winter-bright and silence is broken only by the sound of the Saco, down the notch they come again — Tim, Ben, and The Horse.   END

Author's Note: Although the conversations in this account are fictional and dramatized, Timothy Nash, Benjamin Sawyer, and The Horse actually made this trip in 1771, making them the first, except for Indians, to travel the length of what is today called Crawford Notch. The trip was made in the manner and under the conditions described in the story.

All three disappeared from the pages of history a few years after their accomplishment; The Horse in Portsmouth at the end of his "trials." In 1772, Tim went to Shutesbury, Massachusetts, said to be his birthplace, and married one Mary Powers. In 1773, Governor John Wentworth awarded them a tract of 2184 acres and promised them a fortune in additional land if *they* would build the road through the notch and get five families to settle there within five years. They told him they'd think this over, did, and wisely rejected the proposal. The road was indeed a problem to build, and when repair work was being done, in the 1820s, workmen spent an entire day debating whether or not it should cross the Saco at that particular point.

Certainly, Tim and Ben were just a little apprehensive about the Governor's reaction when his men would come to build that road. They received their tract of land in 1773, and promptly sold it to a James Richardson of Leominster, Massachusetts, for 90 pounds. After that transaction, both men dropped from sight and were not heard of again.

Why I Bit an Elephant

IT was spring and really warm, the day I decided to wear my thin flouncy blue dress, and mini half-slip, for shopping at the Mall. Thinking back on that day, I sometimes wonder how it might have all turned out if I had been the type who is really afraid of animals, underneath a bravado exterior. Probably if I had not been a farm girl and had not experienced pleasurable meetings with all sorts of creatures, I would have hesitated at taking a baby into a traveling zoo — since I knew that goats tend to be cottonivorous, anyway.

But all this is idle reminiscence. Just take it from me: should you ever be moved to enter a kiddie zoo in anything less than long pants and boots, recall this true experience of a lifelong animal lover, and hastily reconsider. Furthermore, when you enter, carry no packages or purses. Keep your hands free at all times, and watch behind you. Should you be followed by more than one creature at a time, keep away from corners. A tour companion would be a great reassurance and might possibly be worth something in an emergency.

My Jennifer was barely a year old, too fat, and an unwilling walker, when I decided we should enter this visiting attraction at the local mall. The sign on the fence proclaimed these animals "the tamest," and the enclosure looked clean. I paid what I considered an outrageous sum for Baby and me, hooked my pocketbook strap over my right arm, and we entered. Husband stayed dutifully outside with our packages.

by Janice Stott Henke

We noted a wide variety of baby things, all anxious to be fed special crackers. For an additional 50 cents, I could later have kept them all at bay, but I lacked the foresight to hoard crackers while we toured. We squatted to pet lambs and llamas, piggies and an anteater. There were ducks, pygmy and regular-size goats, and some sort of little deer. Baby seemed to find them only mildly interesting.

"Good enough," I thought. No bad scares this first time. We were surrounded by soft little friends. Among these, however, was some sort of juvenile ostrich-like bird, maybe an emu. It was black, about Jennie's height, and I noted that it was peering too intently at her face. Emu's long neck S-curved at her when I placed myself between them, and when I pushed its head back a bit roughly, it simply persisted, beak slightly opened, with unwavering gaze fixed on Jennie's eyes.

"Oh well," I thought. "Time to get up out of our crouch and move on, anyway." I stood, slung Baby on my left hip, and noted that the crowd had moved away from in front of the baby elephant pen, which would be the scene of our last encounter before leaving.

Baby Elephant was not allowed to mingle with the other creatures and the visitors, but was behind his own stout fence, adjacent, still inside our main enclosure. He was also chained by one hind leg. Little Elephant appeared truly miserable in there. He was really tiny, as elephants go, all covered with fuzz, and I wondered if he was old enough to be separated from his mother. He looked well-fed, but was rocking from side to side and blowing his nose at us, letting out occasional grunts and a bellow or two.

"Poor fella," I said to him. He quieted down and rolled his red-rimmed, piggy little eyes over at us. Now across the fence came his gooey trunk tip. I figured he wanted a pet cracker, but we were fresh out of those. This was the first time I'd seen Jennie smile wide open at a creature, however, so I thought I'd encourage Elephant's attention a little before we left. With my free right hand, I pulled the trunk over for her to touch.

This was the fateful error on my part. Elephants apparently hate trunk-grabbing by humans. He recoiled mightily and twined all his nose muscles around the pocketbook strap over my right forearm. As we wrestled, the strap twisted, so that my right hand was caught at the wrist. He had me. Piggy red eyes narrowed, and he began to back up, grunting and tugging.

In my close to 30 years, I have successfully out-maneuvered quite a few large, obstinate creatures. Mad heifers, horses, even a bull once, had given up trying to do me dirt because I had kept my cool and either distracted or distressed them so they left me alone. And if all I had had to contend with in that animal pen was one elephant, everything would have been all right. But Jennie was still slung spraddled on my left hip, so my left arm and hand were useless for hitting or scratching on that trunk. And that long-necked, bright-eyed bird was still with us, peering up hopefully, and pressing close to my knee. I couldn't put Jennie down, and at that point she was beginning to squirm.

Elephant continued to wrench and tug. My wrist felt pinched, my fingers cold.

"Don't panic," I thought. "He'll never eat credit cards,

166

just scatter stuff around." This had probably been going on for two minutes or so when I realized the crowd outside the fence seemed to be getting a big kick out of my problem. I smiled weakly and looked around for Husband. There he stayed, leaning on the fence and thoroughly enjoying my predicament. I decided not to scream at him until later. My gaze drifted from the fools outside to the two slouches who stood with scoops and pails, waiting for the usual offerings in the sawdust. Their faces didn't show any sympathy either; they appeared to be pointing at something behind me, and were clearly waiting for me to react with helpless female noises. So far, I had not shrieked, nor said a word.

My wrist really hurt by now, and my attention had just returned to Emu and Elephant when the crowd noises took on a higher pitch. "What do they all find so funny?" I muttered. Suddenly something wet and tickley ran up the back of my bare thigh. One look down behind me, and the horrible truth came clear in a flash. The goat crowd had been eating my dress skirt all this time, gently but firmly wadding and chewing on the back. Now, two had progressed to the mini half-slip, and two more had found my panties. Slip and panties rapidly and surely began inching down over my hips.

I had never felt so thoroughly trapped. Wild kicking did no good. The goat crowd just stamped their feet and continued to wad and chew. I became rather well exposed to some 500 strangers who were all hooting around the outside fence. Elephant wouldn't let go. Emu was still stepping over my left foot, peering up with that same bright interest. People outside began to shove and jostle each other for a better look. More were running in from all over the mall.

Farm girls don't pass out under stress. They act. From

where I stood, there was only one thing to do because no one in the world seemed to care about saving my credit cards, my baby's eyesight, or what might be left of my modesty.

"Damn them all!" thought I, referring to the humans, not to the creatures. I pulled my right arm as close as possible, and drawing back my lips so as not to taste that beast any more than necessary, sank all my teeth into that hairy grey trunk. Piggy red eyes met mine, and elephant nose muscles let go of my pocketbook strap as a pain-enraged bellow filled the mall. Naturally, I quit biting as soon as my wrist was freed. I swung that pocketbook in a wide arc, bashing goat faces violently. They all drew back, including Emu. As gracefully as possible under the circumstances, I stepped out of my pants, which were soggily clinging to my ankles, hitched up my half-slip, which was down only to mid-thigh, and turned to exit out the turnstyle gate. The back of my dress felt soaked, and clung as I strode. I did not run.

After that performance, I expected claps and cheers, but there were none. The laughing faces slowly dispersed, letting me pass. I guess they were disappointed that the show had come to an end.

Husband stood grinning broadly. He took Jennie's weight off my left hip, and squeezed my hand. "I'm proud of you," he said and beamed broadly. "How did he taste?"

Now that you've heard what can happen, I'm sure you'll dress correctly before entering one of those places. This experience of mine probably wouldn't happen again, anyway. But just in case you *should* want to know, elephants taste gritty. END by Carl Goddard

Grandfather's Tricks

G RANDFATHER was full of tricks. Sometimes, out of a clear sky, he performed them at the most unorthodox times. For instance, on his sixty-fifth birthday we were having a picnic for him under the apple trees. When the cake was brought out with all its candles lighted, he turned suddenly to me and said, "Bub, run in and get me a broom."

I wondered what he could want of a broom right then, but it wasn't up to a ten-year-old like me to argue with my elders. So I scampered into the house and was back with a house broom in a jiffy. Grandfather rose from the long, board table and took it from me.

"Well, folks," he said, "as long as you're giving me such a nice party, seems as if I might entertain you a bit. It'll take me just about half a minute to jump over the broomstick, and then I'll cut that cake."

Sure enough, thirty seconds later, his trick performed, he returned the broom to me.

"Put it back where it belongs, Bub." Then, with pride in his voice, "But remember, Grandson, you can tell your sons that you saw their great-grandfather jump over the broomstick on his sixty-fifth birthday."

So that you may know what "jumping over the broomstick" means, take an ordinary broom and hold it in front of you, parallel to the floor, with both hands about twenty inches apart. This forms a rectangular opening —

169

your arms are the sides and the broom handle the bottom. Then jump through that opening without letting either hand lose its grip on the broomstick.

Try it some time! To most people, even the young ones, it is just about like jumping over the moon. Grandfather made it look easy at three score and five. But I found it wasn't. I tried it later, behind the hen house, and barked my shins and skinned my nose before I finally got the knack.

I was a proud youngster when, saying nothing of my practice, I performed for my grandfather. His word of praise was typical.

"That's pretty good, Grandson. Now when you get so's you can do it backward you'll be quite a feller."

He had a lot of little stunts like that. Some of them harder than others, but all of them required an agility that was astonishing in a man who stood six feet two inches and weighed more than two hundred pounds.

I remember one threshing season in particular. Among those helping out for the day was a young fellow named Jabe who was a new farm hand, but very strong and very willing — so much so that it seemed as if he were bent only on showing he was a much better man than anyone else. This made it very difficult for Ed Brown, with whom he was stacking the grain after it was bagged.

Grandfather was keeping his eye on everything, and it wasn't long before he saw Ed was having a bad time of it. The green-hand, in his inexperience and overzealousness, was grabbing at the filled sacks and trying to horse them into place by brute muscle. There was no rhythm in his lifting power. Ed was being thrown off balance by the sudden surges of strength from the young man. The bag stacking was going slowly. Filled and ready grain sacks were cluttering floor space and threatened to slow up the whole threshing crew.

Finally Ed gave voice to his exasperation.

"Listen, young feller, you don't have to lift everything with your back! God gave you strength, but not to waste it the way you are. Just take it easy, roll 'er on your knee and swing 'er with me. Then this stack'll grow just as easy as your grandmaw's knittin' and we'll have some workin' room."

The green-hand, fresh in the full flush of youth, came back pretty snappy.

"Why, what you talkin' about, old timer. I'm gettin' my end up there first ev'ry time. If you can't hold up your end, don't blame me."

Old Ed's mouth drew into a straight line, and nothing more was said for the next ten minutes. About that time Grandfather came around the corner of the ell.

"Hey, Ed! Need another man on the feed belt. I'll work in here for a piece."

I was young and didn't realize just what was going on. It was years later before everything fell into its proper groove, and this whole story became meaningful to me.

Then, I just watched and was proud of how strong my Gramp was. Why he was just tossing those grain sacks up there. That is — when the green-hand came anywhere near getting his end up too! As a matter of fact, looking back, Grandfather didn't give that young fellow a chance to get himself set at all. Gramp, just as innocent as could be, practically had him tied in knots. When the dinner bell rang an hour or so later, young Sampson was just about tuckered out. He also looked a little puzzled.

The crew washed up and hustled in to eat. They had been looking forward to the noon-day meal. Grandmother, for miles around, was famous for the table she set.

Grandfather waited a bit. Then he went into a storeroom off the ell and brought out an empty wooden barrel. He placed it on end at the door of the wagon shed and followed the others into the house.

After they had eaten all of Grandmother's good food that they could hold, the men trooped back to the yard to smoke, talk or rest a bit before going back to threshing.

They had been lounging comfortably for only a few minutes when Grandfather looked toward the wagon shed and remarked. "Say, that's kind of a likely lookin' barrel I got over there. Puts me in mind of something we used to do when we were boys. Remember, Ed, how we used to lay a sugar barrel on its side and then see who could kick it up on end the most times without missin'? That's an almighty pretty barrel. Durned if I'm not going to see if I can still do it!"

With that Grandfather rose to his feet. He brought the sugar barrel out into the yard. Selecting a level spot, he laid the barrel on its side. Carefully backing up to the open end until his heels almost touched the lower edge of the opening, he quickly flicked his heels in a backward kick, both feet rising from the ground together. My heart went up in my mouth. Gramp hadn't done anything! He hadn't even touched the barrel!

I never did know how Grandfather knew I was upset. I hadn't made a sound. But he looked over at me with his quick little smile and a twinkle in his eyes.

"Just warmin' up on that one, Bub. Don't worry. This is the time we do it."

A little shifting of his feet, another measuring glance, the sound of leather against wood, and the barrel was standing up on its proper end.

"Well, I swear, Ed! Makes me feel like a colt to flourish my heels like that. 'Course if I was a young feller like Jabe there," looking at the green-hand, "I suppose I'd have done it right off first crack."

"Yes, sirree," exclaimed Jabe. "I don't think I could miss anything as big as that barrel."

It was then that Ed spoke up.

"Well, young feller, you got just about time to do it once before we go back to threshin'."

"If I remember rightly, Ed," said Gramp, "you used to best us at it most of the time. Go ahead and try it, Jabe, if you want. We got 'nuther minute or two."

The eyes of the older men were quietly surveying Jabe. Nothing abashed, but rather pleased at being the center of attention, he jumped to his feet.

"Nothin' I'd like better than to do just that. I'll set her up on end quicker'n scat."

Jabe was full of confidence. He laid the barrel down on its side. He backed up to the open end with his heels close together against the lower rim and flexed his legs a bit. Then a look of puzzlement came over his face. He looked back at his heels, flexed his legs again, then stepped away to look at the lower edge of the barrel. He suddenly had realized that, with the barrel on its side, the lower rim was only about three inches above the ground. This was of course due to the bellying out of the barrel staves.

He had also realized that three inches was a very short distance to kick with force enough to lift the barrel upright.

With a final measuring look, he backed up to it again, got his heels as far under the lower rim as he could, flexed his knees and kicked backwards — you could almost see the energy pouring from him. Only it wasn't a kick. It was sort of a gigantic, clumsy heave which ended in a frog-like gesture that threw him forward to his hands and knees.

The barrel just rocked a little and rolled sideways.

Jabe looked a little sheepish, but backed up to it again. This time he kept his heels about a foot apart. We could see he was figuring on kicking the barrel farther out on each side to have more kicking room. And he really let fly with everything he had. But if you have ever tried to kick backwards with your feet spread apart, you know what happened. Jabe sprawled forward on his stomach. The barrel moved, but not in the right direction. Most of it seemed to get between Jabe's legs. I wanted to laugh, but all the men were looking on gravely so I thought I had better not.

Jabe was plenty aroused by now. He looked at the barrel for a minute, still meekly lying on its side. His face was getting red. Then he turned to Grandfather.

"Sir, I dunno as I rightly saw just how you kicked this barrel."

Grandfather rose from where he was sitting.

"Guess I did kick fast. You want to stand with your heels close together and so that they will just miss the lower rim of the barrel mouth when you kick. What you really kick is the under side of the upper edge. If you just give her a nice quick little kick with your heels on the under side of the upper rim, she'll come up on her end easy as can be. Now just study that over for a minute before you do it so you'll know how it goes."

"Ho!" exclaimed Jabe, all his confidence and assurance returning. "I won't need to think that over. Hitting that upper edge gives me plenty of room to give it a good kick."

Within the next two minutes Jabe had made another attempt. In the following 30 seconds he was inside the barrel, had barked both his shins, and as a grand climax had fallen over backwards, barrel and all. He was a crestfallen young man when he finally pulled himself together.

Everybody was laughing fit to kill now and throwing

good-natured witticisms at the bewildered Jabe, who still wasn't sure how it had all happened. That is, everybody was laughing except Grandfather, who was just as grave as before, although for an instant I thought I saw a funny little quirk at the corners of his mouth.

Grandfather went over to Jabe and helped him up.

"Don't feel bad, Jabe. That's happened to a good many of these very fellows who are splittin' their sides at you. Here, lemme show you."

Gramp put the barrel in position.

"You kicked just about right that last time. There was only one thing wrong. When you kicked up on the upper rim, you forgot that the lower rim was coming up too. You have to get your feet out of the way almighty fast or else that lower rim catches you right on the shins and you are inside the barrel before you can say Jack Robinson. Here, I'll do it again, and you watch my feet real close."

Gramp's first try put the barrel up on end.

"Try it now, Jabe, and I bet you'll do it."

Jabe didn't have any confidence left, but he was game and, sure enough, on the third try he did it.

Gramp grinned at him.

"Easy enough, Jabe? It's all in knowing how and timin' yourself. Don't need much beef at all."

Jabe grinned back.

"Well, friends," said Grandfather, "what say? Sun looks more'n twelve and a half. Want to do some threshin'?"

As the hands started for the barn, Gramp hung behind a little with Jabe, and I heard him say quietly:

"Jabe, there's lots of jobs like barrel kickin'. You just need to know how and when and save your strength till you need it. Well, enough of that. You and Ed'll be stackin' this afternoon. Expect those bags will pile up there pretty fast and easy now that you fellows got your bellies full."

A little later when I went into the kitchen for a cookie, Grandmother looked up from her baking.

"I see your grandfather was playing children's games again. When he was a young man, he was full of pranks, but he never wasted any time in the middle of the day — threshing time too! I declare, older he gets I think he grows a little foolish."

Even though it was a bumper crop for Grandfather's acreage, the threshing of the grain was finished earlier that afternoon than had been expected. That was good because it allowed the threshing crew to get the threshing machine hooked up to the horses and make an early start for old Mr. Litchfield's farm where they were to work the next day. It pleased Grampa too, because he could do the evening chores at the usual time.

At supper he expressed his pleasure to Grandmother. To her somewhat tart reply that it was none of his doing, what with playing games and all, he replied with a twinkle in his eye. "Just like cookin', Mary. You use sugar to make a green apple pie good. Sometimes, to make a green-hand good, you got to use the sugar barrel."   END by S.G. Mantel

The Bride Wore Gold

YOU know, they raise some mighty smart folk up here in New England. Especially in these parts. Take Henry Flood, for example. I guess you'd say Henry Flood was just about the smartest man ever to come out of the state of Vermont. Leastways, he was the richest — and that's one way to tell. But he married a York State girl he met when he and old Dan Willard were sewing up the big B. & O. deal, and she turned out to be smarter than Henry. Wasn't able to prove it, though, 'til after Henry died.

Not that there was anything wrong with the marriage — no sir! Millie loved Henry, I'm sure; and Henry, he loved her. It's just that, in the long run, she proved a clever woman is smarter than a clever man. Won't find that in McGuffey, I allow — but it's true-for-certain.

Henry was just about nineteen, I recall, when he packed his suitcase and rode the Rutland south to Albany. It was his lucky day. For Dan Willard himself was aboard, sitting in the smoker and holding forth on the state of the Union. Henry and Dan, they hit off fine right away, both being Yankees, and before the trip was done, Dan had Henry working for him.

You know, that Dan Willard was in everything where a man could make an honest dollar — railroads, oil wells, steel mills, the cable — just about everything. And he taught Henry the ropes. The lad took to the business like

177

maple sugar to snow, and before too many years had gone by he was a millionaire in his own right.

One time Dan was involved in a big railroad swap, and Henry went down to Baltimore, representing himself and Dan, too, of course. It was kind of a touchy job, but the upshot of the whole matter was that Henry came barreling back to Vermont with the whole shebang in his pocket.

Dan was staying with T. N. Vail, the telephone billionaire, up in his mansion on the hill in Lyndonville — that's north of here a spell and a mite east — and he came down to the Ville to meet Henry. Sitting right alongside him in his spankin' new rig was Millie Ross. I guess Millie Ross was just about the prettiest girl I ever saw — she's still a right-nice looking woman — and Henry was a handsome, open-looking man. So I don't have to spell out what happened — it was love at first sight for both of them.

Two weeks later their engagement was announced. Made a big stir, all over the world. After all, Henry was a self-made millionaire, and Millie was a rich man's daughter from Utica, over in York State. Her father put up a cure for the mange, and a darn good one. I'm telling you true. But that's another story.

The wedding itself didn't come so fast. I seem to recall there was a wait of about three years. Henry was busy all over the country and he sort of neglected Millie. Not intentionally, you understand, but Millie began to take it kind of personal.

One day, out riding near Utica (I guess Henry had a little time between trips), she says: "My trousseau'll be out of date if I don't get to wear it soon," and she laughs.

Henry, he knew right away what was coming and he headed it off.

"How'd you like to make the Grand Tour?" he asks.

178

"Europe?" says Millie. "I'd love to go back."

"Well, there's nothing to delay us, except the little matter of a marriage ceremony."

"Next month?" asks Millie.

"A simple ceremony would be best, I think," Henry says. "We don't want to flaunt our wealth," and he snaps the reins against the dashboard.

Well, it turned out to be one of the biggest weddings ever held in the state of Vermont. Had it up in Lyndonville — T.N. insisted. They invited half the Social Register plus a lot of people from Milledge and Utica, too. Folks said it was the biggest crowd they'd ever had in Lyndonville, excepting on Washington's birthday when they race the horses in the snow down Main Street.

Like Henry'd promised, they made the Grand Tour. And they had a grand time, too — with everything running smooth until they reached Athens. The way I heard it, the trouble began when Millie came back to the hotel one day from shopping. On her right hand she wore a mighty-fine antique ring she'd just bought. Henry noticed it, right off.

"Now that's a pretty ring," he says.

"It's exactly the same shade of gold as my wedding ring. Don't they make a nice match?"

"Yes," says Henry, "except it don't look right, wearing two gold rings at the same time."

"Why not?" asks Millie.

"Too gaudy."

"Oh, all right," says Millie, a bit miffed. "I'll wear them one at a time, then."

"You mean you'll take off your wedding ring?" Henry was shocked. After all, he'd been brought up in Vermont. So the idea of a married woman not wearing her wedding ring kind of went against the grain.

Now Henry didn't become a millionaire by being

179

stupid. After a while he says; "Will you do your husband a favor?"

"Of course."

"I'm sort of proud of our wedding ring —"

"So am I," says Millie, bridling a little.

"— and I want you to wear it, always."

"But I will. Except when I wear my antique ring."

"That's exactly what I mean," Henry says carefully. "I want you to wear the ring I gave you all the time."

"But I'd like to wear my antique ring once in a while," Millie wails.

"You can wear the antique ring on your right hand," Henry says, switching sides.

"Two gold rings?" asks Millie. "Isn't that gaudy?"

"Gaudy or not," Henry replies firmly, "you have my permission. But I want you to give me your solemn promise, right now, that you'll wear my ring forever."

"I promise," says Millie, not seeing what she was letting herself in for. "I'll wear your ring forever!"

Well, after a few weeks (almost like Henry might've planned it that way) Millie commenced leaving her antique ring in the jewel box, after a while she never wore it again, and the matter never came up again, either, far as I know. Leastways, it never came up while Henry was alive.

Which wasn't long. They came back to Milledge, set up in a fine house on the River Road, and then the tragedy came. In 1912, it was. Henry went down on the *Titanic*, having given his place in the lifeboat to an old woman. You must have read about it. They tell how he stood there on the deck while the ship went down, singing "Nearer My God To Thee." It came as a terrible shock to Millie.

She kept mourning quite a spell; seems to me it was better'n four years. But after a time she opened up the house again and began taking an interest in the town. That was when she met George Plant; he's town engineer now, but then he was just a state surveyor.

Millie was secretary to the Selectmen that year and she saw quite a lot of Plant, who was busy running a new highway through Milledge. First thing we knew, they were engaged, more or less; that sort of pleased everyone in town. Plant, he was from New Hampshire — that's almost as good as Vermont — and he fitted in fine in Milledge. And we'd be glad to see Millie cheerful again, not living all alone in the big house.

But there was a hitch. George was about as stubborn a man as ever you'd meet. Right off, he didn't want to touch Millie's money. This churned up quite a ruckus 'til Millie figured out a way to separate the expenses. Then came the business of the ring.

George hit the ridge-pole when he heard about Millie's promise to Henry. He allowed he'd not marry any woman who wore another man's ring. And Millie turned prideful, too. After all, she told George, she'd made a solemn promise to Henry. They had a big hassle; George said there was a time for mourning and a time for joy; Millie declared he was acting silly and no matter what *he* said, she wasn't going to break her promise to Henry. After a while, they just quit talking to each other.

And that was the way they left it: George went back to Hanover in a spittin' huff and Millie shut herself up in the house and the whole town was upset.

Only time we'd see Millie was when she'd come down here to the post office to get her mail, but I always had to shake my head when she asked if there was a letter from George. And I couldn't cheer her up, either; she said she'd never stop wearing Henry's ring, even if it meant losing George forever.

It looked like the whole thing was over, but it only

shows; you can't count a woman smart as Millie out 'til the last leaf's gone from the tree. Because she finally figured out what to do. Never would have thought of it myself, not in a million years.

First thing we knew, George was back; Millie must've phoned him — I'm certain she didn't use the U. S. Mails. Then an announcement came out in the *Republican* that they were to be married in two weeks at the Episcopal Church. Oh, the tongues were wagging, you can bet! Millie disappeared for a while, no one knew where. Some'll tell you she went back to Utica, but the fact is she spent the time in Boston. My niece, she's a nurse there, and she wrote me she saw Millie in the Medical Center building on Tremont St.

They tried to keep the wedding private — just for George's folks and Millie's, too. But the whole town waited outside the church; after all, Millie *was* the richest woman in town and she was our Henry's widow. Lots of folks got cricks in their necks trying to see if Millie was still wearing Henry's ring, but she had her gloves on when they came out the church. She was solemn, too, as befitting a widow, and she kept her eyes down on the ground and she didn't smile once. They took a hack to the depot and then they went off to the Grand Canyon on their honeymoon.

When they came back to Milledge they sold the Flood house and bought the old Duncan place; that's where they live now, raising the last of three kids and being active in the church. George, he's a big noise in the Rotary; Millie's busy with the Red Cross and the Ladies' Aid. Lots of folks call them Milledge's happiest couple — and maybe they are.

But I suppose you're wondering how Millie kept her promise to Henry and hung onto George, too. Well, everyone in Milledge knows the answer now, but I was the first to find out. Don't mind admitting there was a lot of curiosity about it at the time, though. You see, they rode in on the Flyer, the night they came back, 'bout three A.M. I was down to the depot to pick up the mail and I saw them get off the train. 'Course, I went over to help them with their bags, and I made a little welcoming speech. Just a few neighborly words, you might say.

George, he shook my hand; Millie, she just smiled. You know the light on the platform? Well, it was shining right on Millie's face, and when she smiled I could see a gold tooth shining back. I swear I don't remember Millie ever had a gold tooth before.

You see what I mean? That Millie's a smart one, all right; and the funny part is — she was born over in York State, too!

But I guess you could call her a Vermonter by nature. Leastways, I would.   END

I Wud Knott Dye

I wud not dye in wintur,
  When whiskie punchiz flo —
When pooty gals air skating
  Oar fealds of ice & sno —
When sassidge meet is phrying
  & Hickeri knutts is thick;
Owe! who wud think of dying,
  Or even getting sick?

I wud not dye in spring time
  & miss the turn up greens,
& the pooty song of leetle frawgs,
  & the ski larks arly screem;
When birds begin their wobbling
  & taters gin to sprout —
When turkeys go a gobbling;
  I wud nott then peg out.

in Winter

I wud not dye in summer,
   & leeve the garden sass —
The rosted lamb & buttermilk —
   The kool place in the grass:
I wud knot dye in summer!
   When evry thing's so hot;
& leeve the whiskie Joolips —
   Owe know! ide ruther knot.

I wud not dye in ortum,
   With peaches fitt for eeting;
Wen the wavy korn is getting wripe
   & kandidates are treeting.
Phor these and other wreasons,
   Ide knott dye in the phall;
& sense ive thort it over,
   I wud not dye a tall.

Dinner at the Ritz

BEACON Hill is the place to be when it snows, really snows, giant white flakes frenzied in a somber city. You can see it clearly then, that craggy, aging face of Boston.

And of all the places on the Hill to observe such a grand storm, I recommend the studio apartment of the fifth floor of 3 Woodvine Lane. It looked NNE across the rooftops of Boston to the Charles River and Cambridge beyond. There

by Stephen Austin

was no better view on the Hill, in the city — perhaps in the state.

Having lived there for eighteen months in 1952, I had finally decided to stretch some linen, set it on the easel, and wait through the dull gray days of December for the first snow, a true storm that took itself seriously, a fall that would last at least four hours. And now it was here and the light was right. If I took the phone off the hook and

started immediately, I was certain that what would develop would surely be a masterpiece. Then I should be to snowstorms what Turner is to sunsets. In years to come Webster's 21st Century International Dictionary would record this event succinctly: Austin Storm (1) a snowfall of great mystery, Gothic in essence reflecting the beauty and the power of nature; (2) a religious experience, a term derived from the work of Stephen Austin, a 20th-century painter, genius and mystic.

The trouble was that before managing to get the phone off the hook, indeed even as I reached for it, it rang. To this day I doubt very much if there has ever been a great painting executed since the invention of the telephone.

"Hello," I said.

"Hello, this is Evelyn Austin." My heart sank. It was my mother — the patron saint of interruption, the queen of chaos.

I disguised my voice "Evelyn who?"

"Stephen, don't be rude — it is your mother."

It developed there was no escape. She would be in Boston within two hours, driving, as I knew she would, in second gear the entire way from Walpole, New Hampshire — first over the old Keene road, bouncing and banging along in her '47 Chevy, nose down, tail up. Her mechanic, having finally solved her constant need for shocks, ended the matter one day in a moment of pique by installing two new ones in the rear of her vehicle that must have been meant for a 2 1/2-ton army truck.

Through Keene she would come, her pace slackened only slightly, a token gesture to its pedestrians. "Have you ever noticed that all the people you see in Keene have a funny frightened look?" she once asked my father.

She would take 119 to Rt. 2. The police couldn't possibly catch her on such a winding road. She would make good time because she would cut every corner and jump every amber light.

Her plan was full of detail inextricably cross-hatched with my own near future. I was the center of her focus these days, ever since the announcement of my engagement to Cornelia Gould.

I can't exactly name the person who made that announcement. Indeed, I don't even remember proposing. There *was* one evening when the very wealthy Mr. and Mrs. Gould came to dinner. ("They are the Pittsburgh Goulds," Mother had confided to me once when I was six years old. "A fine family . . .") As usual, they brought their daughter Cornelia with them. I had had, perhaps, more than my share of the wine when the subject of marriage came up on the level of "wouldn't it be jolly if Stephen and Cornelia one day decided to marry." I assumed it was all fairly theoretical — choosing to ignore "Corny's" alternate blushes and giggles, as well as most of the conversation. So when the end of the meal came and Mother turned to me and asked, ". . . the week of the seventh or the week of the twenty-first?" I assumed she was talking about a dinner party.

"Why not the seventh?" I said, sweeping the air with my wine glass. That's when they all cheered except old Corny, whose eyes grew large and soft and . . . fixed on me.

Mother's plans for the late afternoon included a trip to Paine's Furniture. I was to meet her there promptly at five to five. One of her weddings presents would be a bed and there was a problem even in this.

"Well, I don't see why you insist on a double bed, Stephen," she had said less than a week ago. "You'll be much more comfortable in twin beds."

"Double beds are for roommates," I said, "and I'm told that Corny and I are to be married."

Grave then, she looked me in the eye and asked, "You're not marrying Cornelia for sex, are you, Stephen?"

That was the kind of question parents asked offspring in those days. And the whole trouble with answering it was that I wasn't sure exactly what other good reason I might substitute for the one Mother found so abhorrent.

Actually, Corny looked quite striking, a bit over-stuffed here and there but by herself she looked just fine — it was all a matter of scale. She was enormous.

And if she was going to turn out to be one of those violent, passionate lovers, she might end up breaking every bone in my body on the very eve of the wedding.

The painting by now was coming along. In an hour and a half I had blocked things accurately enough. The brush strokes were still honest and solid in character, and the colors were fresh with a wide range. It was more than just a start, I was well into it.

But it was time to leave for Paine's.

The elevator at 3 Woodvine must have been designed by Leonardo da Vinci for the de Medici family — not so much as a means of portage from floor to floor but more as a unique and frightening torture tool. Its twisted baroque ironwork doors were stiff to open and planned in such a way as to pinch something — hands, stomach, knees, anything. For instance, the janitor two weeks before had had to cut my necktie in order to free me from its grasp. And that wasn't exactly the way I had wanted to be introduced to Natalia. Along with all its idiosyncrasies, jackrabbit jumps, horrifying drops (you'd swear the chain had snapped) — its course up through the building took you not *by* but actually *through* the apartment of Natalia Forsythe. That is, it took you right through the middle of her living room. The grill work on both the inner and outer door, while complicated, was open enough for a good view of the entire room.

And such a room! It was painted white as was every other apartment on Beacon Hill and Boston, but that was the end of its convention. The thing that struck you first was the savagery of the patterns in the room. Big, Bold, and Wild — and plants everywhere — giant man-eating plants — and Gustav Mahler, whom I'm not normally all that happy with, booming all around me. But it wasn't until two days later that I saw her as I was passing through her world. She was sitting on her couch or, more accurately, coiled *in* her couch, since she was half buried by it. She was dark-haired and fair of skin — I'd call her twenty-two and remarkably handsome, Sophia Loren handsome.

When the elevator finally came to a stop on the bottom

floor, I just stood there — not quite able to develop either the concentration necessary or the motor control required to open the doors.

I vowed then that I'd meet her one day and devised a scheme of ingenious simplicity. I'd simply stop and ask her if I couldn't take her garbage down for her. Well, I know that's not all that romantic an idea, but *that* was its genius. She'd never suspect that anybody would try to creep into her life by way of her garbage.

And that was the day I got my necktie stuck in the folding ironwork doors and she had to call the janitor.

I felt a little silly talking to her about helping her with her trash with only half a necktie hanging down and the wise old janitor listening in smiling just a little and nodding.

That had all taken place three months ago or twelve trips down the shaft with the garbage.

Sooner or later I was going to have to broaden my relationship with her.

By the time I got to Paine's it was three minutes past five. And Mother was carrying on a one-sided conversation with a floor salesman through the locked door. Reluctantly he let us in and she got right to business.

"My son and I are here to buy a double bed."

The man's eyebrows lifted two inches on his forehead.

"A double bed, madam?"

"Yes, and I've driven all the way down from New Hampshire — it's that important to us, isn't it, Stephen?"

I allowed as how it was indeed.

His eyebrows still hadn't come down. I wondered how he did that. I began practicing with my own eyebrows to see if I could get them to stay up there the way his did. I could hold them for a while but they'd keep dropping back into place.

"I think we should get twin beds but my son keeps insisting on a double."

"Follow me." He gagged a little, then wheeled and walked briskly into the store. Mother was barely five feet tall — proportioned well enough, still her legs weren't long, so she sort of had to trot along behind him. I brought up the rear still working my eyebrows. My whole face was getting the action. I found that if I dropped my mouth open quickly enough, I could shoot my eyebrows a lot higher and, what was more, hold them there longer.

Our little parade had caught the attention now of all the salesmen in the store. Some, in fact, had even fallen in behind us, the shorter ones trotting a little as Mother had to, until finally we came to a sudden and ragged halt in front of a magnificent double bed.

There were beds all over the place but this one was a stand-out. The head- and foot-boards were wrought iron — heavy, too — almost like a gate. The bed was wisely placed in front of a wall of brick painted white. A large plant stood beside it and I thought of Natalia. Just right for her, I decided. Mother by now was bouncing up and down on it, her feet out in front of her. I'd never seen a bed tested that way before but it seemed as good a technique as any. To show my enthusiasm, I went around the other side and bounced there in her fashion. We got sort of a seesaw thing going — she'd be up and I'd be down — I'd be up and she'd be down.

Our salesman was now standing a little bit off, his hands folded together in a distinctly ecclesiastical gesture, his head erect, his eyes closed. Poor devil, he was probably tired.

Well, we bought the bed. It would be delivered to Woodvine Lane next week. Mother paid the bill at the cashier's desk with a check and the entire sales staff showed us to the front door.

They all said goodbye but nobody seemed to want to shake my hand.

Next on the evening's agenda was dinner at the Ritz. We were to meet Corny there, who it turned out had driven down with Mother.

"She seemed fine when we started out," Mother told me, "but by the time we arrived in Boston she was a nervous wreck. She's high-strung, isn't she?"

They had gotten her a room and she was resting. I called her from the lobby at the Ritz and told her we'd be in the dining room, and when she felt up to it she should meet us there.

We were shown to a table for four, one waiter seating my mother, another seating me, a third sweeping the fourth place setting away in a single motion and a muffled clatter of silver. Everything was done that way at the Ritz. Giant menus were brought and then taken away when they heard we were to have cocktails first "to celebrate the occasion."

Then Corny arrived — statuesque but still pale as snow.

Actually the whole thing was pretty stiff. To begin with there was some trouble with Mother's Daiquiri — too much rum. How she could possibly tell that through the sweetness of that drink beats me. She insisted on going out with the waiter to the lounge in order to be sure the "bartender mixes it properly." We could hear her voice above the other guests' even from the lounge. First, there was great protest, and then as she got her way (she almost always got her way) laughter and good fellowship. Once people gave up resisting her, they really quite enjoyed her.

"Stephen," Corny finally broke our silence, "I can't go through with it."

194

"Well, that's all right, Corny." I felt sorry for her. "We could have something light, like soup, sent to your room."

"No, no. I'm not talking about dinner. I'm talking about the wedding."

Oh joy in the evening! I'd have another drink on that. I vowed, however, not to reveal my utter relief. Instead, I looked fittingly concerned and asked, "But why, Corny?"

"It's your family, you're all so ... so ..."

"Crazy?"

"Yes, crazy ..." She laughed gently. "But nice crazy. It's just that my constitution couldn't take it. Your family — my family — they're the ones somehow getting married."

"Well said." I raised my glass to her. "You know, Corny, there's no harm done. But for the rest of the evening let's just keep this under wraps, okay?"

She was greatly relieved and by the time Mother returned with the waiter in tow carrying her rumless drink on a small tray, everything seemed resolved, even comfortable.

"Well, now," Mother said, settling once more at her place, "perhaps it's time we should order."

It was a good idea, but we somehow couldn't even manage that. Mother got in an argument over the vast offering. She wanted somehow to create her own special meal that required borrowing her old favorites from five carefully planned separate dinners. The fight carried itself to the kitchen, she following the waiter through the swinging doors "to have a few words with the cook."

I took the opportunity to slip in an order for another Old Fashioned. Corny took the opportunity to suffer deeply.

We could hear Mother's voice rising and falling as the kitchen doors swung back and forth. Waiters were disappearing one by one into the kitchen — feeling, with some justification probably, that the cook and our waiter might need help in dealing with her.

Hah, I could have told them they were wasting their time — it would take the entire Boston police force.

By this time all in the dining room were dividing their attention between the kitchen door and our table. Now and then I'd smile a little and deliver a shy wave to one or two of the more oppressive gawkers. But the whole thing was beginning to wear me down a bit. Corny was a wreck.

Suddenly from the kitchen came a great and persistent bonging — someone with a steel spoon was hitting a giant kettle. I earnestly hoped it was the cook trying to take charge of his kitchen — and not Mother demanding order in the court.

"Stephen," Corny shouted above the din, "I seem to be developing a little headache."

"I bet — you're a sturdy girl or you'd have worse than that," I bellowed.

"I think I'll retire to my room," she said, rising. The noise from the kitchen had suddenly stopped. I rose. "Oh don't come," she said quickly, "somebody should be at the table when your mother returns."

"I guess you're right," I said, ". . . and Corny, I'm sorry."

"Not at all, Stephen — it's a 'live and learn world' — no hard feelings."

And with that she drifted from the place. She was in tears and I felt lousy about feeling so great.

By now every single person in the dining room was staring at me. So I began to practice my eyebrow routine — popping the old mouth open and shooting the eyebrows up my forehead as far as they would go. I think I was getting the hang of it when Mother reappeared. She'd made up her mind. We were leaving. I paid the bill for the drinks and left a tip. And as we rose to leave the room, all eyes were on us. She led the way out proudly. I walked behind her staggering sideways, my mouth agape, jumping my eyebrows and generally indicating that there was something thoroughly amiss with my central nervous system. Mother got to the hall first and caught my act in a large mirror on the wall. She wheeled then in fury and said, "Stephen, don't *do* that! You're embarrassing me!"

It must have been an hour later before I was able to disentangle from Mother. When I got back to 3 Woodvine Lane and found myself staring at the floor buttons in the elevator, I knew that I had to press ahead with my fine winning streak. So I pushed button number 4 instead of 5. It was a scary ride up. You might say I was in the breach. I didn't have a thing on my mind except beautiful, poised Natalia. No notion as to what my excuse might be to so intrude on her privacy, no grand tactic, nothing. Just me standing there inside the cage looking out at her in her jungle world ... hearing myself saying, "I'm a painter — that's fair. I don't call myself an artist — yet. But I call myself a painter because that's what I've studied and that's what I do ... best. And I have the start of a painting and I'd like your opinion. Here's my contract — I'll give you a glass of wine if you'll come now and give me your opinion."

It was remarkably easy. She didn't say a word but just got up off the couch and walked over to the elevator. I opened both doors for her and held them wide while she slipped lightly in beside me.

By the time we got to my door I was shaking so badly I could hardly unlock it.

We stepped inside and I flicked on a light, an easy light for any unfinished painting to be studied by, soft and yellow. Then I went to get our wine.

When I returned from the kitchen she was still standing in front of the canvas.

"You painted this?" she asked.

"Yes, this morning. It's just a start." My God, supposing she doesn't like my work? It was a new and terrifying thought.

"What do you think?" I asked, handing her a small glass of port, spilling some on the carpet.

"Why Stephen, it's ... it's beautiful. Mysterious — almost a religious experience. I think you may be a mystic."

It was then that I knew that the very essence of her intense beauty was a nature of remarkable insight and great good taste.

And my thoughts returned to my brand-new double bed ...   END by Liam Dougherty

Aunt Birmah

EVERY now and then when I'm feeling puny and my instinct tells me a good quahog chowder would straighten me out, I cut back across Cape Cod to the Bay side to visit a squat little Brewster house with white trim and pewter shingles.

When its proprietor, Aunt Birmah Freeman, sees me coming, she usually makes the same shrewd observation, cocking a gentian-blue eye at the weather for effect, "Wind must have got the word to Ha'wich it's Tuesday." This commentary is a dry reference to a singular coincidence. On Aunt Birmah's calendar, quahog chowder invariably falls on Tuesday; I feel puny on Tuesday.

Aunt Birmah is a small, elderly lady, born and bred to the Cape and ripened in its volatile atmosphere. There is a slight resemblance to the maternal Whistler, except for white hair drawn smoothly back, but a Whistler's Mother with a difference. That difference is "sprawl." Sprawl is an old localism that somehow eluded Webster. It was to the Caper of long ago what the spark plug is to the internal combustion engine. It was gumption, it was git-up-and-go. It was what, after an ordinary twelve-hour workday, trotted out a smoking covered-dish supper to the church basement. A Whistler portrait of Aunt Birmah would have looked like a pinwheel — unless he painted from memory.

Since Asa Freeman died twenty years ago, Aunt Birmah had lived alone and evidently liked it. Both her daughters had "dragged their anchors" (married outsiders). She always refers to her husband as A. Freeman. He spoke of her as A. B. (able-bodied) Freeman. Asa "farmed some and fished some." He was "handy," which is Cape Cod for an honorary engineering degree. He had navigated a boat and a huckleberry-white horse, both of which, by a quaint economy of nomenclature, answered to *Easter Sunday.*

Aunt Birmah's house is "set back a ways" from the King's Highway and above its level on a low knoll. A field, left rough but for its annual scything, lies between. As I cut across this on the particular afternoon I'm speaking of, I could see her talking to a girl over the short, white picket fence that muffles the multicolor explosion of flowers in the traditional Cape dooryard. The girl was wearing green corduroy Bermuda shorts, a yellow T-shirt and red ballet slippers. A purple kerchief imperfectly concealed an away-from-home permanent. White harlequin sunglasses were, of course, the complement *de rigueur.* I at once identified the girl with the gaudy convertible that idled across the road.

When I was close enough to the house to see the lichen on the shingles, I could hear Aunt Birmah, "... you bear East a spell to Orleans, then come about and head due North. If your feet ain't wet, your course is set for P-town."

"I suppose accommodations will be hard to find in Provincetown?" the girl said.

"Wouldn't know about that." Aunt Birmah's eye flicked from sunglasses to slippers. "I never was to P-town. Never had any call to go. I go to Chat-ham reg'lar, though."

Let a summer person make of that what she would as she skipped through the grass to her animated hardware store. Aunt Birmah would probably never see eighty again. Just to see her standing in the bright quilt of flowers before her house, anyone would realize she had been born there — thirty miles from Provincetown as the tourist flies.

Watching her go, Aunt Birmah snapped her apron, turned to me and smiled, "I say things like that to them people from away. They seem to expect it. God-*frey!*" she snorted, "that rig won't stand out none when she fetches P-town."

"Your roses are looking well," I observed neutrally.

"Sweetbrier's on the peaked side," she said, "but the cinnamon's usual. Let's to around back 'til I get them groundapples out of their suits or we'll have to *open* a can of chowder."

Shaken by this cruel jest, I followed her across the millstone doorstep, through the house that would have made a Boston antique dealer thrash in his sleep, and out to the grape arbor. Here I faced her in the green half-light, from one of the old deacon's benches, watching the peelings round from the potatoes as evenly as tape from a ticker. "What will it be today," I mused, "that I never knew before?" For, although the chowder itself was a pearl, the narrative overture during its concoction had, too, always been without price.

The last time I had been there I had absent-mindedly run my finger into a neat hole in the shed's curling shingles about two feet above the ground.

Noticing, Aunt Birmah had said, "Bein' a word-merchant, I suppose you'd like to know about *that* hole."

Being a word-merchant who has learned to play his cards, I said I would. And when Aunt Birmah said, "That's where they run the seaweed through," I'd been smart enough to act becomingly surprised, which almost no dramatic effort.

It seems that back in the days before the Cape Cod

Canal, when shipping went around "outside," Nauset was a wreck-producing, generous beach. A token of this was the keg of rum, flotsam or jetsam, Aunt Birmah's father had brought home one day and locked in the shed untapped — much to the chagrin of the two men who had hopefully lent him a hand. However, being Capers, the men had been skeptical enough to insure against any such deficiency in hospitality by placing the cask snugly against the back wall, where an inquisitive auger could reach it handily.

" 'Course, a little run out at first," Aunt Birmah smiled, "but they cal'lated good and the hole was near the top."

That's where the seaweed came in — the long, hollow, rubbery kind.

"As time went on and the tide went out in that bar'll, why them topers just paid out seaweed and followed it down to the dregs. The first pirate to suck air was a mighty disappointed man, mighty."

Today summer traffic on the highway murmured drowsily behind the more aggressive racket of the July insect world. Our comfortable silence was punctuated by the occasional exclamatory plop of a nude potato into a pan of cold water, until Aunt Birmah suddenly picked her topic for the day from her train of thought, "Them off-Cape folks all got complexions like razor clams." The reference was to her recent visitor, whose skin had been coarsened darkly — no doubt at the expense of much diligent exposure to wind and sun.

"That's a badge the vacationist wears back to the office," I explained. "Home in the city there's a bathroom shelf filled with jars and bottles that will erase the evidence when it's no longer wanted."

"Rubbish!" Aunt Birmah made a noise. "All of them mud-packs and syrups is rubbish — and I'll bet she's got a satchel full right now in the back of that auto-*mo*-bile. Bet I could teach her a thing or two. Why, that complexion lotion I make ..."

"You make?" I studied the pink and white freshness that gave the lie to eighty years of ravaging exposure.

"Certainly I make it — and more besides." Aunt Birmah stood. "Come on into the kitchen 'till I try out that pork and dice up the rest." In the kitchen she said, "All you need is six ounces of quince-seed mucilage, an ounce of glycerine and an ounce of rose water. Into two quarts of boiling water, exactly, in an agate pan, you put that quince seed. Then set it to steep on the back of the stove."

Aunt Birmah gestured with her knife toward the glossy range, backed against a ten-foot square chimney, whose wood fire never went out the year around. Beneath it dozed Quilt, her huge black, white and orange tomcat, fortified against the possibility of a capricious July draught. Quilt's whiskers were white to starboard and black to port, "like a baseball team — nine on each side."

Sneaking out my notebook, I asked, "What else do you make with that Junior Chemistry Set of yours?"

"My best cold cream." Aunt Birmah diced onions on a deal tabletop undulant from a century of knives. "Take ten ounces of albolene — solid, not liquid. Melt it with one ounce each Japanese wax and oil of sweet almonds.

"When you take it off the fire, stir thorough while it's hardenin'. Stirrin' right's the secret of a good article. Just before it's fixin' to switch from liquid to solid, add the six drops otto of rose — that's if you want to smell pretty."

"Where would I get the otto of rose?" I said.

"Why, make it, naturally, like I'm doin'." Aunt Birmah pointed to a two-gallon glass jar, a small vial upended on its top, standing in a sunny West window. "You tamp down the rose petals in the big one and put the sponge full of pure olive oil in the little one. Couple of weeks in the sun and that scent will have rose off them petals and got itself trapped in that sponge. Wring it out, and there's your product."

"So that's what makes you so nice to be near," I said, quoting some hidden persuasion.

"*That's* my cologne water." Aunt Birmah hopped from twig to twig, from table, to sink, to stove. "Take yourself a quart of alcohol, pure, and add the orange flower water, oil of bergamot, oil of lemon and oil of lavender — sixty drops each. Cork it up, shake it good and put it by to set for six weeks. After that, like them clowns say on the air, you won't *offend* nobody.

"Quilt, he always seemed to like my cologne water — him bein' a flower-smellin'cat."

Which, it occurred to me at the time, was probably as good a testimonial as an advertising agency could wring from any polo-playing, society matron.

Later, loaded to the Plimsoll mark, I divorced myself gently from my soup plate. "Good!" I gurgled.

"Good today, but when it sets 'till tomorrow it'll be better," Aunt Birmah predicted. "Won't it, Quilt? Chowder's a godsend to him since his teeth left."

"Well," I said, jokingly, "I guess you had everything in your laboratory but a remedy for falling hair."

"Had tricopherous for that. Sure-fire. Rub it into the roots three, four times a day reg'lar. Used to make it for A. Freeman, but he couldn't be bothered. That's why he went 'round bald as a newel post toward the end.

"All you got to do is to put six drams of tincture of cantharides into twelve ounces of castor oil. Shake. Add three drams of oil of bergamot. Shake some more. Pour in twelve more ounces of castor oil and shake 'till mixed. If you wasn't nervous to start with, you feel like it now. If you want to pretty it up like patent medicine, heat the oil with alkanet root. Strain, and you got a nice pink."

After we had the dishes clean and back in the "butt'ry," Aunt Birmah walked with me to the front door. Looking up at an evening sky beginning to lower, I decided to try out an old Cape word I'd come across recently. "Smurrin' up for a storm?"

"Wind would have to be backening 'round to the North for that. Looks more like a tempest to me."

"What's a tempest?" I asked, back where I'd started.

"You just find that out for yourself." Aunt Birmah smiled privately. "Then the meanin'll stay by you."

Leaving, I turned: "Look, Aunt Birmah, some afternoon why don't I come by early and we'll take a ride up to Provincetown?"

"Thanks just the same," I was told. "I don't hardly go at all any more, now that I got me the television. Sometimes, them people is real comical."

When I stopped at the drug store on the way home, I stepped out into the thunder and lightning of a vivid Cape thundershower — a working model of a "tempest."

I read a little from my notebook to the pharmacist, telling him why when he asked.

"Mister," he said, "now you're talking ancient history. But we've got a nice little up-to-date item here called *My Sin.*"

"No," I said, "that isn't what I'm after."   END

Life Size and Then Some!

by Jay Hutchins

IT was snug, down below, with a warm combination of smells ... of salt and mildew, tobacco smoke, drying socks, and coffee from a battered blue enamel pot on the galley stove. This was the cabin of the *Mildred L. Philbrook*, a Maine coaster for nearly a half century, now proud dowager of the "windjammer" fleet.

She was old, *Mildred*, but her grace was apparent, even in the steamy murk below. The feeble glow of the swinging brass lantern revealed the ample swell of her flanks, hidden as they were by berths and lockers, and the slight longitudinal curve of the dim recess where we sat foretold lean beauty fore and aft.

There were half a dozen of us aboard, back from a gusty sail off Seguin. Lying at anchor in Boothbay, *Mildred* rolled lightly on the soft swell of the harbor, and we sat below, enjoying the warmth and the quiet. Only the pleasant creak of the main boom, swinging a foot or two as the vessel eased back and forth, could be heard before the old man rose from the edge of a berth and took the steaming pot from the stove.

He was my grandfather, skipper of the *Mildred*, tenth or eleventh of her long career on the coast of Maine. He poured each of us a mugful of the old pot's rich contents, then returned to his place in the shadows.

"Bet you never heard about her launching," he said to everyone in general.

"Quite an affair ... but somehow it never made any of

the tourist books, or anything put out by that Boston feller who drops stuff to the lighthouse keepers at Christmas. But it made quite an impression at the time, especially on the girl she was named for.

"It was back in '99, and let's say it was Thomaston ... that's not really the place, but let's say it was ... and Tom Leighton had been back from the Spanish-American War about two years. I remember him from before the war, back when his father's dory was found, and when he worked, after school, to help his mother piece out. He finished high school, Tom did, and afterward went to work in the shipyards.

"This boy was good with tools, and it wasn't long before he was as fine a joiner as there was anywhere on the coast. He read a lot, nights, learned lay-out and lofting, and even at nineteen or so he was bound for a master builder's career.

"It was just about then that Tom began to court the prettiest girl in town. 'Course she was the original Mildred L. Philbrook, banker's daughter, pretty but tempery, I guess, and given to considerable foot-stamping. But as time went on she and Tom got pretty thick, and just about the time everybody expected to hear about wedding plans, he up and joined the Navy.

"Well ... there was quite a to-do, but it got around town that Tom wasn't breaking the engagement, merely postponing the final step for a year or two, and that he'd be back and ready to settle down after he'd helped win the war.

"People in town liked Tom, and could see the sense in this, but Mildred couldn't, and when she stamped her foot that time, she meant it.

"So Tom went off to war, and Mildred never forgave him, never answered his letters, never gave him a pleasant thought, went to picnics, socials, hayrides, and God-knows-what-all with pretty near everybody in town, and married the minister's son about a month before Tom's return.

"It was quite a shock, but Tom straightened out soon enough, and began to see a good deal of another girl. Things went along fine for a month or two, until Mildred queered it by telling Tom's new girl all about how he had run off and left her, and how he couldn't ever be depended on, probably, especially if there was another war, and how she should find a solid, dependable boy . . . maybe her husband's kid brother.

"There was a lot more of this over at the Methodist Ladies' Aid, where Mildred, by this time, had assumed full authority. The immediate result was that Tom's new girl wasn't Tom's much longer.

"This happened several times, with Mildred's blackening Tom's reputation more and more, until Tom ran out of girls, and Mildred ran out of male relatives. Tom was twenty-four, and still single, when he took his savings and started to build this vessel.

"Even her keel was beautiful, and as she took shape, down there on the point behind Tom's house, we were sure she'd be the prettiest schooner ever built. Tom'd work all day in the yards, then half the night on his own craft, and sleep what little time was left. He worked alone, and shaped every plank, and drove every fastening, and later brushed on every drop of paint, until her hull stood finished on the ways.

"But she wasn't quite finished. Her trailboards and figurehead were missing, but they were last-minute touches anyway, and probably Tom was still working on them in his shop.

"It was about then that word got around that Tom had

named her — and this was the big surprise — *Mildred L. Philbrook*. We figured it was quite a tribute for a woman who'd caused him so much trouble.

"Anyway, Tom launched her on a Saturday, when the tide was full, about noon. Town was full of people, and most of 'em were down to watch as the Reverend spoke his piece up under the bows. Tom had flags on the stays, and had draped her bowsprit and most of her stem with red, white and blue, and all this was snapping in the breeze as the minister asked the blessing.

"Tom stood back by the stern, and swung his sledge with the last amen, driving out a block and letting her slide. He watched her go, and when the bow passed, he reached up and grabbed a line that trailed from the stem. He belayed the end quickly to a piling, and as his vessel moved out into the river, the line came taut, pulled away the bunting, and revealed the figurehead.

"What a cheer went up ... because there was Mildred herself, life-size and then some, carefully carved, faithfully painted, completely and gloriously bare."

The old man paused, lit his pipe and looked slowly at each of us, in turn, around the dim cabin. Finally he went on:

"Well ... Mildred and her husband soon moved to Ohio, which they felt was almost far enough from salt water, but for years, as the schooner docked at Camden, Castine, or another Penobscot Bay town, some old Thomaston friend would greet Tom and walk with him up the wharf toward the village.

"Each of these old neighbors from Thomaston had the same thought. They'd glance at the figurehead, then back down the wharf, then peer into the skipper's face.

" 'By Golly, Tom,' they'd say, 'you got her just right!' "

END

Antoine's Choice

EMILE, my beloved son, it is time to teach you about choosing a wife. Some skills, like managing business affairs, are learned by trial and error, and mistakes corrected with little pain. Picking a woman is different. A mistake in this can be for life. The risks are great. You must know what to look for — and you must look! I confess that even I, by neglecting at the outset to make sure of an all-important fact, almost picked a noodlehead. I shudder to think. As a warning, I tell you how it was. Be smart, as I learned to be, and your blessings will be past counting . . .

You already know that I, Antoine de la Montagne, when young, was the big turkey man of the Upper Connecticut Valley. Changes beyond belief have occurred. The railroad came to Brattleboro and beyond. Thereafter, the turkey walked into a fine car, found a good seat, and watched the miles fly by. What a miracle! He rode; and within hours arrived. In my day he walked; yes! it took days, and he wore boots of hot tar and sand, but he walked the scores of miles from his childhood home in Vermont to far-off Boston. He enjoyed that walk, I can tell you, with trees to sleep in each night, pure cold New England air to fill his lungs, and, to occupy his mind, pleasant thoughts about the blue-stocking lady in the Back Bay whom he would make happy at Thanksgiving. His drumsticks, how proudly they bulged!

It was on one of my famous turkey drives, Emile, that I learned about choosing a wife. In that year, Antoine's turkeys should have made him rich in dollars; but who could foresee how rich in wisdom of the sex?

"Look," I said to old Michele as the day to start the drive drew near, "two thousand turkeys, a dozen more or a dozen less, the best ever seen. Have so many so fine ever gone on the march before?"

"Never in Vermont," said toothless Michele.

"Never nowhere," said I. I cast an eye to Mr. John Adams, who weighed twenty-nine pounds and strutted like he was foreman. "Never in Vermont, Michele, never in Boston. Antoine feels proud."

"His pockets will bulge."

"God willing."

"Fine news that will be for the eldest daughter of la Foque!" Only old Michele, my dear friend, knew Antoine's secret feelings for that turtle dove, Françoise la Foque. "Perhaps," Michele gave my rib a small poke, "my friend will bring the fair one with him when he returns this year."

"Tschah!" I pretended such talk was a joke. However, the thought was most amiable.

Even the smartest man may be blinded by the artifices practiced by the sex. I dreamed that this one was without a fault except, perhaps, the giggle, which a man could easily explain was not becoming after she said, "I obey." Françoise played the melodeon beautifully — tinkle, tinkle, tinkle — and was most exciting to hold in the dance.

Whenever I was invited to dine with la Foque, I loved the good smells coming from the kitchen and considered it bad manners to inquire further. During a lonely summer with my birds, I had concluded it would be most intelligent for the fair one to say "Yes!" to the big turkey man with money jingling in his pocket and charms of a personal nature — a man highly thought of, too, in Boston. It was true. Merchants to the carriage trade in that city, I can tell you, did not grab the first birds walked down from Vermont. They eyed the first comers, but their money stayed in their pockets. They said, "I will wait for Montagne." Thus they were able to say truly to customers, "These are Antoine's turkeys, the best."

It was at the granary where wagons were being filled with shelled corn for the drive, that André burst in. The tear was in his eye. "Antoine," he said sorrowfully, "the most terrible thing. Marguerite is with the bleeding again. She says I must stay . . ."

André, you do not remember, Emile. He was old even then. All who knew him, said he was the smartest turkey drover in the Valley. Almost he knew the business as well as Antoine. I was desolated by the news of his woman, and alarmed for the turkeys. "Do you mean you cannot go with the drive?" I asked.

"Regrettably," he nodded. "Yet . . ." hopefully, "André has thought and thought, and thinks he knows who shall go instead."

"Name him, my friend."

"Marguerite's cousin, her great red cousin from Maine."

"The man named Swampscott? I have heard of him, I think."

"Without doubt. He came to Marguerite for the visit. The size of his appetite, you should see! Magnificent! He says he is bound to learn what the rest of the world eats, besides Maine. He even speaks of going where they hunt the buffalo and shoot the Indian. Wherever there is food, he is crazy to go; even gladly he would nursemaid the turkey to Boston to eat some beans. I am glad if he goes."

"He is a good man, André? Your judgment I respect."

"A great roaring man of much strength."

"But the turkey — does he understand him?"

"I almost promise. What he does not know, André will teach him."

"There is little time."

"From André he learns like lightning."

"Send him to me, my friend. I pray the angels make Marguerite well quick."

So, amazing events had their start. With André, the turkey drive would have been like the picnic. But who could guess what a donkey would take his place? Who could foresee that in a hundred and twenty-five miles at the pace of a walking turkey he hardly one time stopped tooting his great horn, doing wrong things, putting his foot in improper places, being a thorn in Antoine's boot? Who could imagine how loud he would talk about logs he rode on fast water (he said), or the rum he drank in quantities past belief (he said), or the bear he wrestled and killed with one small knife (he said)? With the turkey, he — but I spit! With the sex, how disgusting! Antoine could not count how many times he would have given his fine gold tooth on the walk to Boston to buy the last sight of that red face.

Yet Antoine should sink to his knees and thank God for blessings in disguise. At Swampscott I still spit. I pray he eats hash that stinks. But Swampscott ... let the world judge!

A bad place on the turkey drive was a certain covered bridge, now gone. The tollgate keeper would sit all day knitting — tschah! — knitting socks, and roaring at each traveler, "Where's your penny?" Very slow he could be, if he felt so, about raising the gate. The turkeys thought they should walk on the bridge the same as other people. The man would say, "Scat! Get out!" I knew he made good socks, so I always bought two, three pairs. He would smile and say, "What's this? Turkey want to walk on bridge? Gobble, gobble, turkey, go right across!" He even laughed aloud when the last turkey marched past, looked him in the eye, and said, "I go to Boston!"

That way was good. Swampscott did not know this. He came first to the bridge and said in his great roaring voice. "Raise the gate, fellow, and hurry!"

The gateman did not like that. He went on knitting, pretending no big turkey drover was near.

Swampscott laid a hairy fist on his shoulder. "You heard me! Get that gate up before I bust it!"

The man dropped his knitting and picked up the queen's arm, his old flintlock, and pointed it at Swampscott's belly. Antoine would have made money if he shot! "Turkey take *that* bridge," he said, nodding at the river. "He can fly. He does not walk on this bridge."

Swampscott knocked the gun aside, pulled him out of the rocking chair, and held him up by the collar like a thief on the gibbet. Yarn rolled this way, needles that way. *Joie de vivre* in the old gateman went somewhere else.

"Turkey take *this* bridge," Swampscott said, and kicked the gate to smash.

Antoine's turkeys did not understand this, and had the idea to do something original. One flew on the tollhouse roof and looked at the river to be crossed. Others wanted to see too. Quick, the roof was covered with turkeys. Antoine's turkeys weighed twenty-two, twenty-five pounds. The roof was not built to hold fifty sight-seeing turkeys.

Suddenly the old man had no roof to sit under. The turkeys scattered.

I was far back, but came quick. I saw this mess would never improve itself by a small transaction in socks. "Look at my roof!" the old man screamed. "Look at my gate!" he shrieked. "I am ruined!" I showed the color of my money, the best language for smashed roofs. It took many of Antoine's dollars before the old man calmed his voice, smiled small, waved to turkey and said, "Walk across!" But already some turkeys had gone away, maybe two hundred, and given up the notion of going to Boston. At Swampscott I was very angry. Antoine, you know, is as brave as a lion, but also small-built and discreet, so he did not say too much about it to Swampscott personally.

The drive, less some turkeys, went on.

The little poet in Antoine called the village of Three Pines a pearl in a necklace. As we came near, I passed the reins to another and walked ahead to gaze down on it from the hill's eyebrow. It lay beautiful by the small brook which la Foque dammed to make a waterfall to turn his millwheel. I looked down on the dreaming church, the house roofs, the tall mill, and wagons coming with hard little apples to make the good cider. I thought good thoughts. La Foque, long since dead, was a smart man. He was diligent to make the best wine, saw to it that the food on his table was the best and his daughters ... ah! Françoise, who laughed like the meadowlark and had cheeks like October maple leaves and made the heart go pit-pit-pit; Elaine, small and sober, who did not look so much but had other merits; and two little ones, Mimi and Celeste, so small then that a man held them on his knee without shame.

"I eat supper there," I said to Swampscott, pointing to the big house.

"They got a good cook?" he asked. That man hardly thought of nothing else.

"Best in the world," I said, not thinking much.

"Truck in mess pot makes me sick," he said; "I'll go with you."

I was flabbergasted. He was not even invited. I would have liked to point this out, saying, "These are my friends; that, you cannot do." But I thought of the tollgate man, and the bear that displeased Swampscott and became a steak for Swampscott's supper. So I did not say it immediately, but waited to think of something. I knew la Foque would not want this goat at his table to eat like a horse. The best way to explain this was hard for Antoine to think of.

The turkeys soon arrived at the meadow Antoine knew of. Corn was scattered, and when all the turkeys ate enough to suit them, the sun set, they got sleepy and went to bed in the trees. Antoine waved and said, "Good night! happy dreams!" But Antoine himself was not happy. He caught a fine turkey as a gift for Mama la Foque, all the time thinking about something suitable to say to Swampscott. As always, the news that Antoine had come would have gone ahead, and Mama would be expecting him and planning a supper such as he loved. To bring Swampscott without invitation was not polite. But how to tell Swampscott without arousing nasty feelings in him did not occur to Antoine.

"Let's get goin' to where they eat, Frenchy!" Swampscott said. Antoine had to let him go.

Françoise saw us first. Maybe she is sitting at the parlor window in her Sunday dress watching. She flew out of the door and ran to Antoine with the gay welcome. "Antoine!" she cried. Little ribbons fluttered, little bells jingled. Antoine's heart felt good. She looked at what was with him. "Oo-oo-oo!" she said. "Who is this?"

216

I introduced Swampscott, but tried to do it so she would know he was nobody, just hungry. "Oo-oo-oo!" she squealed. "We fix that. Roast is so big, almost it would not go in the oven."

Swampscott shook her hand and squeezed. "Oo-oo-oo!" she squealed again. "You are very strong man."

He strutted like a gobbler when his hen friend is around. "Nothin' to what I could do, missie," he bragged. He looked her over. "Say," he said, "you ain't hitched, are you?" I never heard anything so vulgar and surprising. Françoise giggled and said, "Silly!" And Swampscott slapped Antoine's shoulder so hard Antoine almost dropped Mama's turkey.

"Oo-oo-oo!" said Françoise.

I boiled but did not say so. I smiled like I was amused and said, "My pretty, wait till this — wait till he tells about his bear." I added with the sarcasm, "He will!" I wanted Françoise to know he was a blow of wind with brains like thistledown, and nothing in his pocket, which was hard to explain without privacy.

La Foque roared from the door, "Come in, Antoine, come in!" Already he had filled tall mugs from his best barrel. I, who knew the muscle of that liquor, took a little, then a little. Swampscott did not understand this. One gulp, whoosh! his mug was empty, and he said more of the same would like to go where the first went. I blushed at his manners. I wished to make apologies, and stepped to the kitchen to explain in a small voice to Mama la Foque and Elaine how it happened that great lunk came with me.

Mama waved her fork. "Don't fret the mind, Antoine," she said, and smiled. "Fitchets, we take 'em rough or smooth."

It is hard for Antoine to understand how the woman, so dainty, stands man so coarse.

At table, Swampscott showed his colors like the red bull.

His mouth was never empty and never closed. His mug was filled how many times I could not count. I thought la Foque must run the mill overtime to catch up. Swampscott's plate was piled high one minute and naked the next. He did not learn silence at meals like in the well-behaved lumber camp. He told about his bear, which I had heard so much, about log jams, and fish, and Swampscott this, Swampscott that, Swampscott-God-knows-what till the ears ached. Not always were his stories delicate for females. He made jokes that shocked even a man, and it seemed to Antoine some of those females were not shocked. Once Françoise laughed till tears came; this I did not admire. His most bad story was about a woman in Maine. "She made fun of my manners," he said; "she told me I was worse than a bear. I said, 'Bear? I show you what a bear does, miss.' So I grabbed, and she shrieked, like this . . ."

I blush to remember. Françoise sat next to him. He grabbed her and squeezed till I thought something would bust. "Oo-oo-oo!" Françoise squealed; "let go!" She pushed, not very hard. He let go, not very quick. My face burned with shame. I would have liked to kill. I hoped Françoise would slap him. She just unmussed, and giggled.

Elaine, very quiet, sat across where I looked in her face. She lifted the eyebrow, did not smile; her head shook a little. She saw this thing as Antoine did, she told me with her eye before her eye dropped.

When supper was over I had to walk back to camp with that great codfish, though my stomach objected. Swampscott, full of cider, roast, and pie, gurgled at every step. He talked, sang, roared till I thought he would shake the turkeys out of their trees. I reminded him that turkeys like to sleep quiet, but he gave no goddam about that.

"That pussycat back there," he said, "—she's my style."
I remained completely silent.

Never was a turkey drive more hoodooed than that one.
No turkey has a big brain, but once he understands some
situation, he uses the brains he has to his personal advantage. Many times I have explained to the uninformed that
to drive the turkey, it is necessary to be a little more smart
than the bird. Swampscott flunked this test. He never
learned how a turkey, on a long walk with friends, may
leave them a while and take a little walk by himself. This is
not bad. He wants to think about his problems. Leave him
alone, and he soon comes back. Swampscott didn't think
turkey thoughts. He allowed no goings-on like that. The
turkey must march like a British redcoat, tramp, tramp. If
Swampscott had a drum, the turkey must keep step. No
turkey thinks like that.

A day or so later we were going to pass Hate-Evil
Bodley's big farm. This was a bad place. Hate-Evil himself
raised many turkeys. Antoine's turkeys liked to get acquainted with Hate-Evil's, and Hate-Evil's enjoyed seeing
new friends from Vermont. One turkey looks much like
another, so we had to be careful not to get mixed up. I re
minded the drovers of this. Swampscott was maybe thinking about his bear or his belly, and paid no attention. I
said plainly:

"Never mind if one turkey takes a little walk by himself.
He will come back. If many go, this is bad —"

Swampscott belched like a volcano, yawned, said he was
sleepy. He picked the best place with his feet near the fire,
and soon his blanket shook and he snored like the earthquake. Away from the fire the night was cold and still, and
Antoine went for a last look at his turkeys. The trees were
so full the branches looked like they'd break. Clouds scudded across the moon, snow crunched underfoot, and it felt

good to be on the turkey walk. Antoine thought of the money that would dance in his pocket in Boston, and how happy his turkeys would be to make kitchens smell like Thanksgiving Day and pumpkin pie, and the man of the house would take his sharp knife to carve and say very stern to his wife:

"Martha, is this Antoine's turkey?"

And Martha would say, "John, you know I buy only Antoine's turkey."

And all would bow their heads and say, "Thank you, God; thank you, Antoine."

Swampscott did not feel good next morning. He said his belly did not like its food, so he only ate three times more sausages and pancakes than anybody. A man could go to the poorhouse filling that belly. Turkeys ate breakfast too, but civilized, not too much corn, and started to march, hunting bugs and beechnuts to save Antoine money, getting fatter as they went. Mr. John Adams was the proudest of all. He must have weighed thirty pounds by now, and should have carried a pocket mirror to admire himself, he was so handsome, the lady turkeys liked him so much. His beard was biggest, his wattles reddest, and when he put his wing down and tail up and strutted, nobody thought anybody else was the boss. When he gobbled, everybody said Mr. John Adams made a fine speech.

This turkey was keeping an eye on things when he decided it was best for him to take a little walk alone. We were now near Hate-Evil's, and Antoine's eye was anxious. Swampscott observed Mr. John Adams leaving, and said, "Hey you, come back here!"

Mr. John Adams pretended not to hear: he would attend to his own affair the way he thought best.

Swampscott yelled louder. Mr. John Adams kept going, but had an eye on Swampscott. Swampscott liked to have people pay attention to his law. He set out to teach that big turkey the rules, and he chased Mr. John Adams. Mr. John Adams walked faster. Swampscott started to run. Vermont turkey did not look like a speed man, but when he decided in favor of a race, he could go like the wind for a ways. Swampscott chased and chased, yelled and yelled, and did not notice this tree root. He tripped and plowed his big red nose in the dirt with some stones in it. At another time it would have made Antoine laugh to see him so bloody. But Antoine remembered Hate-Evil and was worried. Swampscott, he saw, was not going to let one old turkey get away from him, you bet, but how about two hundred turkeys? He got up cussing, with dirt and blood all over him. He told bear to get out of the way or get hurt, and bear must mind or be eaten. He told turkey to get back there, and turkey better mind. *He* thought. Mr. John Adams didn't think so.

The turkey ran very fast maybe a quarter-mile, but he was fat and puffed and got tired, and Swampscott caught him. This started the fight. Swampscott did not know it, but a big tom turkey can fight good. He has spurs to rip with, wings to flap in a man's face so you can't see to think. He has a beak to bite with, toenails to scratch. Mr. John Adams used all these tools and some more he happened to think of, and I bet Swampscott wished that turkey was a bear and easy to lick. He got more bloody, hot, tired, his shirt was torn, his hat was lost, he was a mess.

Now, turkeys like to keep up with the latest news, and when Antoine's other turkeys saw what was going on, they hurried to see the fight and guess who would win. It is sad to tell. Where they came from, Antoine does not know, but Hate-Evil's turkeys also heard about the fight and came to watch. They thought it was nice to see so many fine strangers from Vermont. Soon, who knew which was Hate-Evil's turkey and which was Antoine's? Hate-Evil's turkeys told Antoine's about a place in the swamp they liked to go to. "We show you," they said. Antoine tore his hair, Mr. John Adams tore Swampscott, and many of Antoine's turkeys went off never to be seen by Antoine again.

It was a tragedy. While Swampscott was still bloody and Antoine too angry to remember caution, Antoine spoke like the lion: "So many turkeys lost, you big bear-fighter, you got no more job. Here is your wage. There is the road! Go! If I see you no more, my eye is dry."

Swampscott said he was not fired, he quit. He went. I hoped to see him no more.

Life has sadness. Antoine never got back most of his beautiful turkeys, though he hunted and hunted, and Hate-Evil, with a little smile for having some new turkeys, helped, but not much. He pretended he was sorry, but when we met a big turkey, he'd say, "That's mine; I know that one." How Hate-Evil, who was a deacon in church, knew, Antoine could not guess. Antoine did not tell him he lied, but what Antoine thought, he thought. However, time was flying; to hurry was necessary. Antoine took the turkeys Hate-Evil did not claim, and resumed the walk. It was peaceful without Swampscott, but sad that two thousand turkeys now were not even one thousand.

Even these were too many. Antoine reached Boston very late. As the time had come nearer for the housewife to buy her bird to give thanks with, everybody said, "Antoine maybe does not come this year." They were disappointed, but had to make the second-best do. When Antoine did come, turkeys were plenty, buyers few, and prices down in the cellar. Antoine, who should have pocketed hundreds of dollars, had not many left after he paid his drovers and settled his bills. It was sad.

But his heart was stout, and Antoine smiled bravely and said, "Better time comes." Always he had hope like the lighthouse. He remembered he still had a couple dollars in a snug place in Vermont. Another day, another turkey. Françoise la Foque he would see on the way home, forgive, and God willing, she would say yes when he spoke. So Antoine went to Carter on Tremont Street, and said, "Louis, you are my friend. You know what a gentleman must have in his pocket when he kneels and says to his lady friend what he thinks of to say. Show me, please." Louis winked and brought a tray with the most beautiful rings. Antoine picked the best, and when Louis said, "That costs twenty-seven dollars!" Antoine did not bat one eye. Who would think cheap when the best woman was about to make him the happiest man?

This and that took much time, and snow was deeper on the hills when Antoine came again to Three Pines town. He saw ice on the river. La Foque's mill had gone to sleep, not to waken till summer. It was beautiful. The world was beautiful. And how excited was Antoine's heart! He came in the wagon now, and Françoise did not sit by the window to see him and come running. This was nothing. Smoke flew from the chimney. He knocked, and soon the door was opened one little crack by Celeste, the smallest la Foque.

"Oo-oo-oo!" she squealed like Françoise. "Mama! Is Antoine."

She forgot one little thing. Mama was not there.

This Antoine discovered. He went in, but the house was not laughing. Nobody was home. No good smells came from the kitchen. Antoine said to Celeste, "Where is Papa? Where is Mama? Where — ?"

"I have whooping-cough," Celeste said. She whooped in my face to show me. "They not let me go," she said; "I very angry." She stamped her foot to show how angry.

"Where did they go?" I asked.

"Oo-oo-oo!" she whooped; "to see priest."

"Priest?"

"Si! Big sister marry."

Something went plunk in Antoine. "Marry? Sister?"

She nodded. "Oo! is he funny man. He tickles Celeste, tosses her to ceiling, catches her. Celeste squeals."

"Elaine is married then?" I said bravely.

"Oo-oo-oo! Big sister, Françoise."

My heart stopped. "Who —," I saw a chair and sat,"— who she marry?"

"Oo-oo-oo! Bear man from Maine."

"S-Swampscott?"

She nodded, giggled, and whooped.

It was past belief. Just weeks ago, Antoine regretfully brought that great grasshopper to eat la Foque's food without being asked, and before a man could say jack, he makes Françoise the wife. What was he, magic? What was she, crazy? Man who squeezes till he busts something, fights Mr. John Adams, has nothing but a great appetite? How could Françoise so soon forget the man of large turkey affairs? It was past contemplation. "Celeste," I said and heard my voice tremble, "please go somewhere and whoop. Antoine must rest."

Celeste was smart like all women, even little ones. "Antoine sweet on Françoise too, no? Si!"

I made no reply. She went, and Antoine sat in la Foque's chair and covered his eyes to be sad. Almost the tear came, maybe one or two. How long he sat with the lump in his throat, who knows? It began to get dark. His world was tumbled down. He saw no lighthouse.

He did not hear the door open and someone steal in, quiet like the mouse. A little hand touched his shoulder. He uncovered the eye, and heaven opened his mind. In one quick minute he knew what he must have known before but did not know he knew.

"Elaine!" he said. "Little darling!"

He rose like the gentleman and opened his arms. She slipped in and fit like the hand in the glove. He stood and enjoyed this a little. All was beautiful again like the rain bow. "See!" Antoine said as soon as he could think to "See what Antoine brought Elaine from Boston." He showed her the ring Louis had sold him. "Antoine asks if he may give it to Elaine?" She smiled shyly and held out the little hand. The ring fit perfectly. Bells went jingle-jangle in Antoine's head like St. Mark's. The sadness he thought he had vanished like a bear down Swampscott's gullet.

You understand now, Emile. In choosing the wife, what matters is knowing what to look for — and looking. Forevermore Antoine could laugh at Swampscott of the great belly. For the woman he got could never prepare one small potato so it was fit to eat. Elaine, the shy little wood-cock, was the la Foque who could cook!   END

The·Immortal Wilfrid

Much has been said and written by critics about the evils of our computerized civilization. Here, in one man's report, there is evidence that computers are sometimes not without their redeeming social values.

I had been with Westward Ho Conestoga Wagon Co., East Epithet, R. I., for twenty-seven years when it was taken over by Consolidated Motors, Sporting Goods & Ice Cream Co., an up-and-coming conglomerate. Shortly afterwards I was laid off, and while I had no cause for complaint since I was one of the more junior executives of Westward Ho, it was still a heavy blow. You see, when I took the job my wife warned me that Conestogas had had their day and that there was no future for me with the company. I dreaded hearing her contralto "I *told* you so!"

So I postponed telling her. Instead, I reported for work as usual the following day. Much to my surprise, a card with my name and number was in its usual place in the rack beside the time clock. When no one was looking, I punched in, half expecting to be collared as I did so. I quickly decided that if I was caught I would say I was suffering from amnesia. That might also serve as an excuse for not informing my wife too, I concluded.

Several of my old colleagues looked at me with mild surprise when they saw me, but as they were all chaps who had been with Westward Ho fifty or sixty years and considered me something of a Johnny-Come-Lately

by Edward Stevenson

R. Smeach

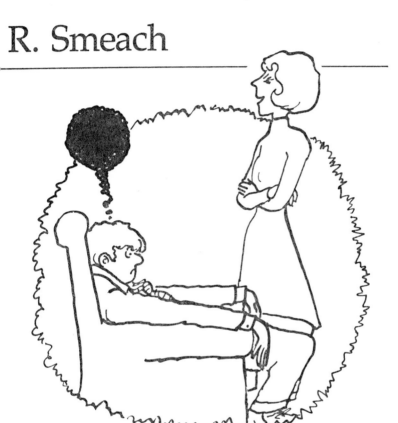

I dreaded hearing that contralto "I told you so!"

upstart, they didn't stoop to question me. And of course the newcomers from Consolidated, who swarmed all over the place like locusts in a cornfield, didn't know me from Adam, as the saying goes.

There was one initial difficulty. My old desk, which had

been built in the early part of the 19th century, had been carted away and burned as a potential death trap. That left me without a base of operations, so for several days I divided my time between the men's room, the company cafeteria, and that area around the water cooler where a little group of parched employees was always gathered.

Like all companies, Westward Ho had its share of absenteeism, so when I could endure being on my feet eight hours a day no longer, wandering about like some landlocked Flying Dutchman, I began looking around for unoccupied desks. These I took over in the absence of their rightful occupants, and was able to enjoy my idleness in relative comfort without coming home each night with a low back pain — a disability which I passed off to my wife as a sign of approaching middle age. My sudden, almost miraculous recovery was a little more difficult to explain. I said I guessed I was a quick healer.

Occupying other people's desks was not without its perils and moments of drama. Sometimes the regular occupants were simply late for work, and when they showed up and found me in residence, so to speak, they regarded me with suspicion and hostility as I hastily evacuated, mumbling explanations so unintelligible that no one dared to question them.

And one time, a high-strung late arrival, seeing me in his place and assuming he was the victim of another of Consolidated's instant purges, became so emotionally upset at not having at least received notice and severance pay that he created quite an uproar in the office. I sneaked away in the ensuing confusion and joined some of the water cooler regulars, of whom I innocently inquired, "What ails *him?*"

But the acid test of my audacious escapade — and I must say that at times I felt like Robert Redford (for whom I

... he created quite an uproar in the office.

have sometimes been mistaken) in one of those spy thrillers — came on the first payday after my return. What if there was no check for me? Then the whole game would be over and I would have to go home empty-handed and confess to Theodora — that's my wife — that her gloomy premonitions about Westward Ho had been correct.

I acted daringly. As soon as I saw Gloria-Jean the payroll clerk come into my department — or *former* department, if you want to be a stickler about it — and start passing out checks, I approached her and said, bold as brass, "Hi, G-J! I probably won't be at my desk when you get there, so would you please give me my check now?"

Gloria-Jean looked at me in surprise. "Geeze, Mr. Smeach," she said, "I thought you got canned!"

I winced at hearing my predicament so rudely expressed. "Whatever made you think *that?*" I asked, as if butter wouldn't melt in my mouth.

"Damn it all, Smeach, I swear I chipped in half a buck to get you a farewell present!"

"I saw a 'Terminate' notice on you go to Data Processing."

"Must have been my brother, G-J."

"I didn't know you had a brother, Mr. Smeach."

"Howard. Used to be in Conestoga convertibles." I was inwardly shriveling as I watched G-J flip through the fistful of envelopes. What would I do if there wasn't one there for me? "Actually, he's only my *half* brother and spells *his* name *S-m-double e-c-h,* the way they do in the Southern branch of the family."

"Guess you're right," Gloria-Jean muttered with a puzzled frown, "because here's *your* check, all right," she added, handing it to me with a mine-not-to-reason-why shrug.

I hastened to the men's room and tore open the envelope with trembling fingers. There was my old familiar check! *Smeach, Wilfrid R. SS No. 045-20-8051* — all the familiar old landmarks were there. The computer had apparently misfired, and I was still gainfully employed!

I checked out the numbers. Everything was the same as usual except for one item. For some reason, there was a two-dollar deduction for charitable contributions instead of the one dollar I had pledged, but I decided not to make an issue of it. When Theodora questioned it — she had the instincts of a CPA — I explained, "I decided to increase it. After all, my dear, we have much to be grateful for!"

All of the foregoing took place months ago, and I'm still on the Westward Ho Division — as our branch of Consolidated is now known — payroll. There are occasional bad moments, such as the one the other day at lunch when one of my senior colleagues suddenly exclaimed, "Damn it all, Smeach, I swear I chipped in half a buck to get you a farewell present!" But minor incidents such as that aside, things go rather smoothly.

Some weeks ago, I received my annual raise. It was not a great deal, to be sure, but it did prompt Theodora to concede, "You know, Will, I guess maybe I did Conestoga an injustice."

But my proudest moment came last week when I was named Westward Ho Division Worker of the Month and awarded a $25 U.S. Savings Bond!

END

The Man Who Beat the

ITS not that Great-grandfather really wanted to delay
progress in New England — nor can you blame the
New England Telephone Co. — heaven knows they tried.
They sent a new man out every six months to explain the
problem, but Great-grandfather would not be convinced.

When the New England Telephone Co. was founded, it
solicited some of the better known businessmen to try the
new device in their homes. Great-grandfather, the head of
Boston's most prominent import-export firm, lived way
out in Wakefield Junction where there was not yet a single
installation. It would surely be a feather in the cap of any
telephone company to extend its service into such a rural
area of Massachusetts.

Soon there appeared on Great-grandfather's immense
front porch a sprightly young man. Fresh out of school
and anxious to close the first telephone account in
Wakefield Junction, the young man asked to see Mr. Ruggles, and was admitted to the impressive frame structure.
From a ladder-back chair with a horsehair-stuffed seat he
extolled the virtues of the telephone:

"And, Mr. Ruggles, you already have a telephone at
your business, so you could call home from work."

"What in the world for?" asked Great-grandfather.

"Well," the young man coughed, "perhaps you'd prefer
to call your friends — and avoid having to go visit them
only to find them not at home." He smiled. He was proud
of this point.

by Jeremy W. Gorman

Telephone Company

"My friends don't have telephones," observed Great-grandfather.

"Well, Mr. Ruggles, think of the times your children are ill — you could summon the doctor."

"If," Great-grandfather reminded him, "he had a telephone."

"Oh, but Mr. Ruggles, Dr. Dutton in Wakefield is considering a telephone right now." His eye fell on the grand piano. "The Miller Piano Factory in Wakefield is already installing a telephone. You can call the Smith and Anthony Foundry. The telephone is the coming thing. Everyone will have one. Bonney's Drug Store is considering a telephone. Mr. Hathaway wants one in his stables. Why, you'll even be able to order groceries by telephone!"

"Order groceries?" glowered Great-grandfather.

"Oh, well, not you, sir! I mean your wife, sir."

"My wife? Order groceries?"

The young man looked furtively around the huge immaculate house. "Well, ah, the cook, sir?" The horsehair seat suddenly seemed extremely prickly. He stood up. "In fact, Mr. Ruggles, I believe that you will not only have the first private telephone in Wakefield Junction, but one of the first outside of Boston proper. Mr. David Darling has a private telephone in Wakefield, and several other people are interested."

Now Great-grandfather was fascinated by new things — particularly mechanical ones. He had already made up his

233

mind to have a private telephone. He wanted to assure himself of all the ramifications.

"How do I know you'll keep up the service? What if it breaks?"

"Oh, we'll supply a contract guaranteeing service and repairs."

"What kind of a contract? Suppose your company goes broke, or is bought by another? What about costs?"

"Our contract will cover every detail. It will be binding in case of merger or acquisition."

Great-grandfather thought about this awhile. "How much did you say it costs?"

And so in 1883 there was installed on a wall in Great-grandfather's house a wooden box. It had a crank on one side, two bells on the top, a slot for coins, a metal horn to speak into, and a hook holding an earpiece where you heard the voice of your distant conversationalist. The process was simple. You picked up the "receiver" from the hook, turned the crank which rang the bells, and waited. Soon a voice on the other end of the wire said "Operator." You announced whom you wanted to call, and the operator did the rest. When he connected you to your party, you put your money in the slot and talked to the person you called. When finished, you put the receiver back on the hook to turn off the instrument.

Since the telephone message was carried by wire, this box was accompanied by a long row of poles that marched away over the horizon, bearing a single wire. In addition, after three rejections and several harsh words, there finally arrived a contract satisfactory to Great-grandfather, and bearing a very official-looking seal. Thus began Wakefield Junction's private telephone service.

The young man was right. Telephones sprang up everywhere. Soon the doctor was summoned, the groceries were ordered, and friends were contacted on Great-grand-father's telephone. Soon, also, those poles were supporting dozens of wires leading to various surrounding houses.

But the New England Telephone Co. was busy in other ways too. They were building a network of telephone lines and tying them into other telephone companies all over the country. Within four years Great-grandfather could talk directly to New York, and in another twelve years directly to San Francisco. By the time overseas service was available, Great-grandfather was extremely pleased with his investment.

Great-grandfather, however, was as busy as New England Telephone. He involved himself in many hobbies as he approached retirement. Paramount among these was the study of heraldry. He traced family ancestry, drew family trees, and located relatives and coats of arms. In fact he became an international expert in genealogy, and provided his expertise broadly. It was in this endeavor that the wooden box on the wall found its most cherished service. The convenience of calling foreign countries to find out immediately the source of someone's ancestry was positively invaluable. As his interest and reputation developed, his international telephone calls increased.

Assuredly it was these latter calls that initiated an increasing procession of bright young men dispatched by New England Telephone to visit the whitehaired octogenarian. Each in his turn tramped up Charles Street beside that row of poles which began supporting ever fewer wires until at long last they again supported but a single one. Other poles nearby were laden with cables.

"Mr. Ruggles."

"Yes."

"I'm from New England Telephone. I'd like to tell you about some of the wonderful new inventions we have made to help improve your telephone service."

"My service is fine the way it is."

"But Mr. Ruggles, our modern phone is light and portable. It has a long wire so it can be moved about. You can have it installed at your desk."

"Really?" observed the old man.

"You don't have to ring for the operator. You get her automatically without waiting. And to speed the service, we have a book of local telephone numbers and space for special numbers outside your local area."

"I don't need them. The operator has those."

"But Mr. Ruggles, the new system is much more convenient. You don't have to turn any crank to get . . . ."

"Can your numbers find my friends when they're not at home?" interrupted Mr. Ruggles.

"No, sir, but . . . ."

"Well, the operator usually can."

"But Mr. Ruggles, you have the only private operator left in the Greater Boston area!"

Great-grandfather looked at him in silence.

"And another convenience with the new system is that you don't have to keep all that change handy. We automatically keep a record of your calls for you, and send a bill at the end of the month the way we've been doing for all our other customers. They really enjoy that feature."

"Why bother? Cash is fine!"

And so on and on it went, year after year from about 1920 until 1934 when Great-grandfather died at the age of ninety-four, thus terminating a 51-year old contract which kept a wooden wall phone in Wakefield Junction, on which he could call anywhere in the world and talk as long as he wanted for one nickel!　　　　　　　　END by Everett S. Allen

Capt. Ulysses and the Sea Serpent

THERE exist two interesting accounts of the Great Serpent. One is to be found in Pontippidan's *History of Norway*, published in 1747. This is a record of the statements concerning the Serpent by a Captain de Ferry, who describes the head as being on the order of two to three feet wide.

The next account of the Great Serpent is found in an extract of a letter from Cheefer Felch of the United States Navy *Schooner Science* dated Gloucester, Massachusetts, August 26, 1819. Here again the description conforms more or less to the sketch of the Serpent made at the time by James Prince, Esq. The head is described here as of about three feet circumference.

The present writer, a reporter on the New Bedford, Massachusetts, *Standard Times*, has recently been favored with a third description of the Great Sea Serpent. This was given him recently by eye-witness Captain Ulysses Pettibone, now retired. It arises in his experience during a voyage with the bark *Hempstead Grange*, from Newcastle to Durban, on April 13, 1890.

"It was a bit after midnight, and I had the watch. No clouds in the sky, the moon as big as a bucket, and too hot to sleep in the foc's'le; most of the crew was curled up on deck, for'ard.

"I was aft, leanin' and spittin', and occasionally hummin' pieces from a tasteful tune I heard dished up one time by a blond from Battersea.

"Well sir, suddenly, there was a terrible odor, like the sea breakin' from the bottom — brings up all the mud, you know? Gear started slattin' aloft and we began to wallow, harder and faster and them below came pilin' up in a hurry. Because there wasn't a breath of wind ... not a breath. But we rolled 'til I thought she'd twist herself inside out as well as heavin' everybody overboard.

"Then there was a great splashin' and a kind of suckin' noise that only happens when somethin' big comes to the top o' water. We all crowded along the starboard rail, not a word out of any manjack among 'em; we squinted out over the black water, watching for whatever it was ...

"It was longer than the ship, near as we could make out, and shaped kinda like a big worm with wrinkles. As it come closer, we could see it had two horns and a head somethin' like a kid's rockin' horse. And it had spots with white circles along its sides — like a waterline, as it were, and it had sharp-white stripes all along, like chevrons on a drum major.

"Nobody made a move. Nobody talked. We could see it was makin' for us, slowly finnin' up alongside. Even the Old Man had his jaw on his chest and you could have knocked his eyeballs off with a boat hook and he wasn't one to get stirred up for nothin', either. I figured it was the end, and I just wished I hadn't been in such a hurry to pay back the tobacco I borrowed off the bos'un.

"This thing raised up its ugly head, all scaly and shining like silver light in the dark, it was, and eyes like bulls-eye lanterns. And its head came clear to the maintop, and glowered down at us, weavin' like a drunk snake. And then it groaned and it sounded like "Boom-Tackle" Jernegan with the colic the night he drank his way out of a hogshead of calvados in Carentan ... only worse. All hands shrieked and swore and wished they'd been better to their mothers and they hit the deck face down, bellerin' for mercy. Me, among 'em, I might say.

"Then came this voice, like somethin' out of a history book sung through a sewer pipe ...

" 'What shippe is thatte? Speake uppe you dogges, or I'll spitte you like anne haddocke and boyle you in oyle!'

"Bein' what you might call the only readin' man aboard, I knew he was talkin' a brand of old-style English, probably because he was about seven years older than Moses. Rattled though I was, I figured somebody better answer his hail in a hurry or he'd probably have us all for dinner, and he'd do all the eatin'.

"So I jumped up, and sung out, 'Sirre, we are the barke *Hempstead Grange*, for Durban, may't please you.' It came hard, saying 'sirre' to a blasted, goggle-eyed swimmin' snake, but still it wasn't too difficult being polite to anything that big and that close.

"Then he groaned again, somethin' fearful, and purple fire came out of his nostrils. It singed one whole side of the galley cat and sent her to the masthead with a bushed-up tail for a week; she just sat up there and snarled and wouldn't even come down to eat. It peeled all the paint off the top of the after house, makin' a horrible smell. There was a pair of the Old Man's pants hangin' on a clothesline aft, and it burned 'em off short right up to the galluses they were hangin' from. I've seen Vesuvius and St. Elmo's fire, and I tell you they wan't one, two, three to this.

"He finned right up alongside and laid his big ugly, bony chin right on the rail, just forward of the main shrouds. Just the weight of it put the ship down at least two feet, I reckoned, and you could hear her standin' rig-gin' strain, and everythin' was still so quiet you could hear some crockery in the galley go by the board with smashin' sounds like pay night in a Hong Kong saloon.

"An' he smiled at me, like a blood brother! Smiled, mind you! He curled back his lips and opened up his mouth and it was more or less like stickin' your head in the firebox of a Channel packet buttin' home in a blow. The whole insides was lit up and hot and filled with teeth like stockade posts, and about as big. I dunno now why I didn't turn to stone, right there.

"He leered at me with one bloodshot eye as big as an Englishman's tea saucer. I thought to myself, 'Well, Ulyss, one more blast of that purple fire, and you'll go to your Maker well done on both sides.'

"The beast evidently noticed I was sufferin' from the heat of its breathin' and turned its head somewhat.

"'May't please you, sirre,' he purred to me, 'an I would do you no harme, nor your shippe. Prithee, list then to my tayle (he looked at his tail and smirked horribly, thinkin' to make a joke) and I will tell thee what has come to pass!'

"With this kind of talk, more friendly-soundin', all hands got up off their faces and gathered 'round for a horrified look at what God had wrought, as it were.

"'This harshe talke which I employed at the beginninge was just a bluffe,' the creature sighed. 'While still a youthe, I fell in, alas, with gaye, but eville companions. In soothe, you may have heard of themme — Billy Bones and Captaine Kydde?'

"'I don't think it's spelled "themme,"' I said rather sourlike. I was gettin' somewhat fed up with his airs, which were more than somewhat for an overgrown water bug, especially if he wan't goin' to chew our heads off. 'Any place I ever read it, it was just "them".'

"He looked at me for about as long as it takes an idea to

240

get through the rockbound skulls of one of them things, and then he just sort of licked out the littlest belch of purple fire that nonetheless took all the hair off the back of my right hand and melted down the gold watch fob shaped like an eagle that Father gave me when I was twenty-one. I subsided.

" 'I swam with themme,' he resumed pointedly, 'for some yeares, and although I understoode notte their kinde of trayde, I didde acquire some uncouthe talks.

" 'Your pardonne, thenne. And to more urgente thynges. You maye have hearde me groane, alack!'

"I was going to suggest that anybody this side of Capricorn that hadn't heard him 'groane' had better be buried right off, but I didn't.

" 'Odds bodkins, but I have an achynge toothe; prithee, gette thy carpenterre to haule itte oute for me, and I shalle be your fryende for lyfe, as sure as my nayme is Cholmondely.'

"An' a lifetime for you, my over-aged grub, is a darned long spell, I thought to myself.

"Well sir, one and another, we took a fresh chunk of cut plug, kind of pulled our innards together, once we got used to the situation, and went at it, for he showed no signs of leavin' and we certainly couldn't leave him without a breeze stirrin', so there was nothin' else for it but to have a go at the job.

"We rigged some heavin'-down falls, the biggest we had aboard, and we got a timber hitch around the bottom of the tooth that hurt. There was four men in the beast's mouth, trumpin' on his rubbery tongue and sinkin' up to their knees like walkin' through swamp grass. Considerin' everythin', they went in there quite willin' after the Old Man batted them once or twice with a bung-starter. But the carpenter, name o' Mudge, refused to go in without his shoes even though the serpent said they tickled. Mudge said barefooted, he'd just as like to slide right on down the thing's gullet, and 'Who's comin' down after me in that case I'd like to know?' he yelled. I wan't, that's for sure.

"Well, Mudge was in there, rushin' around with a half-barrel of augers and pry-bars, and swearin' like the mate of a Yemen dhow. He propped the critter's jaws apart with an extra spanker bcom so nobody would get et by mistake, and he hung a pair of lanterns from the spar so they could see to work. It was eerie, I tell you, and all this sloppin' and slushin' and cursin' goin' on in there. Every once in a while, somebody in there'd jab at his sore tooth and sort of heave 'round on it, and the most unearthly groan would set us all back to loo'ard, and the creature would thresh the sea for half a mile into the most awful foam.

"Anyway, finally they got things ready in there, and Mudge came out, makin' a great show of countin' the other three men to make sure everybody was there. Miserable man, Mudge. Unreasonable. They brought all the gear out, pulled the prop out from between the thing's jaws, and I sung out to him: 'Keepe thy mouthe open!' He grunted, and blew water out of one nostril. I wondered afterward how you could blow fire and water out of the same nose. Peculiar.

"All hands got on that tayckle, and a bowlegged Belgian — whose wife ran off with a Sunday School teacher, and whose name escapes me — struck up 'Five-Aces Gray, the Pride of Tiger Bay' and we swung to it with a will. 'Pull and bust!' yelled the bos'un and we pulled, with an eye on them tayckle blocks, comin' closer and closer. Somethin' had to give.

"About the time I had the wild idea that maybe we could capsize the ship, all tarnation broke loose. First, the tayckle went slack, and spilled men, blocks and line into the scup-

242

pers in a mess of gear and profanity. I figured it must have parted, but I looked up, just in time to see the tooth ...

"I'd say it was ten feet long if it was an inch. It was pearly-white and glistened in the dark, especially the part where it came out of the gum. It was twisted, like a unicorn's horn, you know what I mean? I remember thinkin', Ulyss, your share of that fine curio will bring a pretty penny ... and I meant to have a share, too, because after all, there wan't anybody else aboard could even talk to the critter, and if it hadn't been for me ...

"Wasn't to be, however. 'Fore I could get to my feet, that tooth slipped out of the hitch and overboard. Musta weighed five hundred pound; made a terrible splash.

"The Serpent had tears as big as fryin' pans down both cheeks; anyway, I guess you could call 'em cheeks, he was so pleased to be rid of it. 'I amme youre obdt. servnt.,' he said, tryin' to bow with his chin still on the rail. 'I shalle not forgette what has passed this daye, norre the debt of honour thatte I owe.' With that, he oozed out of sight in a mess of bubbles that covered half an acre, and last I saw, he still was trying to conjure up that awful smile ... worse than before, because of the hole where the tooth had been.

"Some days later, the beast appeared again, to warn us, he said of a Great Blow. Good thing he did — the *Hempstead Grange* was the only ship to survive that blow — six other ships all larger than we were, taken by surprise, went down in it. Odd way to pay a dentist's bill but I guess a sea serpent doesn't have much choice." END

Highway Robbery

by Priscilla Harris

THIS very minute as I look out my kitchen window which faces south, I can see five men and two large trucks out in the field. The trucks are making deep tracks in the sodden earth, and the five men are engaged in taking down a very large snow fence which they put there last fall. They have done this for the past two years since I've been living back in my family homestead, and how many years before that I don't know. Perhaps at some time they asked someone's permission, but they have never asked mine, and I feel a bit resentful about the whole procedure. I'm sure if I were to complain I would be told that the snow fence must be there "for the general good," just as the conservation people say when they devise means of taking land or pass by-laws to make it valueless, or the state claims, when it takes land by eminent domain to build a road "for the general good." There *was* a time when people didn't take this sort of thing sitting down. At least my father didn't.

Back in the '30s, when I was a child, one fine spring day a group of men appeared on our farm. They busily arranged tripods and spread themselves over a large area of the field. My father fairly flew out of the house and ordered them off his property. They practically ignored him, and went about their business. He came back in the house, crestfallen.

"They're from the State, and they're going to build a road." A few days later a large envelope arrived in the mail.

"They're offering me $1400 for eight acres of my land! That is highway robbery. I'm going to fight it."

He made several trips to the State House in Boston and gave us a blow-by-blow description of what went on in there.

"I'm dealing with a bunch of fools and dummies, not only in Boston but out here too. They told me that I was the only one who has complained, and that if they gave me more money for my land, they'd have to give more to everyone."

One day he came back from Boston unusually sad and weary. "I've made a settlement. They won't pay me a cent more, but I got them to agree to move the road 100 yards nearer to the woods and not to split my henhouse in half. I told them it would be a hardship to have my farm split in half, so they're going to build me a cow-pass."

"A what?" we all chorused.

"They're going to build a tunnel under the road."

"Did you tell them you have only one cow?"

"They didn't ask me how many cows I had."

"But it's going to cost a lot of money to build a tunnel, just for one cow. It doesn't make any sense. Why won't they pay you the money it's going to cost for the cowpass? Would you settle for that?" my mother asked.

"Of course I would, but they won't do that."

For weeks bulldozers and all sorts of heavy machinery made hideous noises and raised clouds of dust. Every morning my father woke up fuming. When the men came to the kitchen door and asked for water, he wouldn't speak to them. My mother gave them water, and sometimes homemade root beer. My father often mumbled, "It's getting more like Russia all the time, when the State can come and take away a man's land."

They finally got a rough layer of stone laid, and left the rollers on "our property." My brother and I found where they hid the keys, and I drove a roller and he a grader back and forth one Sunday afternoon when my mother and father were having their afternoon nap.

Then one day some different-looking equipment came lumbering along the road, stopped, rolled off the hard surface down a steep grade and started digging. We ran into the house to tell my father, and for the first time in weeks he brightened a bit and showed some interest in what "they" were doing. "They're starting to build the cowpass," he said.

"Are they going to build it there?"

"They've had engineers testing the soil for several days now, and that's where they've decided to put it," my father said.

I couldn't understand any of it. The preceding summer we had had a drought, and our barn well was getting dangerously low. A minister friend of my father's was visiting us, and he said he was sure he could find a spring on the farm. I followed him around while he looked for a willow tree; I watched as he cut off a branch with a fork in it and hurried to a low pasture. Holding the forked end, he walked around for awhile, and I stood spellbound as the end of the branch bent slowly toward the earth.

"*There* is the spot to dig your well," he said. I remember what a thrill it was when he let me hold the branch and I actually felt the pull of the earth. Sheer magic. My father and brothers started digging immediately. In a very short time the earth became soggy muck, then water gradually began to seep into the hole. All that summer there was plenty of water in the new well, long after the barn well went dry. When we didn't need the well any longer, my father filled it with rocks so no person or animal could fall into it.

What I couldn't understand was: why was my father standing idly by, watching the men from the State dig a tunnel *there*, so close to the very spot where just the year before the willow branch had found us a spring? When I tried to question my father, he said, "They're supposed to know what they're doing. They chose the spot. I didn't."

All the kids in the neighborhood and some of the men gathered to watch. I felt very important. The huge shovel lifted an amazing amount of earth the first day. Men rushed around building forms to hold up the road. A cement mixer joined the other heavy equipment. Such noise and activity!

They quit work around noon on Saturday, and that afternoon it started to rain. It rained all night, and most of Sunday. On Monday morning when the men came back to work, there was about a foot of water in the tunnel.

"You must have had a cloudburst down here," one of

the men said to my father. I'm sure my father knew that most of that water didn't come from the sky. "Well, we'll just have to get a pump," the man said. Then I heard him exclaim, "Good God, what the hell's happened here!" We went to the other side of the road where the big digger was, and one side of it was about a foot down in the mud. Soon another big piece of machinery came lumbering along the road. It was a huge crane. It groaned and shuddered as it tried to lift the hind end of the digger out of the mud. All day long the men ran around shouting orders to one another, and the crane tried time and again to move the digger. The men were up to their knees in muck. All the time the pump was gushing water to the drier side of the road.

At the end of the day the tunnel was almost free of water, and the crane looked exhausted. The next morning another crane arrived, and the two of them managed to get

the digger out of the mud. A cheer went up from the crowd. Then someone shouted, "Look! The tunnel's full of water again." They started the pump, and it gushed away all day long. When the men came back the next morning, they shook their heads when they saw the tunnel with at least a foot of water in it. They started the pump again — and this time they kept it going all night. As I lay in bed I could hear its steady chugging, like a heartbeat.

The next morning when the men came to work, the boss said, "Now that's more like it. Now we can finish the cementing." The tunnel was dry. They worked really hard all day. The cement mixer whirled around, trucks came and went, children dashed up and down the banking. At the end of the day the boss said, "Tell your father his cowpass is finished. We'll be back in the morning to get the equipment."

Early the next morning the men arrived. From the house

we could see them standing in a sort of semi-circle, looking down into the tunnel, like people looking into a new grave. We ran, and got there before my father. The engineer looked up and said to my father, "Goddammit, Mr. Swanson, you'll just have to teach your cows to swim." They didn't start the pump or anything; just started up the engines and left.

No cow ever used the cow-pass. The only animal that did, that I know of, was our Newfoundland dog. He loved to swim, and we children would watch him start on one side of the road and come out dripping wet on the other. The following year, the water became sort of scummy, and frogs took over the tunnel.

Last summer as my brother-in-law was heading towards Boston along Route 53, he saw several men and a cement mixer stationed near the old cow-pass. He stopped and asked them what they were doing there, and they answered, "We're going to fix up this old cow-pass. It's one of the few left in New England, and they say it has historical value." How many more hours they spent on it I have no idea. I do know that if they had paid my father somewhere near what he wanted for his land, the State would have saved itself a lot of money.   END by Wendell White Secrest

In Search of
Rare Species

PROFESSOR Roger Digby — B.S., M.S., Ph.D., Sc.D., noted author, lecturer, scholar, and butterfly collector — emerged from behind a bayberry bush and gazed out across the meadow toward the trees along the fringe of the woodland. The look in his eyes was that of a man who had just witnessed something extraordinary.

"I have just witnessed something quite extraordinary," said Professor Digby, pointing toward the treetops.

"A purple-spotted woolly-winged harvester," said Mrs. Abigail Moonstone.

"A gold-banded brushy-backed olympian," said her husband, Mr. Theobald Moonstone.

"A spiny silver-crested metal-marked aphrodite," said Colonel Percy Caruthers, USAF, Ret.

"A grizzled velvet-winged variegated swallowtail," said Mrs. Edwina Sedgewick.

"A flying saucer," said Professor Roger Digby.

The members of the South Tewksbury Chapter of the Digby Lepidoptera Society leaned forward and gasped in astonishment, struggling to maintain their balance beneath the weight of their kit bags, lunch pails, map cases, and butterfly nets.

Mrs. Sedgewick adjusted her gilt-rimmed pince-nez and began thumbing through the index of Professor Digby's definitive work on the subject of butterflies, *The Digby Guide to Rare and Familiar Lepidoptera.*

"Oh, dear," she said, lowering her pince-nez to her ample bosom. "I'm afraid I can't locate that particular variety in the index of common names. Perhaps, Professor Digby, you would be kind enough to supply the genus and species ..."

Professor Digby remained silent for a few moments, his gaze still transfixed upon the trees in the woodland, beyond which the strange flying object had descended from view.

"Felix qui potest rerum cognoscere causas," he said.

Mrs. Sedgewick closed her eyes and opened them again. "What?" she asked.

Presently Professor Digby turned, his eyes narrowing upon Mrs. Sedgewick, who blinked back at him, the folds and crevices in her face knotting into an expression of befuddlement.

"Madam," he said, "I trust you will forgive the omission, but the identity of the aerial phenomenon to which I refer will not be found in *The Digby Guide to Rare and Familiar Lepidoptera.*"

"Perhaps if we look in the revised edition," she said.

"I think we will have better luck if we look beyond those trees — in the upper end of the meadow," he replied. He pointed toward the promontory of dense woodland, which concealed the upper half of the crescent-shaped meadow.

"See here, Digby," said Mr. Moonstone, a frown pulling at the corners of his mouth. "If one of those infernal contraptions has put down on my property ..."

"A UFO," corrected Colonel Caruthers. He struck a

match and lowered the flame to the bowl of his pipe.

"Precisely," said Professor Digby. "A UFO, piloted by aliens, I suspect."

"Good heavens," sputtered Mrs. Sedgewick. "Aliens!" She fluttered her eyelids spasmodically and spread her chubby fingers at the base of her throat. She looked as though she might faint.

Mrs. Moonstone turned to the unsteady Mrs. Sedgewick and began fanning her solicitously with a silk handkerchief.

"The nerve of the scoundrels," she snorted. "Trespassing on private property like a band of common vagabonds!"

Mr. Moonstone looked at his wife, his salt-and-pepper brows arching above his spectacles and disappearing beneath the visor of his pith helmet.

"Every acre of my property is posted," he said with mounting indignation. Then he shook his gnarled fist in the direction of the woodland. "I'll notify the sheriff!"

"Sounds like a military matter to me," said Colonel Caruthers, puffing leisurely at his pipe.

"I'll prosecute!" said Mr. Moonstone.

"*Facta, non verba,*" said Professor Digby.

Mr. Moonstone blinked. "Come again, Digby?" he asked.

Professor Digby stroked his white moustache thoughtfully for a few moments. Finally his lips moved: "Rather odd, these UFOs. We must investigate straightaway." He paused briefly and then continued, his voice rising spiritedly, "For science!"

"For material evidence!" bellowed Mr. Moonstone.

"I don't feel well," said Mrs. Sedgewick.

Professor Digby shifted the bulk of his field equipment until it hung as comfortably as possible about his portly body; then, raising his butterfly net and thrusting it forward like a guidon to point the direction of march, he tramped off into the kaleidoscope of wildflowers that painted the meadow. The members of his entourage blinked quizzically at each other and then hurried after him, striding loosely militarily.

On the other side of the meadow, near the terminus of the promontory of woodland, Professor Digby caught a glimpse of something that sent a quiver of excitement leaping along his spine. He halted abruptly and turned back to the others.

"Sh-sh!" he whispered, pressing a forefinger against the tip of his nose. Then he pointed to a spot several yards away where, balanced upon the blue petals of a periwinkle, sat a frosted crimson-crested dagger-winged elphin, an extremely rare species, normally sighted only in the south of France. In Italy, perhaps once in a decade, but in New England or anywhere else in North America — never! Scarcely able to believe his eyes, he decided to capture it before it flew away.

He drew a long deep breath and crept forward until he was within range; then he swung his net and, with a single expert pass, picked off the unwary butterfly in a shower of periwinkle petals. Slowly, carefully, lest the rare prize escape, he transferred it from the muslin netting into a specimen jar and screwed down the cap.

Trapped, the butterfly fluttered violently among the long, slender strips of paper which, moistened with ethyl acetate, curled like deadly spider fingers along the glass walls of the jar. Presently, however, it grew weaker and sat quietly, its wings rising and falling in a slow, measured, dreamy cadence.

Professor Digby held the jar to the blueness of the sky, turned it slowly in his fingers, and peered at the tiny creature within, noting the dark, intricate striations, the bright swirls of white and crimson embossed upon the delicate translucent fabric of its wings.

"Most irregular," he whispered. "I've never seen a member of this species in these parts." As he pondered the contents of the jar, it occurred to him that he might not be seeing what he thought he was seeing, that he might be having a delusion.

"But that's impossible," he said aloud. "How can I be having a delusion? The little beggar is right here in front of my eyes, hermetically sealed inside the specimen jar."

He blinked several times in rapid succession and squinted into the jar. Identity confirmed.

"Ergo, one frosted crimson-crested dagger-winged elphin," he said. He tilted the jar and the butterfly tumbled over in lifeless polychromatic splendor.

Flourishing the jar above his head in a gesture of triumph, he shuffled back toward the others, who stood knee-deep in wildflowers, outlined against the green leafy tangle of the woodland.

"Congratulations, Digby," said Mr. Moonstone, eyeing the specimen jar. "Good work!"

"It's beautiful," said Mrs. Moonstone. "What is it?"

Mrs. Sedgewick blinked through her pince-nez at the butterfly inside the jar. "I think it's dead," she said.

"I seem to have nabbed this little fellow while he was off on holiday — from the south of France!" said Professor Digby.

"Probably sucked over the Atlantic by that UFO," said Colonel Caruthers, more to himself than to anyone else in particular. He was gazing past the trees toward something in the upper end of the meadow.

"An excellent possibility," said Professor Digby, "depending, of course, on its direction of travel."

"Offhand," said the Colonel, "I would say it's traveling in *this* direction."

Everyone turned and gaped in awe at the huge oval object that was just emerging into full view from behind the promontory of woodland. It was following the contour of the meadow and moving directly toward them.

"Zounds," said Professor Digby. "It's the UFO!"

Mr. Moonstone's expression of awe darkened to ire. "It's ruining my meadow!" he cried. He pointed toward the broad swath of crumpled grass and wildflowers that delineated the object's path through the meadow.

"The aliens appear to have spotted us," said Professor Digby.

"Seem friendly enough," said Colonel Caruthers. "Perhaps they want to make contact."

"I'll demand full compensation for damages," said Mr. Moonstone indignantly.

The great ship loomed before them, its gleaming silver dome rotating slowly, spinning off bright ribbons of reflected sunlight. It proceeded to within several yards of where they stood and then stopped and sank down against the earth. It sat there — still, mute.

Professor Digby strolled casually over to the ship and rapped on the hull with the handle of his butterfly net.

"Professor Roger Digby here," he said. "On behalf of the Digby Lepidoptera Society and the United States of America, welcome to Earth." He swung his arm back in a broad gesture to indicate the others, who stood in a semicircle, staring at the ship.

There was no response from inside — only silence.

Colonel Caruthers poked the curved stem of his pipe between his teeth, then clasped his hands behind his back and began pacing back and forth, his eyes wandering over the ship appraisingly, as though he were looking at a used car. He kicked the base of the hull. The sound was an odd thud.

"That's odd," he said. "It looks like metal, but it sounds like — what *does* it sound like?"

"It appears to be a rather sophisticated alloy," said Professor Digby, running his fingers over the sleek surface of the hull. "Most remarkable, these aliens."

"Why don't they come out?" asked Mrs. Moonstone.

"Perhaps they don't speak English," said Mrs. Sedgewick.

"Nonsense," said Colonel Caruthers. "If they are civilized enough to build this extraordinary machine, they are certainly civilized enough to speak English."

Mr. Moonstone took a few steps forward and glared at the ship; then he cupped his hands to form a megaphone. "Are you there?" he shouted. "I demand that you come out and present yourselves at once!"

Something flashed in the sunlight atop the dome of the ship.

"Look," gasped Mrs. Moonstone, pointing toward the flash of sunlight.

"It's moving," said Colonel Caruthers.

"I'm scared," said Mrs. Sedgewick.

A silver shaft, crowned with a spheroid of the same brilliant hue, peeped periscope-like above the silver dome and spun slowly upward until it stood as straight and tall as the mast of a sailing ship.

Mr. Moonstone gaped at the gleaming silver spheroid. "On second thought," he said, lowering his eyes to address the ship, "I might be inclined to forget this entire matter if you fellows would just toddle off back where you came from."

The shaft pivoted on its base and dropped forward a few degrees, the spheroid turning, pointing, sensing. The mechanism moved like the proboscis of a giant insect.

"Amazing," said Professor Digby.

Suddenly the shaft dropped forward a full ninety degrees, the spheroid opened, and something silver and dark hurtled forth, uncoiling like a ribbon, unfurling like a sail, billowing outward like an enormous web.

Professor Digby gazed up at the thing that was rapidly filling the sky, his lips moving, struggling to form the words that would give it a shape and a name:

It's — *a net!*"

And it descended upon Professor Roger Digby and the members of the South Tewksbury Chapter of the Digby Lepidoptera Society. It swept them into its deep silver folds and closed upon them as smoothly as an eyelid closing upon an eye.

As the shaft quivered and drew back, the spheroid whirled with the furious precision of a reel, drawing the retrieval cable taut, hauling the bulging net aloft where, for a moment, it hung suspended like a huge bloated tetherball. Then the net opened and deposited its contents through an open hatch into a glittering crystal compartment deep within the dome of the ship.

The hatch cover slid closed, the retrieval mechanism descended back into the dome, and the great silver ship began to tremble in the eye of its own violent whirlwind. It rose, hovered briefly above its crater, then whirled away in a long catenary of flight above the patchwork pattern of rivers, fields, and forests. It soared like a streak of silver light above oceans, islands, continents, up, up toward the high, thin cirrus, toward the dark of space, toward the alien stars.   END by Lael J. Littke

Till the Cows Come Home

ALL the trouble started, Ivy Turner speculated later, because her husband Sylvester liked to name his cows after the men from whom he bought them. Hence in his sizable herd, along with the Muleys and Bossys and Rosies which he had raised himself, he had a Bill Higgins, a Walt Adams, an Asa Bell, and a Harvey Thompson. No one in town minded Sylvester's calling his cows by these names, least of all the men concerned. As a matter of fact, the men considered it kind of a mark of distinction, and they all had a good time about it when they gathered at the Owl Billiard Parlor in nearby Burnsville each Saturday night.

Things would have gone along peaceful and happy if Sylvester hadn't bought two cows from Thaddeus Cooley. Since he couldn't name two cows Thaddeus Cooley, he up and named the second cow after Thaddeus' wife, Viola. Right from the first Viola didn't take much to the idea, but she didn't say much of anything about it until Sylvester started noising it around that Viola Cooley was going to have a calf.

Ivy was out hoeing in her lettuce garden one morning when Clyde, the mailman, beckoned her over to where his car was stopped by her mailbox.

"Hear tell Viola Cooley's fit to be tied," Clyde told her.

"Oh?" Ivy said. "What's the matter with Viola?"

Clyde cleared his throat. "Don't especially like Sylvester's naming a cow after her. Says it ain't fittin'."

Ivy nodded. "Well, it isn't. I told Vest it would stir up a ruckus, but nothing would do but that he name that cow 'Viola.' I'll tell him he's got to change it. Though 'Viola' does seem to fit that cow so well. Her pretty eyes remind me of Viola Cooley's somehow. Well, I'll just tell Vest he's got to call her 'Beauty' or something."

Clyde sent Ivy's words along the line as he went on his rounds, only by the time it got back to Viola, after being filtered through Blanche Neiderhauser and Millie Higgins and Nell Olsen and Althea Thompson, the only thing that remotely resembled Ivy's original words was that Viola had eyes like a cow.

Now, even though the bovine Viola Cooley was a cow of uncommon attractiveness, being a russet-colored, small-boned Jersey with gentle manners and large, intelligent brown eyes, no woman takes to being likened to a cow. In any respect.

"Look like a cow, do I?" shrilled Viola to Millie Higgins, further altering Ivy's intent. "Well, I always did think Ivy Turner had it in for me. I'll just bet it was her that put Sylvester up to naming that cow after me. It was her, that's who it was. She hasn't been friendly at all since I got my new maroon overstuffed set. She's jealous, that's what she is. Jealous. Naming a cow after me and all."

Viola's speech was duly transmitted to Ivy, whose first thought it was to run over to Viola's and get the matter straightened out before any more rumors started turning the air blue. But the truth of the matter was that she *was* a little jealous of Viola's new maroon overstuffed set, especially since Viola, in a spirit of generosity with only just a tinge of pride, had offered Ivy her old brown set, thus implying that even her old castoffs were superior to what Ivy had. So after she thought about it, Ivy decided she wouldn't be caught dead going over to Viola Cooley's.

There were those ladies in town who were on Ivy's side. After all, Viola *had* been a little uppity since she got that new furniture, although it did seem a mite harsh to run around saying she looked like a cow. But if that's what it took to bring her down a notch or two, then it was all right.

Of course there were other ladies who lined up with Viola, claiming that Ivy Turner was not one to have a run-in with, since what she did was name all her farm animals after people she didn't like.

"Why," said Millie Higgins, "I heard somewhere that she even named one of their hogs after Reverend Ballew after he called her down for making raspberry jam on Sunday." Millie had heard no such thing, but it fit well into the conversation.

It wasn't long until Opal Smith, who was on Ivy's side, recalled that Eldora Meacham, a chum of Viola's, had once beaten her unfairly in a spelling bee in the fifth grade, and Marge Carter remembered that Blanche Neiderhauser's grandfather had once sold her grandfather a spavined horse, not to mention a cow who up and died two days after the purchase. It wasn't long until the ladies of the town were in full battle. The men stayed out of it, looking at it as a hen fight which didn't concern them except to provide a source of amusement for their weekly gatherings at the Owl Billiard Parlor.

Viola got so mad at Ivy that she took to walking backwards out to feed her chickens since if she walked normally she would be facing Ivy's house and might catch a glimpse of Ivy out hanging clothes or working in her garden. One day she tripped over a milk bucket Thaddeus had left on the path and broke her leg. Nothing would do but that she blame it on Ivy. After all, if Ivy hadn't up and called her a cow, she wouldn't have been walking backwards, and if she hadn't been walking backwards, she wouldn't have tripped over the milk bucket and broken her leg.

The county newspaper compounded the problem by printing a short article on page 5 stating that Viola Cooley, a cow owned by Sylvester Turner, had kicked over a milk pail and broken her leg. It further stated that the cow would probably have to shot. Such errors were to be expected in the weekly *Grouse Valley Tribune* since it was a well-known fact that Art Haskins, publisher, editor, reporter, and printer, kept a bottle hidden under the press which did not contain printer's ink.

Naturally Viola Cooley took it hard, being laid up with her broken leg and all.

"I can't abide a woman who would stoop so low," she wept to Millie Higgins, blaming the article on Ivy, too. "You can just pass it along that I'm sitting here with my busted leg just waiting for her to come and apologize."

"Apologize!" Ivy was indignant when Clyde told her the news. "In a pig's eye, I'll apologize. If I'd of done anything, I'd march these two feet right over there and apologize my head off. Viola should be the one to apologize. Thinking I'd do a thing like writing that article. No, sir, she'll sit there with her busted leg and wait till the cows come home before I'll go apologize."

And so the battle raged. The womenfolk hadn't had anything important to talk about since Soren Ernstad's wife Helga ran off with the Italian linoleum salesman, so they made the most of it.

No one knows how Viola ever got Thaddeus to take a hand in the fight, whether it was her everlasting dinging at him or whether his conscience smote him as he looked at her lying there with her leg all encased in plaster. It was unheard of for a man to interfere in a hen fight, but interfere he did. At least he went over to speak to Sylvester about it one evening.

"The wife's all het up about it," Thaddeus told Sylvester, hanging over the bars of the fence while Sylvester replaced a broken post. "You understand how it is, Mrs. Turner." He directed that remark back over his shoulder to where Ivy was working in her lettuce patch. Ivy made like she didn't even hear him.

"Vest," Thaddeus continued, "do you reckon as how you could call that cow by some other handle? Maybe Rosie or something?"

"I already got me a Rosie," said Sylvester.

"Well, Bossy then. It's not me that objects to it, Vest. Why, I kind of take a personal interest in that cow named Thaddeus Cooley. But womenfolks, they're different." He looked back over his shoulder. "You know how it is, Mrs. Turner."

Sylvester tamped the dirt around the new post and leaned on his shovel. "I'd sure like to oblige you, Thaddeus, but look at it this way. That poor little heifer is due to have her first calf just any day now. She's got used to being called 'Viola'." To emphasize what he said, he called softly to the pretty little cow who was placidly grazing on the other side of the fence. She raised her head to gaze at him, then ambled over to the fence where she allowed Sylvester to scratch behind her ears.

"Thaddeus, I never did rightly understand women," Sylvester said, "but I do understand cows. Now, if I was to switch names on Viola right now she'd go plumb off her feed and no telling what would happen to her when her time comes. I'd sure hate to upset her right now."

" 'Course not," said Thaddeus. "She's likely to be a good

milker, and it would be downright crazy to do anything to put her off her feed. I'll just tell Viola to forget about the whole thing."

Having done his duty, Thaddeus bade Sylvester goodbye, tipped his battered hat to Ivy, and strolled across the field toward his home.

Ivy had pretended not to hear any of the conversation, but after Thaddeus left she discovered that she had hoed off an entire row of young lettuce plants.

When Viola, the cow, finally produced her calf, as pretty a little creature as you ever laid eyes on, Art Haskins, still befuddled about the whole situation, put a short filler at the end of a column reporting that Viola Cooley had given birth to a calf and was doing fine in spite of her broken leg.

There was speculation as to whether Sylvester would name the calf 'Gladys' after the eldest Cooley daughter, but he said he'd never hang a handle like that on a defenseless calf. Everyone expected fireworks about that, but Viola, to the disappointment of all, had subsided into morose silence. Ivy was a bit disturbed about the silence, wondering if Viola had gone into a real decline, but Clyde reported seeing her hobbling around her yard tending her rose bushes. He said she didn't want to talk and he figured as how she had got to the point where she just didn't care what happened any more.

It wasn't long until Viola the cow began attracting attention in a new way. For such a small cow, she gave enormous quantities of milk which consistently tested remarkably high in butterfat content. The owner of the local creamery allowed as how he'd never seen a cow test so high, and told Sylvester and Ivy that they had a champion on their hands in that Viola Cooley cow. "I say let's blab it around a bit," he said. "You might have the butterfat champion of the state." With Sylvester's consent he inserted an article in a state agricultural newsletter and contacted the state agricultural college. Sure enough, Viola was a champion, and pretty soon interested parties from all over the state came to see the pretty, gentle little Jersey and offer Sylvester large sums of money for her.

The townspeople, torn for a while between continuing their interesting feud or uniting in pride at the attention the cow was bringing to their community, finally forgot about the fight. The main topic of conversation switched from Viola the woman to Viola the cow.

Sylvester turned down all offers to sell Viola since Ivy said she couldn't part with the gentle creature. Of course the attention and prestige which they enjoyed as a result of Viola's prowess might have influenced her just a little bit. She felt that owning the cow gave her a decided edge over Viola Cooley whose only claim to fame was the maroon overstuffed set.

It was a big day in Grouse Valley when the Cherry Milk Company from upstate sent a representative down to talk to Sylvester about using Viola for their mascot. Her picture would appear on every can of Cherry Milk and her name would be used in all the company commercials, to say nothing of personal appearances on TV and maybe an occasional tour of state and county fairs. She would be allowed to live at the Turner farm since the slogan of the Cherry Milk Company was "Cherry Milk comes from cheery cows," and they didn't want to take a chance of making Viola unhappy by moving her to unfamiliar pastures.

"We'll retain her name," said Mr. Trumbull of the Cherry Milk Company to Sylvester and Ivy and most of the people of the town who had assembled for the big event. "It's a good name for a cow."

Sylvester nodded and Ivy was about to give assent, too,

when she happened to glance over toward the Cooley farm. There stood Viola, leaning against the corner of her house. She looked lonely and forlorn as she watched the gathering at the Turner place.

There stands a woman who never did a really mean thing in her life, Ivy thought, except maybe get too prideful over a new overstuffed set, a thing any woman has a right to be proud about. Then Sylvester had to go take all the shine off her pleasure by naming a cow after her and stirring up a regular hornet's nest. And now she's over there all alone while everybody, even Millie Higgins and Eldora Meacham, are here enjoying themselves and not a one even thinking of her. And all the trouble was because menfolks thought more of cows than they did of women.

"No," Ivy said all of a sudden. "No, you'll have to change her name. It's just too much to do that to her."

"I don't understand," stammered Mr. Trumbull.

"There's a limit," insisted Ivy. "Call the cow Elsie."

"But another company has Elsie," said Mr. Trumbull.

"Well, Bertha then. But not Viola. It's bad enough to call her Viola around here, but to advertise it all over the world — NO!"

Mr. Trumbull cleared his throat. "Mrs. Turner, it won't be all over the world. We're a small company. We'll do well to advertise in the next state." He tried a conciliatory little laugh, not understanding what the problem was.

"Now, Ivy," Sylvester began.

"Don't 'now Ivy' me. You've had your little joke all these months and look what it has done to poor Viola."

Mr. Trumbull glanced at the cow who stood cheerfully chewing her cud, a perfect advertisement for the Cherry Milk Company. "She looks fine to me," he said.

"I'd best explain," said Sylvester.

"You'd best do just that," Ivy said, "while I go over to the Cooleys'."

Viola was still standing by the corner of the house when Ivy arrived. She opened her mouth to speak as Ivy approached.

"Now don't say a word," said Ivy. "Let me have my say, first. It's a sad day when the womenfolks get all afire over something the men haven't got any better sense than to go and do. It's a wicked thing Sylvester did, naming that cow after you, and it got us all riled up toward each other. Us, who have been good neighbors all our married lives and who have helped each other with new babies and have borrowed back and forth who can count how many times." Ivy paused.

"I heard about how the milk company wants to use that cow for a mascot," said Viola softly.

Ivy hung her head. "I figured you had."

"They name roses after people," Viola continued softly. "You know, the Eleanor Roosevelt Rose and all. But this would be the first time that there'd be a famous cow named after an actual person. I'd be right proud."

Ivy stared at her friend in stunned silence.

"Just imagine, my name being used on TV and everything," Viola said. "And can't you just see what Art Haskins will do to it in his paper? 'Viola Cooley, champion butter maker of the state and wife of Thaddeus Cooley, was chosen by the Cherry Milk Company to have a picture of her broken leg appear on all their cans of milk.' Or something else just as garbled. Ivy, I never saw my name in print before all this fracas. It kind of pleasures a body."

Ivy broke into a laugh and put her arm around her neighbor. "We'll all be famous," she said. "Us for owning the cow and you for having her named after you." They giggled together like schoolgirls.

Ivy sobered a little. "Viola, I really am sorry about all

that mess. I guess I *was* just a teeny bit jealous of your new overstuffed set."

"Don't even think about it," Viola said. "You'll get enough from the Cherry Milk Company to buy ten over-stuffed sets."

Ivy frowned, foreseeing new jealousies and feuds.

"Oh, I won't mind that at all," Viola said. "If you'll just do one little thing for me."

"Anything at all," Ivy assured her.

Viola leaned over to pick a ladybug off a leaf and sent it flying away. "Well," she said, modestly, "do you think you might name that calf 'Violette'?"

Ivy grinned. "I think that could be arranged," she said.

END

by John Gould

The Insiders

WHEN it was suggested to me lately (by a non-resident) that Yankees are given to a smug vanity far in
excess of reasonable self-estimation, I was about to deny it
when I reflected that to do so would be rather snobbish.
There is a restraint and a delicacy involved which is extremely illusive, until it takes considerable art to be snobbish without appearing so — and while this has caused me

much meditation on the subject of Yankee snobbisms, I think it is exactly what led my friend to bring the subject up. I remember asking a member of the Tavern Club, one time, what he did, and he answered, "I carve ducks." This intuitive debasement of personal merit spared him an enumeration of the banks of which he was a director, and the corporations on whose boards he sat, but it also reprimanded me for bringing up a mercenary thought in a social context. An illusion of shyness is part of it, but mainly to emphasize his success, good breeding, modesty, and to reassert that a true gentleman is never proud. Above all, the remark possessed wit, and derived from his firm opinion that whatever he did was all right. Only from a position of security and satisfaction could such a remark come.

I have concluded this to be the warp and the woof of Yankee snobbery. It depends on a pleasant willingness to let everybody else be different, which is not at all like being different yourself, and with an inner approval that permits a gentility of comparison. Yankee snobbery never seems to be harsh, and is often subtle rather than than quiet; a Texan, thus, may be a braggart, but he can't be a snob. Texas stories, you see, are born of the unpleasantness of being a Texan, whose spirits must be lifted to create an illusion of superiority. There is nothing unpleasant about being a Yankee, and consequently our snobbery has sincere motives. It thus has a regional charm. Had I asked a Texas millionaire what he does, he would have described his spread.

"There is no culture," said Henry Beston, "west of Framingham."

"We might have had ye Pilgrims in Mayne," wrote Sir Ferdinand Gorges, "but we didn't want them."

"Goodness," said the Boston lady when the *Transcript*

ceased to publish, "whatever shall the country do now for a newspaper?" She was, of course, the lady who toured to San Francisco via Dedham, and while there wouldn't eat fish so far from the ocean, and once remarked that the menu at the Bellevue was construed in the pluperfect. She said that her husband, who was in the Antarctic for a six-year scientific expedition, was "out of town." And when Boston society expanded beyond its decent limits she was careful about offending anybody from the Back Bay, and always kept Faneuil distinct from Allston and Brighton. Mr. "Perce" called her punctually, and personally, every forenoon at nine to take her grocery order, and she would bow to her friends but otherwise maintained calm dignity in the elevators at R.H. Stearns.

The legendary snobbery of Beacon Hill is by no means the invention of counter-snobs. When William Randolph Hearst founded the Boston *American*, his journalistic reputation prevented enthusiastic acceptance of the idea. There was blue-blood resistance amongst the *Transcript* trade. One day a morsel of gossip seemed noteworthy, and the *American* wanted a photograph of a Louisburg Square dowager. The *Post, Globe Herald,* and *Journal* knew better than to try to assault the bastions in such an impossible desire, but the *American* reporter pushed her doorbell and boldly asked if she would give him her picture.

"I'm from the *Transcript*," he lied, thinking, hoping, that this might carry him through.

There was one fallacy in his approach; the *Transcript* had never printed anybody's picture.

"My good man," said the dowager, "I happen to know that our *Transcript* does not use photographs!"

"That's right," he said. "We're starting tomorrow."

"How nice," she said. "Then I would be the first."

Her picture and the juicy details of the gossip can be

found in the files of the *American,* and the files of the *Transcript,* of course, can be found in the Boston Athenaeum, where the meticulous obituaries are being tediously entered in the genealogy records. If you were anybody, you didn't die until the *Transcript* had reported it. The Boston Athenaeum being, you very well know, the best place to look your family up. If you step in, the clerk will probably ask, knowing very well that you are not, if you are a member. Members, he knows. But in the gradations of snobbery, you *can* step in. It is not so with the Tavern Club.

Some snobs proudly assert they have never been in the Tavern Club, while a higher class of snobs will tell you they have been "kicked out" of it. This is an unfortunate phrase, because they really mean they were asked to leave. The true gentility of Tavern Club snobbery is perhaps best demonstrated by the directions for getting there. If you are invited to lunch with a member, he will explain that the club is on Boylston Place, but that "not above two or three Boston cab drivers know where that is." This is even better than not knowing where the Tavern Club is. Passing through the door, for gentlemen who have succeeded in doing so, is far more estimable than being accepted for Harvard Dental School, or gaining admittance to the royal bedchamber at Buckingham Palace. Upon entering, of course, one finds oneself amongst congenial company in the warm democracy of impeccable equality, scholars and gentlemen all, hail fellow and welcome. However, if a member asks what class you were in, the answer is "Sorry sir, but I went to Bowdoin."

Otherwise, if you simply say, "1931, sir," he will begin naming Harvard members of 1931, and there will be no later time for you to extricate yourself from the snobbery of "The Yard." There is one story that shows the snobbery of the Tavern Club can be out-snobbed.

At the death of Jacob Wirth, the immigrant German whose *bierstube* became a Boston tradition, certain members of the Tavern Club who frequented his restaurant prepared a memorial booklet with several essays extolling the man and his food. One of them was in Latin. This, on the face of it, seems to smack of snobbery, but it was not so considered. The snobbery came when diners at Jake Wirth's picked up the booklet to peruse it along with their knuckles and kraut, and would comment, "And very good Latin!"

The snobbery of being a Jake Wirth fancier likewise was out-snobbed. When prohibition was repealed, the loyal supporters of the venerable restaurant on Stuart Street presumed that Jake would get his traditional "License No. 1." They assembled, but Jake's man didn't come back from City Hall with it. They waited and waited, in parched patience, not knowing that the pendulum of snobbery had shifted in the meantime, and that No. 1 had been issued to Purcelle's over on School Street. The politicians in City Hall had fun with this for some hours, and then Jake got No. 2.

And the legendary snobbery of Boston is by no means that of New England. As snobbery fans out, it becomes more elusive, and loses the cohesion and the volume of the Boston kind. It is riddled with nuances until its freemasonry needs initiation. But, if its cypher is mastered, it is like Mount Washington on a clear day. The Pattersons have been coming to Starfish Cove every summer since old Grandfather Patterson bought the Coombs place in 1842 and built the stone wharf. But when the first Patterson shows up each June, some rubber-booted fisherman wrings his hand warmly and asks, "You down for the season?" There is no animosity or disdain — in fact everybody is glad to see the Pattersons, who are "nice people" — but the Pattersons will never belong, and they will forever be reminded that they can't. They must forever console themselves in their own kind of snobbishness — of going back to Baltimore to tell about their wonderful summers on the Maine coast, and of paying the biggest tax in Starfish Cove.

This particular kind of snobbishness has been endemic since the Monhegan fishermen referred to the Pilgrims as new-comers. Joseph C. Lincoln did all right with the "rusticators." On the Maine coast they are "summer complaints," except on the islands, where they are "off-islanders." On Beal's Island, Chebeague, Vinalhaven, and suchlike ramparts of preferment, they will impress this truth by asking, "Did you come from the main?" The only other place to come from is the open ocean, so the snobbery is evident, but those who come by yacht gain one-upmanship by calling their sneakers "topsiders." And "Do you charter?" is the snob question from a "summer mahogany" sailor who owns his own boat. The proper way to out-snob *him* is to have your boat documented. But the best of such out-snobbing, as it soars, is always brought to earth again by some genius who, for instance, will tell the summer lady always to use female lobsters in her stew. "Always," he says. So she comes to Trefethern's wharf and wants six female lobsters. This, she presumes, will make her sound like an experienced hand, and Trefethern will see that she knows a thing or two. Snobbery, trying to make like a native. She is dashed when Trefethern says, "That cussid Walt Skinner — he pulls that on ten-twelve summer complaints every year!"

The first, the biggest, the best, the tallest — whatever the glory, it has its snobbery. Even on highway signs:

The Only Henniker In The World

Wiscasset — The Prettiest Village in Maine

Carrabasset — Your Life Will Never Be The Same Again

Thomaston, using that intense restraint that smooths the best snobbery, slyly rebukes the public's misinformation about Colonial truths by hanging out:

Thomaston

1605

But this snobbery was easily outsnobbed by some wag whose name should be known — he nailed a sign to a tree on a Scott Paper Company Road, far up in the woods above Moosehead Lake:

Twp.2, R.3

Pop. 22

Then he crossed out the 22 and painted on 21. The snobbery of all the fastest growing communities can only bow, there is no other answer to the snobbery of declining excitement.

Do you know that in Vermont the towns of Corinth and Charlotte are pronounced c'RINTH and ch'LOTTE? Distinction must be achieved somehow; and a man in Ridgefield, Connecticut, boasted that he lived at the farthermost point in New England for commuting by train to his New York office. It meant at least four hours a day on the railroad, a snobbery hard to beat unless you have seen the little snack shack at Oquossoc, Maine, with the sign that says:

The Place Duncan Hines Missed

And are you aware that at least six places in New England claim to be the first place in the United States to be touched by the beams of the rising sun?* You have seen it and heard it a thousand times, but probably never knew that

---

*See "Where Does The Sun Shine First," by Blanton C. Wiggin, *Yankee* Magazine, Jan., 1972, p. 59.

THE STATE OF MAINE is itself snobbery on exhibition. In 1820 the makers of the new constitution thus set it down, to let the whole world know they would have no further truck with any snob commonwealths! But Rhode Island goes one better — the smallest state has the longest name: Rhode Island and Providence Plantations. That is the *official* name of Little Rhody, and *official* snobbery is hard to beat.

In meditating on these examples, I find instances of smugness and superiority (or opinions of superiority) which are not snobbishness. Such as that of the little boy from New Jersey who was admiring a new pack basket. "Gee," he said, "that's a swell pack basket!"

The little Maine boy who owned the pack basket said, "You don't know much — that's my Kennebecker!"

Now, his mother reprimanded him for being rude to his visitor, and in a whisper she said, "Nobody from New Jersey would know that!"

The incident has all the elements of accomplished snobbery, except those of grace, charm, and wit. Against it, I would balance the Vermonter who was asked directions by a tourist:

TOURIST — I want to get to Orange.

VERMONTER — Don't know a thing to hinder.

Logical positivism has its own nuances, but it is not the dominant element which makes this colloquy properly snobbish. The most difficult role for a Vermonter is to play a Vermonter, just as Robert Peter Tristram Coffin found it taxing to go about all the time being Robert Peter Tristram Coffin. The tourist, being a willing straight man, expects *something* when he is in Vermont, and it is the duty and privilege of true Vermonters to supply it. And the tourist certainly does not expect something as flat and unpalatable (to go back to the previous example) as the news that Kennebecker is the Maine word for a knapsack. In short, snobbery is to some extent forced upon us as the consequence of an established reputation. If that Vermonter had said, "Ten miles, straight ahead," the tourist could not have gone home to Delaware to exercise that counter-Yankee snobbery which says, "On my vacation up in Vermont I met some dandies!" Nor would that have given his friends a good laugh. But, now his friends can say, "That's great! They sure do have some grand characters up there!"

We sure do, but as Doc Rockwell says, they all go home on Labor Day.

Before leaving the subject, I think I should explain that I meant nothing, really, by referring to my friend as a "non-resident." I intended merely to indicate that this subject was brought up by a person not basically qualified to have a sound opinion on our purely regional virtues. It was not intended to be snobbish. But he does come from "away," or as the folks in Aroostook County phrase it, "outside."

END

Malcolm My Horse

by Gayle E. Steed

"THERE are no poisonous snakes in New Hampshire," I repeated from the inside of the raspberry thicket. A moment ago I'd said that. A moment ago I'd been astride my horse. "That is," I added, being a truthful person at heart, "there are a few timber rattlers, but only a very, very few. In fact, there are so few that the State Conservation Agency reports that not one of its rangers has been bitten by a rattler in the last ten years. I read that only last week in the *Ecology News Bulletin*. The most dangerous creature you would be likely to come across is the snapping turtle, and the turtle is only dangerous if you were to pick it up, which is something you wouldn't even have to think about . . . ."

Malcolm, who hadn't read the *Bulletin*, snorted and moved off to nibble the goldenrod.

"There are no poisonous snakes in New Hampshire," I repeated hopelessly. "There are raspberry thickets, to be sure, and while these are not a deadly menace, they are quite uncomfortable, especially when entered at high speed from above. There are also pheasants in New Hampshire. You will probably notice the next time, Malcolm, provided you look before you leap, that pheasants do not actually resemble snakes at all. Pheasants are rather round, have both feathers and feet, and they fly. It might be a good rule for you to remember: if it has feathers, feet, or it flies, it is probably not a snake."

Malcolm began to roll his eyes in dread of being left behind with only me and a raspberry thicket full of snakes. From under the raspberries I could see Tulip, the pony, with my youngest child aboard, disappearing over the hill towards home. A moment later I could also see Malcolm disappearing over the hill towards home. Tulip was much closer to the ground and always walked with his eyes on his feet, so Malcolm considered him an ideal snake-spotter and was loath to be caught anywhere without him.

On the lonely walk back to the barn, I consoled myself thinking that Malcolm was just as foolish to trust his safety to Tulip's scouting ability as he was to fear snakes at every step. A child and a pony too diplomatic to notice that I had been catapulted into the raspberries would not be very likely to notice something as casual as a snake. On the other hand, I reflected with chagrin, since we'd broken Malcolm to saddle, my sailing into thickets had become much more common than even garden snakes.

I would not, I insisted, give up my intention of turning Malcolm into a first-rate saddle horse simply because of his sleight of mind over reptiles. I had raised him from a foal, had I not? I had survived his youthful attempts at fence-jumping. I knew who his parents were. This tiny mental aberration about snakes could be overcome and was in all likelihood temporary. I comforted myself with memories of Malcolm's dear, if somewhat homely, mother, her patience and good nature towards my novice attempts to learn to ride. Surely some of that good-temperedness had passed on to her offspring. I remembered how delighted I had been with Malcolm when he was born. To my untutored eye he was a reasonable facsimile of the proud and handsome horse I'd always dreamed of owning and probably never would have acquired had my neighbor not owned a Morgan stallion that was an incurable fence-jumper.

I cheered myself by recalling that Malcolm was attractive to more skilled judges of horseflesh, too. Donald Fairbrother, who owned quite a few fine horses, had seen Malcolm only once and forthwith made an offer for him. Flattered beyond belief, I turned him down. I would never part with my beautiful young horse.

"If you ever change your mind, let me know," he said. I had promised that I would, confident that the occasion would never arise. This was the horse I had always wanted.

Walking home from the raspberry thicket, I realized that Fairbrother had made that offer three years ago and many things had happened since then, mostly to Malcolm. For instance, there had been that episode of fence-jumping when he was a yearling. It wasn't "jumping," but we didn't know what else to call it.

During his first year we had made the mistake of treating Malcolm to a taste of the sweet corn we grew in the garden beside the house. He spent the remainder of the season trying to get at the rest of it. He would begin by racing at the fence with the Morgan grace of his sire; but when he reached it, something short-circuited at the crucial moment and instead of sailing over it he crashed into it. It was nerve-wracking to watch. He made all the right motions and had all the style of a steeplechaser except that he never left ground level. He smashed against the wooden pasture fence so often that he wore all the hair off his chest and lower lip. But he persevered. Eventually he developed a method of hitting the fence at a half leap sideways that rolled him over the barrier like a pole vaulter and plopped him dizzily on the other side. In the face of this accomplishment, we surrounded the garden with barbed wire to discourage him, but he only fell into it as though it were a net and ended up spending more time at the vet's than did his fence-jumping father who lived there.

Now he had contracted an insane fear of snakes.

"I won't give up," I said over and over in time with my march across the meadow.

That evening I called a family conference, as was the policy when someone had a problem. Whenever I called a conference I always had the same problem: the unanimous verdict was to accept Fairbrother's offer. Two of my sons preferred riding a snowmobile to riding a horse, and my eldest daughter felt we would do better to trade Malcolm in for a second car. The youngest complained that Malcolm was getting on Tulip's nerves. I dismissed the meeting in a huff and phoned my neighbor, Frank Hall. Frank was the veterinarian who owned the fence-jumping Morgan.

"Just talk to him calmly and truthfully," he told me. "Horses respond to a calm and reassuring voice."

"That's what you told me before, and I've tried it. It won't work. My best riding pants are covered with raspberry stains and my ankle is swelling. I have two children in the kitchen shouting the going price of snowmobiles plus shipping charges and another who claims her pony is coming down with anxieties. Think of something else."

"Hang a snake in his stall," he said, confidently. "I understand they train polo ponies not to shy by hanging mallets in their stalls until they grow used to them."

I reconvened the family meeting, outlined the strategy, passed out several lengths of rope, each with a knot at one end, and thanked the boys for the loan of their very good rubber likeness of a snake. The ropes were scattered skillfully about the pasture and along the creek bank where Malcolm would be most likely to meet the real snake. The rubber snake was impaled on the stall door, and Malcolm was shut inside with it.

In the morning we found a nonchalant Malcolm and no trace of the snake.

"He probably ate it," said Frank Hall over the phone. "It probably won't hurt him, but I'd keep an eye on him for a couple of days if I were you and call me if you need me. By the way, you had better use something he can't swallow as a snake from now on."

We replaced the rubber snake with a metal one, ingeniously bent and painted to look like the real thing. This time Malcolm was properly horrified, and all day we could hear him thrashing about and whinnying for us to rescue him. During the night he grew quiet and finally we fell asleep dreaming that we were making progress. The next morning the metal snake was in the stall but Malcolm wasn't.

"At least he didn't eat it," said my youngest, cheerfully.

"He didn't eat the snake," I said to Frank Hall over the phone."What he ate was the board from the windowsill. After that he pushed out the screening and climbed out."

Frank suggested that we put tar on the windowsill to keep him from gnawing on it, and after we had done that we dragged the kicking, screaming Malcolm back into the stall.

The following morning, with the phone in my hand, I decided not to call the vet again to tell him that Malcolm had eaten the tar and all. I asked myself, Why am I following the advice of a man who can't even train his own horse to stay home and charged a $50 stud fee when it was his horse who jumped into my pasture? If I simply waited, perhaps Malcolm would overcome his fear of snakes.

We waited the whole summer. By the next spring I had

to admit that Malcolm had changed a bit even if he hadn't improved. He was still afraid of snakes, especially imaginary ones, but he had less time to bother about them because there were other things on his mind. He had fallen in love with Jamie Forrester's sorrel filly at the bottom of the road.

"She's quite lovely," I complimented him, "and she seems to be somewhat taken with you too."

At first I thought it was only a passing fancy — something to do with the new green meadows and the first robins. I had forgotten that Malcolm had been in love once before, with my sweet corn, and had stopped at nothing to get it. By the time the trees had blossomed they were calling their endearments to each other night and day, until the whole hillside rang with their embarrassing enthusiasm. I learned to sleep with Malcolm's anguished cries pealing through my dreams. I began to appreciate the merits of having a second car and to worry about my nerves as well as Tulip's.

"He'll get tired soon," I assured everyone. "Think how sweet and sad it is that they will never meet."

"Oh, for heaven's sake," said my youngest — and she spoke for all of them. I was afraid to call a family meeting. They had taken to carrying the snowmobile catalogues around with them.

Malcolm's noisy enchantment grew. Then one morning when the dew was still on the grass and his love for Forrester's filly was in full and sleepless bloom, he gathered himself together and ran at the fence. Why the fence didn't snap I'll never understand, for Malcolm was no longer a slender colt. It didn't collapse and it didn't ease him across it. What it did was flip him into a spectacular somersault onto the other side, where he landed dazed and unhurt and, best of all, free to pursue his romance.

And pursue her he did — down the road and down the hill, bugling his joy all the way. At the bottom of the hill between him and his lady-love, the creek tumbled into a deep drainage ditch that funneled the creek water and general runoff under the road through a huge culvert. When he came to the ditch, he threw himself into his horizontal leap. The result was that Forrester's filly found herself being pursued up and down her own fence row by an invisible suitor as Malcolm, now trapped in the ditch, ran the length of it back and forth. Scared out of her wits, the filly bolted for her own barn, whereupon Malcolm, in the ditch and hearing her hoofbeats departing, raced along straining his neck to catch a glimpse of her and ran into the culvert.

We found him in the giant pipe, lodged sideways, his head bent at an uncomfortable angle, his love long since flown, and his trembling legs straddling the trickle from the creek. Dark, wet places, he seemed to know, were probably full of snakes.

"We'll save you, Malcolm, old boy," we encouraged him, and we did after three hours of prying and pushing and dislodging him inch by inch. The rescue operation was hampered by Malcolm's trying to lie down every time we nudged his hooves. We spent most of our energy holding him up. Pushing and dragging him out of the ditch was almost as bad. He didn't stop trembling for two days afterwards, and ever after that whenever we wanted to examine his feet, we had to tie his head tightly to the top rail of the fence. So vivid was his memory of the experience that his knees would begin to tremble and he would try to lie down. His dash into the culvert ended his love affair. The filly was forgotten or associated in his mind too clearly with the dark and damp of the drainage culvert.

He did quiet down a bit that summer, but he began to

develop more and more curious fears. I had looked forward to pleasure-riding down the autumn country roads. Now that Malcolm was quieter, I felt secure about riding him outside the pasture for the first time. But as soon as he took his first step onto the pavement he pounced back onto the grass and refused to budge. I found I could convince him to walk on the road only if I dismounted and walked before him stomping loudly to show him that it would support my weight. My dream had not been to stalk down the autumn roads followed by an animal who was absolutely fascinated by my every step. I began to lose my enthusiasm for riding.

Winter and Christmas were just around the corner, and I put Malcolm's training out of my mind for the year. To brighten the season I bought myself a long awaited new coat — a beautiful, fun, pretend fox fur coat. As soon as I brought the coat home strange things began to happen. I wasn't the only one who thought the coat was attractive. Though I had lost my enthusiasm for him, Malcolm developed a new enthusiasm for me. Whenever I appeared in the coat outside the house, Malcolm fell over the fence and galloped up prancing and curious and very interested. I was baffled and somewhat taken aback.

"Your coat is the same color as Forrester's filly," my youngest said.

"Thanks a lot," I replied, "and besides, horses are color-blind."

She shrugged as one who had given her best and left me and my coat to Malcolm's attentions. It was unnerving, to say the least. I couldn't enter or leave my own house wearing the coat without being admired, followed, sniffed and stepped upon. I began to sneak the coat out of the house in a grocery bag and only put it on when I was well out of Malcolm's sight.

One late fall morning after everyone had left for school with their snowmobile catalogues, I dressed to go on one of my rare shopping trips. At the front door I paused to scan the pasture fence, hoping to slip away unnoticed.

"I am crazier than he is," I told the doorjamb. "Why would a rational adult allow herself to be haunted by that idiotic animal? This is, after all, my own home, and if I want to wear my own coat, I will wear it." I put it on and stomped defiantly into the yard.

In a flash I was surrounded by Malcolm. It was embarrassing. Every time I tried to get past him he blocked my path. I began to retreat. Malcolm followed, dancing around me` with growing excitement. I began to run. Down the hill we went, me in my good dress and shoes splashing through the soggy spots and recalling something I'd once heard about an explorer escaping from a polar bear by discarding articles of clothing as he ran so that the bear stopped to examine each one, and the man escaped. I refused to part with my new coat. I remember shouting. I can remember that Malcolm was shouting too, and the next thing I remember was being in the culvert, sitting in a fine puddle of muck while Malcolm scrambled around outside, growing frantic as the culvert threw his own rival echo back out at him. His anger at being bereft of his love a second time overcame his fear of the culvert. Besides, being something less than a superb jumper, he couldn't get out of the ditch.

Exasperated, I wondered how long it would take someone to miss me. I wondered if I wanted to be missed and found trapped in a rain culvert by a giddy horse that was in love with my coat, now bedraggled beyond belief. I began to wonder where the culvert came out and how long I would have to slosh in the dark to come out at the other enc. My hand fell on a piece of dirty rope — one of the "snakes" from the summer before (Oh, how simple the problem had seemed then!), washed down here by the creek. I took a deep, resigned breath.

"Malcolm," I said calmly, being a truthful person at heart, "there's a snake in here with me."

I tossed it out into the sunlight and listened with grim satisfaction to Malcolm's making perhaps the only successful upward leap in his life. I peeked out. The ditch was empty. Hoofbeats faded away towards the barn. I scrambled up the embankment, took off my once beautiful coat, and retrieved the length of rope.

The snake and the coat and I limped peacefully back to the house and made the long overdue phone call to Fairbrother.   END